Off the Plan

THE URBANISATION OF THE GOLD COAST

Editors: Caryl Bosman, Ayşın Dedekorkut-Howes and Andrew Leach

PUBLISHING

National Library of Australia Cataloguing-in-Publication entry

Off the plan : the urbanisation of the Gold Coast/Caryl Bosman, Ayşın Dedekorkut-Howes and Andrew Leach.

9781486301836 (paperback)
9781486301843 (ePDF)
9781486301850 (epub)

Includes bibliographical references and index.

City planning – Queensland – Gold Coast.
Urban policy – Queensland – Gold Coast.
Gold Coast (Qld.) – History.
Gold Coast (Qld.) – Planning.

Bosman, Caryl, editor.
Dedekorkut-Howes, Ayşın, editor.
Leach, Andrew, 1976– editor.

307.7609943

Published by

CSIRO Publishing
36 Gardiner Road, Clayton VIC 3168
Private Bag 10, Clayton South VIC 3169
Australia

Telephone: [+613] 9545 8555
Email: csiropublishing@csiro.au
Website: www.publishing.csiro.au

Front cover: (background) GCRT 2031 Corridor Study (Gold Coast City Council and HASSELL; imagery by Doug and Wolf); (foreground) Modified from Mantra Circle on Cavill, Surfers Paradise, Gold Coast, Australia, by Phalinn Ooi. Available under a Creative Commons Attribution 2.0 Generic licence (https://creativecommons.org/licenses/by/2.0/) at https://www.flickr.com/photos/phalinn/6874989458.
Back cover: Coomera to Tweed Heads motoring map, late 1920s (New South Wales Government Tourist Bureau and NRMA). Reproduced with permission of Universal Publishers Pty Ltd.

Set in 10.5/12 Adobe Minion Pro and ITC Stone Sans
Edited by Karen Pearce
Cover design by Andrew Weatherill
Typeset by Desktop Concepts Pty Ltd, Melbourne
Index by Bruce Gillespie
Printed by Ingram Lightning Source

Feb26_RP_ILS

Contents

Acknowledgements

This book has been an idea some years in the making. Initially a project of GoCART, the Gold Coast Area Research Team of Griffith University's Urban Research Program, its remit has expanded to capture several strands of the research around the Gold Coast's formation and operation as a city. This research is anchored to Griffith University, especially the activities on its burgeoning Gold Coast campus, near Southport. It describes, too, a research community that extends to several neighbouring universities. The editors wish to acknowledge the ongoing support of colleagues in the Urban Research Program and, in particular, Brendan Gleeson, Jago Dodson and Paul Burton, who have each served as directors of the centre while this book has been under development. Aspects of this book document research funded by the Australian Research Council as Future Fellowship project FT120100883. We are grateful for the support and encouragement of Lauren Webb at CSIRO Publishing, who has shown remarkable tolerance as well as expertise in guiding us towards publication.

List of contributors

Caryl Bosman is a senior lecturer and Head of Discipline Urban and Environmental Planning at Griffith University and a member of the Urban Research Program. She has a PhD in urban planning and a Bachelor of Architecture. Her research interests focus on the planning and development of past and present suburban landscapes. Caryl's current research centres on the residential landscapes of the Gold Coast and planning and provision of housing for an ageing population, particularly in relation to ideals of community, 'the good life' and placemaking.

Matthew Burke is Deputy Director (Nathan campus) and an Australian Research Council Future Fellow at the Urban Research Program at Griffith University. His research explores transport and land-use planning and transport policy, with particular focus on how the built environment and transport systems influence travel behaviour. Matthew worked in transport and land-use planning at all three tiers of government in Australia, before joining Griffith. He is presently exploring the impacts of the Gold Coast's new light rail system.

Paul Burton is Professor of Urban Planning and Management at Griffith University and Acting Director of its Urban Research Program. He directs the City of Gold Coast/Griffith University Growth Management Partnership and is a founding member of Regional Development Australia, Gold Coast. Before moving to Australia in 2007, Paul was Head of the School for Policy Studies at the University of Bristol, a director of the charity, Support Against Racist Incidents (SARI) and served as the chair of the Bristol Democracy Commission, which recommended the adoption of a directly elected mayor for the city.

Jason Byrne is an Associate Professor in Urban and Environmental Planning with Griffith University's School of Environment, Gold Coast campus, where he has taught since 2006. A geographer and planner, Jason's research interests include urban nature, parks, green-space, environmental justice and political ecologies of climate change adaptation. He is a member of Griffith's Urban Research Program and Environmental Futures Research Institute. Jason previously worked as a planning officer, environmental officer and policy writer with the Western Australian Government. He has over 70 scholarly publications, including an edited book *Australian Environmental Planning: Challenges and Future Prospects.*

Eddo Coiacetto is an Associate Professor in Urban Planning at Griffith University. His research and teaching are motivated by an interest in improving the effectiveness of planning practice, especially by focusing on the challenges of implementing planning in market-based economies and by basing it on a more sound understanding of the realities of urban development. Eddo is particularly interested in the nature of real estate development, the strategies of developers and their implications for urban development, urban planning and sustainability. His research also focuses on planning education and the preparation of students for the challenges and realities of planning practice.

Ayşın Dedekorkut-Howes is a Senior Lecturer in the Urban and Environmental Planning Program at Griffith University's Gold Coast campus, a researcher with the Urban Research Program and the co-convenor of Gold Coast Area Research Team (GoCART). Her current research focuses on urbanisation and growth management in subtropical areas. She conducts historical research on the development and urbanisation of the Gold Coast as well as current issues and problems the city is facing such as climate change. Ayşın has a background in city planning and has previously worked in Turkey and the United States.

Sarah Gardiner is a Lecturer in tourism and hotel management at Griffith University. She has a PhD in Marketing from Griffith University and has published in several high-ranking tourism journals. Prior to that, Sarah worked for more than 15 years in the private and government sectors of the Gold Coast tourism industry, managing several marketing and product development strategies. She has provided consultancy services to industry in the areas of tourism, events, marketing and community engagement. Sarah's current research interests are consumer behaviour and tourism destination marketing and development.

Donna Houston is a Senior Lecturer in the Department of Geography and Planning at Macquarie University. Her scholarly interests are concerned with environmental and social justice in a time of global environmental change. She has recently published research on storytelling in environmental justice activism, urban political ecology in Australian cities and planning for climate-just, more-than-human cities.

Michael Howes is an Associate Professor at Griffith University's School of Environment and Urban Research Program. Michael's research explores how governments try to make society more sustainable and resilient with specific projects on climate change, sustainable development, environment protection institutions, public environmental reporting, eco-efficiency programs and environmental policy. Before becoming an academic Michael worked for several years as an industrial chemist and technical manager in the manufacturing sector. He has also been a member of the Queensland Conservation Council board and chaired the Technical Advisory Panel for the Australian Government's National Pollutant Inventory.

Daniel O'Hare is Associate Professor of Urban Planning in the Faculty of Society and Design at Bond University on the Gold Coast. He holds a PhD and MA (Urban Design) from Oxford Brookes University, UK, and a town planning degree from the University of New South Wales. Danny's research interests include urban cultural landscapes, urban walkability, knowledge-based urban development and the transformation of coastal tourism areas into sustainable urban regions. His publications on these topics have appeared in journals including *Urban Design International,* in book chapters, and conference proceedings published by Australian, UK, Chinese and US universities, government departments and professional organisations.

Andrew Leach is Professor of Architectural History at Griffith University, where he holds an Australian Research Council Future Fellowship and is Deputy Director (Gold Coast campus) of the Urban Research Program. Andrew's work concerns the intellectual history of twentieth-century architectural culture. He has published widely on this theme, including the books *Manfredo Tafuri* (2007), *Architecture, Disciplinarity, and the Arts* (2009), *What is Architectural History?* (2010) and *The Baroque in Architectural Culture 1880–1980* (2015). His inaugural lecture was published as *The Gold Coast Moment*, and his survey of the Gold Coast Architecture Awards as *GC30+*.

Ruth Potts completed her PhD at the Queensland University of Technology in early 2015. Her PhD research focused on evaluation of decision-making for natural resource management planning in Far North Queensland. Her PhD was nominated for an outstanding PhD award by both thesis examiners. Ruth's research interests include governance, natural resource management, planning theory and city identity.

Sacha Reid is a Senior Lecturer in the Griffith Business School, specialising in the areas of real estate, property development and event management. Prior to this role she was the Foundation Research Director for DTZ (Queensland), a global property consultancy full service agency. Her research interests focus around vertical communities, multi-owned properties and high-rise living.

Noel Scott is a Professor in the Griffith Institute for Tourism at Griffith University. His research interests include the study of tourism experiences, destination management and stakeholder organisation. He is a frequent speaker at international academic and industry conferences. He has over 200 academic publications, including 13 books. He has supervised 18 doctoral students to successful completion of their theses. Prior to his academic career, Noel worked as a senior manager at Tourism Queensland and Research and Planning Manager at Suncorp Building Society.

Severine Mayere is a Senior Lecturer in Urban and Regional Planning in the School of Civil Engineering and Built Environment at Queensland University of Technology (QUT). Her research interests include comparative urbanisation, land-use planning, and regional planning and governance. Severine holds degrees from the University of Paris-Sorbonne and Florida State University. Prior to joining QUT she held research positions in the United States (Florida State University) and Germany (Technical University Dresden).

Chapter 1

Considering the Gold Coast

Ayşın Dedekorkut-Howes, Caryl Bosman and Andrew Leach

The subtropical, Pacific-edge Gold Coast city-region, abutting the New South Wales border in the Australian state of Queensland, is famous for its sun and surf. Although the country's sixth most populous city, it is popularly viewed as an overgrown resort town. Its glittering image as a vacation destination – with long stretches of white sandy beaches, a skyline of resort skyscrapers, an enduring legacy of such gimmicks as the gold lamé bikini-clad Meter Maids, and the now century-old figure of the tanned and carefree surfer – dominates representation of the city in policy and publicity alike. Cultural analyst Patricia Wise (2006, p. 185) sums up the general perception of the Gold Coast accurately when she observes:

> *The city continues to be characterized in the national media as a 'cultural desert'. Its neighbour, the state capital Brisbane, is represented as having 'matured' into a 'metropolitan centre' with a 'vital arts life' and definable 'cultural precincts', like Sydney and Melbourne. But in the Australian cultural imaginary the Gold Coast's total identification with leisure, popular cultural excess and dispersion is taken to signify a sort of perpetual adolescence. There is no expectation that it will 'grow up' into 'a real city' where 'culture' occurs.*

As Grahame Griffin (1998, p. 286) noted nearly two decades ago, 'the Gold Coast isn't an easily definable place with a singular identity'. A survey of its caricatures bears this out: Michael Jones borrowed from Noël Coward's snipe at the French Riviera to describe it as 'a sunny place for shady people' (Jones 1986, p. 1); the pages of the *Brisbane Sunday Mail* cast it as 'sin city' (Griffin 1998, p. 285); urban sociologist Patrick Mullins held it as an example of 'tourism urbanization' that is physically, demographically, socially, economically and politically distinct from other Australian cities (Mullins 1991); local historian Alexander McRobbie has called it 'the most heterogeneous region in Australia' (McRobbie 1991, p. vi); the city's own *Gold Coast Heritage and Character Study* has it as 'the most postmodern of all Australian cities' (Allom Lovell Marquis-Kyle *et al.* 1997, p. 4); for sociologist David Holmes the Gold Coast is 'an urban setting that has already achieved many of the conditions towards which post-industrial urban centres are moving' (Holmes 2001, p. 179); while for Paul Burton it is a city still in the throes of an urban 'adolescence' (Burton 2009, p. 1).

At the same time, with a population of more than half a million people, the Gold Coast is one of the fastest growing cities in Australia, already far larger than some of the state and territory capitals. It is the country's most populous non-metro city, occupying one of the largest urban areas outside the major state capital conurbations. Thanks to the peculiar history of local government amalgamations in Queensland, it is home to the second most populous local government area (LGA) in Australia. After Sydney, Melbourne and Tropical North Queensland, the Gold Coast is the nation's fourth most popular destination for international leisure visitors (Tourism Research Australia 2008). It is a substantial and complex city. Economically and socially it is no longer limited to the characteristics of a resort town. A real city has for some time been emerging from behind the glittering façade. More than a mere tourism destination, it is a city with two universities (three, if you extend the Gold Coast across the state border to include Tweed Heads; and more if you include the 'branch' campuses of other institutions), an international airport, national sports teams, two major regional hospitals and many other amenities. It is a city that is preparing to host the XXI Commonwealth Games in 2018. Indeed, as sociologist David Holmes (2006) has suggested, the Gold Coast is now looking for the balance within the dual identity of a city and a destination. Robert Stimson and John Minnery have gone further to suggest that the Gold Coast presents at least four different images to the world: 'a city of leisure; a city of enterprise; a city of tourism; and a city in its own right within the South East Queensland 'sun-belt' growth metropolis' (Stimson and Minnery 1998, p. 196).

This book draws these characterisations of the Gold Coast into conversation with one another, subjecting this city-region to a sustained regard under the multiform lens of urban history. It sets about to unsettle the assumptions with which the Coast is treated out of habit, asking how – from starting points as varied as environmental history, the history of housing and the histories of media and tourism – various factors conspired to make the city of Gold Coast. There is, of course, some basis to the assumptions that commentators bring to any fresh reading of that city, and this book sets about to demonstrate the origins of those assumptions as well as those moments in which they depart from the reality of the situation the Gold Coast describes. To recall the title of an earlier attempt by two of the present authors (Dedekorkut-Howes and Bosman 2011), this book addresses through history 'The Unbearable Lightness of Being Gold Coast'. Through a series of iterations this book examines the historical evolution of the Gold Coast, its urban development, its environment, the structure of its development, urban form and urban systems (including transport), its population and history of population change, its demographic composition and housing, its economy and significant industries, its governance, its image and its opportunities. In these many respects the city can sustain comparison with state and national trends, with the Australian state capital cities and with the nearby city of the Sunshine Coast, which – being the second major tourist settlement in the state of Queensland – shares some of its preconditions while presenting us with a decidedly different urban history.

Historical evolution

A few key observations serve to orientate the reader among the individual contributions that follow. As Jason Byrne and Donna Houston observe in the following chapter, the area now called the Gold Coast has been continuously occupied by members of the Yugambeh peoples, and especially the Kombumerri saltwater people, along with the Wangerriburra, Minjunbal, Gugingin and Numinbah peoples, since around 23 000 BC. Following the British occupation of Sydney in 1788, the southern coast of what became Queensland in 1859 was sighted and surveyed from 1823, the time of John Oxley's landing at Mermaid Beach, and charted in 1840 by the New South Wales Government. The area of Moreton Bay was drawn by Robert Dixon in 1842. The Gold Coast region witnessed the difficult progression of British settlement from the middle decades of the nineteenth century onwards, with the earliest British settlement, Nerang, surveyed in 1865. While the city would be orientated towards the Pacific by the turn of the twentieth century, the area's first settlements supported agriculture across the region defined in its westward extension by what Michael Jones (1988) called the *Country of Five Rivers*. Coolangatta and Tweed Heads (straddling the colonial and then state border) and Southport (to the north of the Nerang River) emerged as the major service towns in the late nineteenth century, supporting inland sugar plantations, logging activity and dairy production (Mullins 1984; Jones 1988).

The first railway line from the colonial capital of Brisbane to Southport (a distance of less than 80 km) was completed in 1889 to support the farming industry. The line also allowed for more democratic access to the beach, thereby encouraging the development of a holiday centre. With the extension of the railway to West Burleigh in 1901 and to Coolangatta–Tweed Heads in 1903, what was then called the 'South Coast' in relation to Brisbane began to sustain development as a regional leisure destination (Longhurst 1995). The area was connected to New South Wales and Victoria by rail in 1930. Throughout the 1940s and 1950s most of its visitors were from its immediate neighbours in the south-east corner of Queensland (Prideaux 2004). Increased private motor vehicle ownership complemented rail mobility, and from the mid-1930s onwards automobiles became a popular way to travel to the region from Brisbane or northern New South Wales. The sale of land parcels at Southport, Surfers Paradise and Coolangatta offered many from Brisbane the opportunity to establish second homes on the 'South Coast' – an opportunity famously taken up by Queensland's Governor Sir Anthony Musgrave in 1884, who set an example that was widely followed.

The introduction of passenger air services in 1947 and direct flights from Sydney to Coolangatta in 1956 made the city easily accessible to the national tourism market (Prideaux 2004). Following these developments, and the lifting of the post-war construction restrictions, the large-scale sale of coastal building plots began in earnest from 1952 onwards (Hofmeister 1988). Improvements to the interstate motorways, responding to rising car ownership, described a major change to the way in which visitors were getting to the Gold Coast, and heralded the closure of the Brisbane to Gold Coast rail line in 1964 (Longhurst 1995). In the following decades the attractions and services offered on the Gold Coast developed and diversified to respond to the changing profile of its tourist markets. These markets underwent a major shift from being primarily domestic to primarily international during the 1980s, with direct airline connections from Brisbane to Europe and Asia enabling the city and its beach to become an international tourism destination. The rail link to Brisbane was restored in 1997 (Nightingale 2006), but rather than following the coast as its predecessor once did, the new link followed an inland line parallel to the Pacific Motorway – reflecting as it did the Gold Coast's emergence as a commuter satellite to the capital.

Between 1934 and 1995, the area administered by what has since 2013 been rebranded as the city of Gold Coast expanded by means of a series of amalgamations, connecting a string of once-independent coastal resort towns, including Labrador, Southport, Surfers Paradise, Burleigh Heads and Coolangatta, and inland settlements, such as Nerang and Mudgeeraba, into a single urban system. In 1958, the South Coast Town Council adopted the informal but more marketable name used widely, if informally, by the local and national media – the Gold Coast. The region was bordered to the north and west by the alluvial plains and hinterland hills of the Albert Shire until March 1995, when the amalgamation of the two LGAs rendered the Gold Coast a 'super city' (Stimson and Minnery 1998, p. 199), and the nation's most populous municipality after Brisbane.

(A technical observation: the contiguous urban area of the Gold Coast region extends beyond the state boundaries to the south and only a street separates the suburb of Coolangatta, which is part of the city of the Gold Coast, from its twin city Tweed Heads in New South Wales. If the Gold Coast is defined as a region rather than an administrative jurisdiction, Tweed Heads is viewed as part of the region. The Australian Bureau of Statistics (ABS) has recognised the contiguous urban areas of the Gold Coast–Tweed region as a single urban conurbation since 1966.)

Population growth and demographic structure

The trajectory of the Gold Coast's growth is one of the more astounding episodes in Australia's demographic history. While the 2011 census confirmed its ranking as Australia's sixth largest major urban centre (urban area population 557 822, LGA population 494 501: ABS 2013b), it has grown from a few sparsely populated settlements over a large area. In 1933, for instance, the Gold Coast had a population of 6602 (Council of the City of Gold Coast 1969), which had grown more than five-fold in three decades to become 33 716 (including Tweed) in 1961. For more than five decades, the Gold Coast has been one of the fastest growing urban regions in Australia (see Table 1.1), doubling its population between 1954 and 1966, and again between 1966 and 1976, when it passed 100 000 (Mullins 1979). The city registered the largest population growth among all LGAs in Australia with 74 200 additional people reported and an average annual growth rate of 4.8% between 1991 and 1996, during which time Queensland was the country's fastest growing state or territory (ABS 1997). Since this time, it has consistently registered the second highest growth levels after Brisbane, with an average annual growth rate of 3.6% between 1996 and 2006 (ABS 2007). Despite having a more moderate rate of growth in recent years, in the decade up to 2011 the Gold Coast–Tweed conurbation still topped population growth levels among Australia's major cities with a 2.8% annual growth rate (see Table 1.2).

While Australian urbanisation tends to differ from that of other Western societies in the concentration of its population in capital cities, Queensland, in turn, tends towards a higher degree of decentralisation (Hofmeister 1988; Mullins 1988). The recent growth of the Gold Coast has been challenging the primacy of the state capital of Brisbane to an extent not experienced by the other Australian capitals, where second cities beyond the immediate conurbation of the capital proper are much smaller and located some distance away. In fact, the Gold Coast is more populous than Canberra, Hobart and Darwin.

From 1991 to 2012 the most prominent population growth in Australia outside the capital cities was along the coastline. Table 1.1 shows that of the 10 largest urban areas in the country, the coastal cities of the Gold Coast and the Sunshine Coast are the fastest growing. However, this growth might not solely be due to the factors identified by Mullins (1991) as being proper to tourism urbanisation, but rather to a more generalised trend of sunbelt growth, 'a regional development phenomenon resulting from basic shifts in comparative economic advantage' (Abbott 1987, p. 8; compare Stimson 1995; Guhathakurta and Stimson 2007). The term 'sunbelt' originated in the United States in reference to 'those South and South-western states that, because of geographic position, enjoy a natural advantage over places in the North' as opposed to the 'frostbelt', and 'implies that climate is mild, the air clean, and sunshine copious' (Raitz 1988, p. 14). The concept of sea change (Stimson *et al.* 1996) reflects the concentration of this migration on coastal communities. Australian sunbelt migration is evident in changes to the rank order of cities and towns in Australia's national urban hierarchy between 1961 and 2011, and especially from the 1970s onwards (see Fig. 1.1). Within the comparatively faster growth of coastal sunbelt cities –

Table 1.1. Population change in major Australian cities, 1961–2007 (%) (ABS 2008)

Ranked urban areas	1961–1971	1971–1981	1981–1991	1991–2001	2001–2007	1961–2007	Per cent of national population (2007)
1. Sydney	28.6	14.1	14.6	12.4	5.0	98.5	20.5
2. Melbourne	30.9	8.8	15.9	10.0	9.6	99.0	18.0
3. Brisbane	39.6	18.5	32.0	20.0	14.0	198.8	8.8
4. Perth	67.4	27.8	32.2	17.2	11.6	269.9	7.3
5. Adelaide	43.3	10.6	13.4	4.9	4.5	96.9	5.5
6. Gold Coast–Tweed	**120.2**	**138.8**	**57.6**	**69.9**	**22.9**	**1631.2**	**2.8**
7. Newcastle	68.5	10.7	14.3	10.7	6.3	151.0	2.5
8. Canberra–Queanbeyan	164.8	50.9	33.9	12.3	7.7	547.0	1.8
9. Wollongong	51.1	11.8	10.1	10.1	3.9	112.6	1.3
10. Sunshine Coast[a]	27.3	164.3	61.6	55.81	23.6	947.1	1.1

[a] Estimate only

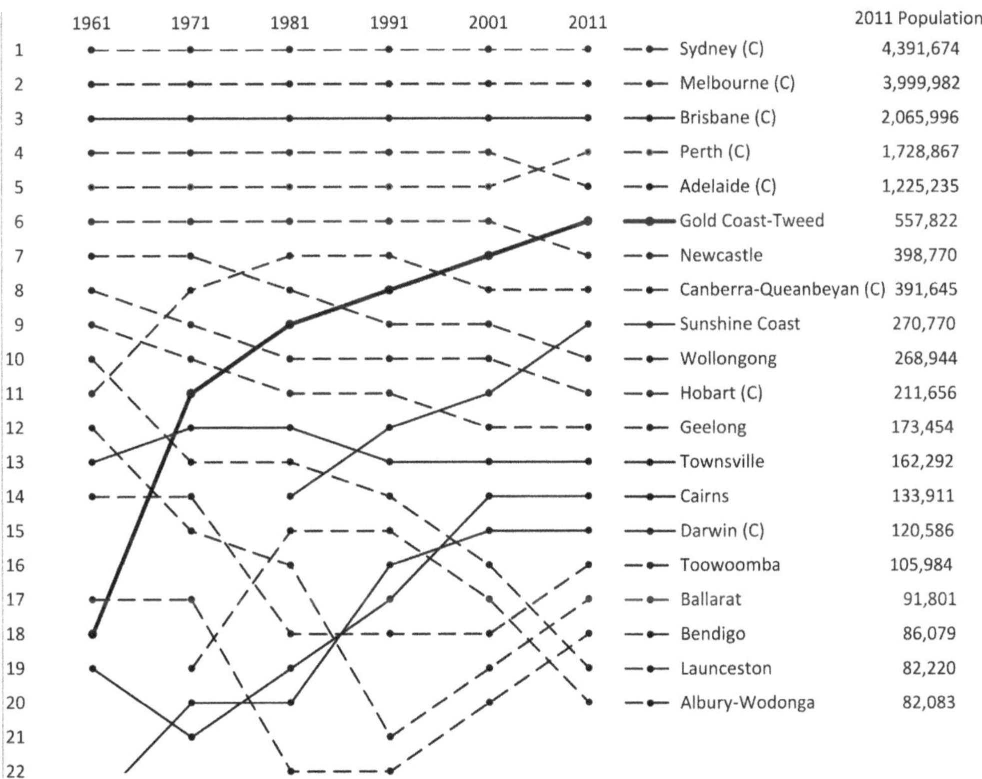

Fig. 1.1. Changes in the rank of Australia's 20 largest urban centres, 1961–2011. Capital cities are marked with (C) and solid lines indicate sunbelt cities. (Data sources: ABS 2008 (1961–2001), ABS 2013a (2011))

Table 1.2. Comparison of Gold Coast demographic structure with other Australian cities, Queensland and Australia[a]

Area	Annual population growth rate 2001–11 (%)[b]	Aged under 15 (%)	Aged over 55 (%)	Aged over 65 (%)	Median age	Population density (persons/km^2)[b]	Born overseas (%)	Internal migration (persons who lived at a different suburb 5 years ago) (%)[c]	Persons with post school qualifications of population aged 15 and over (%)[d]
Australia	1.6	19.3	25.6	14.0	37	-	30.2	34.5	45.1
Queensland	2.4	20.2	24.8	13.2	36	-	26.3	41.1	43.3
Brisbane GCCSA	2.3	20.1	22.6	11.8	35	918	23.1	42.0	44.8
Gold Coast-Tweed SUA	**2.8**	**18.4**	**27.5**	**15.7**	**38**	**553**	**33.2**	**44.7**	**45.5**
Sunshine Coast SUA	2.6	18.8	31.6	18.3	42	848	25.0	42.0	45.5
Sydney GCCSA	1.1	19.2	23.7	12.9	36	2037	40.1	33.1	48.1
Melbourne GCCSA	1.7	18.5	23.8	13.1	36	1566	31.0	34.3	47.0
Perth GCCSA	2.4	19.2	23.7	12.5	36	1213	40.4	39.5	46.6
Adelaide GCCSA	0.9	17.7	27.5	15.5	39	1374	29.8	33.0	44.2
Canberra-Queanbeyan SUA	1.5	18.7	21.4	10.6	34	1081	28.2	41.7	51.9
Greater Hobart GCCSA	0.9	18.8	28.2	15.4	39	1027	17.9	32.9	44.6

[a] ABS 2013b unless noted otherwise**:** Urban area statistics are for Greater Capital City Statistical Area (GCCSA) or Significant Urban Area (SUA),
[b] DIT MCU 2010, [c] DIT MCU 2012 These figures are based on 'urban centre' for capital cities and 'statistical sub-division' for regional cities, [d] ABS 2013a

excepting Townsville, which does not have a tourism-based economy – the Gold Coast–Tweed urban area shows the most remarkable rise, from eighteenth place in 1961 to sixth in 2011. With the exception of Darwin, the cities experiencing highest population growth are located in Queensland. The Gold Coast's growth is consistent with state and nation-wide trends. Examining the proportion of the Australian population living in major cities, the 2012 *State of Australian Cities* report (DIT MCU 2012) concluded that the rapid growth of the Gold Coast, the Sunshine Coast, and to a degree, Cairns and Townsville, reflects Australia's version of the sunbelt migration that swept much of the developed world in the 1960s and 1970s.

The Gold Coast's significance in the Australian landscape does not only stem from its role as a large and rapidly growing regional urban area, but also from being part of the wider conurbation of South East Queensland (Stimson and Minnery 1998), extending from Noosa to Tweed, which Peter Spearritt (2009, p. 87) has called 'the 200 km city'. He argues that the economies of the Gold Coast and the Sunshine Coast 'are no longer simply dependent on holidaymakers and retirees, but have merged into the wider metropolitan economy that now dominates this coastline' (Spearritt 2009, p. 88). At the centre of the conurbation, Brisbane played a crucial role during the early days of the Gold Coast as a source of tourists and daytrippers. The city's dependence on Brisbane has, though, greatly diminished. In 2011, 77.9% of all Gold Coast residents were working within the Gold Coast–Tweed area, with only 8.2% commuting to Brisbane and 9.6% working outside South East Queensland (City of Gold Coast 2013d). In recent years (2010–14) only 22–25% of overnight visitors to the Gold Coast were from Brisbane (Tourism Queensland 2010, 2011; Tourism and Events Queensland 2012, 2013, 2014).

Demographically, the Gold Coast is below the national and state averages in the percentage of population aged under 15 years, as one might expect. This proportion is only higher than that of Adelaide but is almost the same as Melbourne. Between 1996 and 2011, however, the Gold Coast and Cairns were the only major Australian cities not to experience declining numbers among children and youths aged 0–14, and likewise the Gold Coast and the Sunshine Coast for population aged 15–24 (DIT MCU 2012). The commonly held belief, fed by the aforementioned change in retirement circumstances, that the Gold Coast is a city with a larger than typical older population is not accurate. In 1981, 26% of the Gold Coast's population was aged 55 years or more (Mullins 1984) and this figure has not changed much since (26% in 2006 and 27.5% in 2011). Currently within 2% of the national average, it sits on a par with Adelaide and lower than Hobart and the Sunshine Coast. In fact, Hofmeister (1988, p. 151) reports that only 14% of residents were 65 years or older in the bicentennial year of 1988, which was only 4% higher than in Brisbane (since maintained at that level), and concludes that '[i]t was not, as assumed, a great influx of interstate retired people that made for the rapid growth of the Gold Coast'. Stimson and Minnery (1998, p. 212) question 'the validity of the popularly held view that "sunbelt" migration to the Gold Coast is dominated by retirees' and report that Gold Coast migration flows for the period from 1986 to 1991 are characterised by an increasingly balanced age distribution as well as a relative increase in the proportion of migrants with advanced qualification and higher incomes. The 2011 *State of Australian Cities* report (DIT MCU 2011) confirms that the age profile of the Gold Coast–Tweed area largely reflects Australian averages, with the population aged 65 or over currently at less than 2% above the national level. The median age (38) is lower than that of Hobart, Adelaide and the Sunshine Coast, and is only one year older than the national average. In fact, between 1996 and 2011, the Gold Coast was the only major Australian city where the proportion of the population aged 65 and over has declined (DIT MCU 2012). The Gold Coast is no longer 'God's waiting room' as once claimed in the *Gold Coast Bulletin* (Jones 1986, p. 71) but is getting younger, with younger people who are looking for opportunities moving in.

Data on population densities likewise tends to confound the city's popular image. The overall population density on the Gold Coast is lower than all the other cities against which it is compared. While parts of the Gold Coast, such as Surfers Paradise and Broadbeach–Mermaid Beach, have much higher densities (3728 and 3910 persons per square kilometre respectively, by statistical local area) and transit-oriented developments (TOD) such as Varsity Lakes are reaching 2475 persons per square kilometre (BITRE 2013), beyond the coastal strip and TOD areas the city reflects the historically dispersed, low-density pattern of urban development characteristic of South East Queensland.

The Gold Coast also has an increasing multicultural profile and is becoming a major destination for international immigrants. The percentage of residents born overseas increased from 27.6% in 2006 (Dedekorkut-Howes and Bosman 2011) to 33.2% in 2011 (ABS 2013b), which is much higher than the national and state averages and surpassed only by Sydney and Perth. The percentage of persons with post-school qualifications (45.5%) is higher than national and state levels and exceeds the levels of Adelaide, Brisbane and Hobart. Information on individual mobility, measured as the number of people who lived in a different suburb five years earlier, confirms the transient nature of the Gold Coast population, with the city claiming the highest percentage nationally. It is interesting to note, however, that the Sunshine Coast and Brisbane follow the Gold Coast closely in this indicator, and the comparatively higher percentages in Queensland and Perth suggest an alternative explanation for this trend: these areas are among the fastest growing in the country and are receiving constant streams of internal migration due to the job opportunities they offer. In 2010 and 2011, the Gold Coast–Tweed region had the third highest net gain of domestic migrants after Perth and Newcastle, and was followed by the Sunshine Coast (DIT MCU 2013).

Economy

The Gold Coast is a classic sunbelt city, with its economy almost from the beginning being based on tourism and residential development. By the 1910 census almost 80% of employment in Southport was related to the tourism and building industries (Vader and Lang 1980) and little has changed since, with construction, retailing and service industries still underpinning the city's economy (see Table 1.3). Construction is the most productive industry in the city, generating $2593 million (12.2%) of the region's gross regional product, and also has the largest output (the total gross value of sales generated by the selected industry sector over the four quarters of the selected financial year), generating $8393 million in 2013/14 (City of Gold Coast 2015) – a dominance of construction industries typical of sea change cities (DIT MCU 2010). In the same time period, the retail sector was the city's largest employer, generating 35 363 local jobs.

Its economy, however, rests squarely on tourism. The Gold Coast attracted more than 11 million visitors in the 12 months to September 2014. Of these, 62.3% were domestic day visitors. The number of daytrip visitors to the Gold Coast in 2012/13 increased by 2.4% and overnight visitors decreased by 4.6% compared to the previous year. Of the total 4 234 000 overnight visitors, 19% were international, 40% were interstate and 41% were intrastate (Tourism and Events Queensland 2014). With regular services to destinations throughout South-East Asia and New Zealand, the Gold Coast Airport at Coolangatta is Australia's fourth busiest international airport (Gold Coast Airport 2010).

Table 1.3. Industry sector contribution to the Gold Coast City 2013/14 (City of Gold Coast 2015)

Industry rank[a]	Sector	Value added ($M)	Per cent of gross regional product	Per cent of total employment
1	Construction	2593.4	12.2	10.4
2	Health care and social assistance	2165.2	10.1	12.7
3	Manufacturing	1830.1	8.6	7.3
4	Retail trade	1642.6	7.7	14.6
5	Financial and insurance services	1558.4	7.3	2.2
6	Education and training	1362.6	6.4	7.7
7	Wholesale trade	1345.1	6.3	3.9
8	Accommodation and food services	1260.1	5.9	9.8
9	Rental, hiring and real estate services	1255.8	5.9	2.5
10	Professional, scientific and technical services	1250.1	5.9	6.4
11	Public administration and safety	935.7	4.4	3.7
12	Transport, postal and warehousing	900.3	4.2	3.8
13	Administrative and support services	753.5	3.5	4.5
14	Information media and telecommunications	633.3	3.0	1.4
15	Electricity, gas, water and waste services	524.4	2.5	0.7
16	Arts and recreation Services	440.9	2.1	3.3
17	Mining	163.9	0.8	0.3
18	Agriculture, forestry and fishing	102.5	0.5	0.3
	Other services	620.8	2.9	4.5
	TOTAL	**21 338.7**	**100**	**100**

[a] Industry rank is by per cent gross regional product

Nevertheless, Mullins's (1990, 1991) observations that a large tourism economy tends to have a high proportion of low paid service jobs, resulting in overall low incomes and high rates of unemployment, bears out in the Gold Coast case. Table 1.3 illustrates the predominance of service jobs in the city's economy. Median household income and average taxable income are below national and state averages (see Table 1.4); unemployment data show that the city is less stable in this respect than other Australian cities. In 2009, the unemployment rate was below the national average, as well as that of the metropolitan centres of Sydney and Melbourne, and was much improved from the period from 1976 to 1986 when it had reached 16%, almost double the rates of Brisbane and Sydney (Mullins 1990). However, by 2011 the unemployment rate was again up to 7.5%, the highest among all areas compared. Mullins (2000) explains these fluctuations in terms of the seasonality of tourism industry and the wildly fluctuating construction industry, which is highly susceptible to economic shifts at regional and national levels. The drop in the number of dwelling unit approvals from 7130 in 2007 to 2776 in 2011 doubtless contributed to rising unemployment (ABS 2013c). The number of building approvals on the Gold Coast in proportion to its population is, however, among the highest in the nation. The number of tourist

Table 1.4. Comparison of Gold Coast economic indicators with other Australian cities, Queensland and Australia[a]

Area	Unemployment rate 2009 (%)[b]	Unemployment rate 2011 (%)	Service jobs (clerical, trade, service, sales) 2006 (%)	Median weekly household income 2011 ($)	Average taxable income 2008 ($)[b]	Building approvals (total dwelling units) per 1000 (2009)[b]	Hotel motel serviced apartments (5 or more rooms) per 10 000 (2009)[b]
Australia	5.0	5.6	48.0	1234	53 603	6.06	2.79
Queensland	4.4	6.1	49.4	1235	50 591	6.54	3.48
Brisbane	5.9	5.9	48.7	1388	52 909	6.31	1.12
Gold Coast	**4.9**	**7.5**	**53.6**	**1125**	**48 485**	**8.53**	**3.53**
Sunshine Coast	5.3	7.1	52.8	1011	46 236	8.43	5.63
Sydney	5.6	5.7	46.2	1447	60 617	3.11	0.97
Melbourne	5.0	5.5	47.3	1333	54 813	7.98	0.98
Perth	3.7	4.8	50.1	1459	59 095	8.38	0.73
Adelaide	5.9	5.8	50.0	1106	49 674	6.98	1.09
Canberra	2.9	3.5	46.0	1891	59 575	8.17	1.71
Greater Hobart	4.2	5.7	51.3	1065	47 926	6.78	3.49

ABS 2013b unless noted otherwise: [a] Urban area statistics are for Greater Capital City Statistical Area or Significant Urban Area, [b] ABS 2010 accommodations in proportion to population is likewise much higher than in most Australian cities, even if on a level with Queensland as a whole and much lower than the smaller city-region of the Sunshine Coast.

The Gold Coast's heavy economic reliance on tourism and construction has left the city vulnerable to boom and bust cycles. The effects of national and global economic shocks have been observed in the city in recent years (City of Gold Coast 2013a). Recognising the vulnerability of the city's narrow economic base dependent on the success of tourism and construction industries, the Gold Coast's *Economic Development Strategy 2013–23* has aimed to diversify the economic base of the city into other sectors, such as education and health (City of Gold Coast 2013a). This increasingly diverse economic base is reflected in the increased contribution to the gross regional product by health care and social assistance, education and training sectors, and both retail and wholesale trade (City of Gold Coast 2015). Such initiatives as the Gold Coast Health and Knowledge Precinct, described as a fully integrated health, medical, technology, research and innovation centre for learning, innovation, knowledge creation and commercialisation; the Robina Health Precinct; and the Varsity Lakes Business and Innovation Precinct (Business GC 2013) have lent structural support to these rising sectors. Looking forward, the Southport Priority Development Area aims to position Southport as the central business district of the Gold Coast, addressing a long-standing sense that a city without a centre is no city at all.

Urban development

Back to history. With its developmentally driven growth, the Gold Coast exemplifies Harvey Molotch's (1976) growth machine theory. Among the reasons for the rapid growth that the Gold Coast has experienced is the coincidence of a pro-development Queensland Government (Morris 2004) with pro-growth populist local politics (Mullins 1979, 1984). Mullins (1984) further argues that the Gold Coast's rapid development occurred through the entrepreneurial initiatives of the local 'petit bourgeoisie' and small-scale capitalists. Among their activities, land speculation looms large in the Gold Coast's image.

From the 1930s, domestic tourism in Australia was stimulated by the prosperity of a modernising economy and a growing cultural attachment to the outdoors, to the beach in particular. The Gold Coast benefited from these trends, which bolstered land speculation among developers who tapped into Australia's post-war prosperity to feed a widespread desire to own a holiday house by the beach. This trend towards second home ownership stimulated the development of construction industries and property services, and their high concentration on the Gold Coast in particular seeded the city's decades-long property boom. By the end of the 1959 financial year – the year in which the Gold Coast received its charter – the value of Gold Coast building approvals had set an Australian record (*The South Coast Bulletin* 1959), a position the city has maintained with relative consistency throughout the second half of the twentieth century.

The city's image began to change dramatically in the early phases of this boom. Until that moment the Gold Coast (or, better, South Coast) had been 'Brisbane's traditional seaside resort' (McRobbie 1984, p. 81). There was nothing fancy or flash about the place; it was an affordable escape (Davidson and Spearritt 2000). The beaches offered adequate camping grounds and many of the holidaymakers participated in communal games and festivities (Condon 2003). But in the setting of widespread property speculation and in the wake of a 'recreation' culture left by Australian and Pacific servicemen during World War Two, Surfers Paradise was, by the early 1950s, criticised as 'tawdry, vulgar, [a] clip joint, millionaire's mile, garish, brassy, Americanised' (McRobbie 1982, p. 81). Architect and critic Robin Boyd argued in 1960 that it exemplified the new and troubling advent of 'Austerica' (Boyd 1960, p. 71). This image was fuelled in part by the extended opening hours of shops and cinemas, which were restricted elsewhere in the state (or country) (McRobbie 1982). In 1965, the local council installed parking meters in Surfers Paradise, to which the local progress association responded by introducing Meter Maids who were charged with inserting coins into meters that were running out of money. These girls, clad in gold lamé bikinis, became a symbol of the city and its tone. Alongside them, surfing legends and legendary 'pyjama parties' helped to consolidate the Gold Coast's saucy reputation (Davidson and Spearritt 2000; McRobbie 1984). According to the editors of a special Gold Coast issue of *Architecture in Australia* (1959, p. 47) these practices contributed to 'a chaos of the worst type of commercialisation ... [and] ... a wild jungle of indecorum'.

As for the populous, so too for the city: the changes to the Gold Coast's physical form were rapid and significant, especially along the Pacific edge. Many of the summer and weekend homes that had been economically constructed along the coast in timber, iron and fibro-cement sheeting were demolished and replaced with motels, which were soon thereafter demolished in turn and replaced by higher yield towers containing apartments and hotel units. Ann Green (1982, n.p.), a local Gold Coast resident at the time, writes of this phenomenon:

> *[When] the American inspired Motel craze hit the coast in the late 1950s ... peppering our already littered highways with neon-lighted promises of tea-bag [convenient, standardised] accommodation the Coast's wonderful old guest houses went into gradual decline, and with them the last traces of Australian individuality.*

The motel phase was soon overtaken by the growing popularity of apartment accommodation. The new modern 'American' serviced apartments proved so popular that many other holiday accommodation types, including the rapidly dated Googie style in which roadside motels were draped, were left vacant for much of the year (Burchill 2005; McRobbie 1984). This change of use proved significant in years to come. As land on the coastal strip became scarce and property prices soared, these humble holiday units, by now homes mostly to elderly pensioners, became the focus of the economic growth machine and were fodder for entrepreneurs and developers.

During the 1960s and 1970s there were no effective town planning schemes in place to deal sufficiently with the extent and pace of growth on the Gold Coast. Development approval was gained, for the most part, by obtaining a 'single' and 'simply granted' development permit (Burchill 2005, p. 126) regardless of infrastructure issues such as adequate water supply, sewage disposal, urban context or road amenity. Consequently, new residential estates flourished in the Nerang area, together with a boom in the commercial, service and light industries. Because of the size of the LGA during the 1960s and 1970s boom years, then mostly limited to the coastal strip, land was at a premium and developers – known as the 'white shoe brigade' and whose reputations were not always without blemish – increasingly looked beyond the city's official limits for residential development opportunities. Nerang and environs, and in particular the Nerang River floodplains, were perfectly located to accommodate the ever expanding development push from the Gold Coast city proper. The 1974 floods put a temporary stop to development along the Nerang River floodplains. Geoff Burchill (2005, p. 218) describes this period of growth and the effects it had on the township of Nerang, which was replicated in various ways on several inland settlements:

> *Fried egg shopping centres [a retail yolk with car-park whites] were built on both sides of the river. In less than 10 years, Nerang changed from being a genuine country small town with a saddler, a feed store and a pet vet that served hinterland farmers and rural residents.*

By the 1980s the opening of the international airport, the proliferation of high-rise hotels and residential towers, and the development of extensive canal estates along the length of the coast consolidated the Gold Coast as a landscape of consumption (Stimson and Minnery 1998). The opening up of the Gold Coast to foreign visitors also stimulated the rise of unparalleled international investment in the city's property sector. By the 1990s the city had established itself as 'simultaneously brash, trendy, sophisticated, relaxed, overdeveloped and overurbanised' (Stimson *et al.* 1996, p. 196). Its image is one of spectacle, hedonistic consumption and competing moralities. But this was nothing new. As Jim Davidson and Peter Spearritt (2000, p. 146) observe, the Gold Coast continues 'to offer sun, sand and sex, as it has always done … [but the] marketing ploy of … the 1960s [has] been replaced with an aggressively commercial air, where shops and restaurants and accommodation providers [vie] with each other for market share'.

Structure of development and urban form

Mullins (1991, p. 331) defines tourism urbanisation as 'an urbanization based on the sale and consumption of pleasure', being marked by seven distinct features: it is spatially different; symbolically distinctive; distinguished by rapid population and labour force growth; operates as a flexible system of production; draws from a form of boosterist state intervention; demonstrates both mass and customised consumption of pleasure; and has a socially distinct resident population. This distinctiveness included a high population growth rate, relatively fewer children and greater numbers of elderly residents, higher residential densities and greater levels of transient residents; the population would evidence low job skills, concomitantly lower incomes and a high unemployment rate. Mullins found these characteristics to hold on the Gold Coast at the start of the 1990s, even if they have since shifted as we have seen.

In an essay, Mullins (1984) argued that hedonism, which is the locus of resort tourism, had fuelled the growth of the Gold Coast and resulted in a city unlike any other in Australia. He claimed that with its condominiums, canal estates, shops, restaurants, amusement centres and related infrastructure, the city had responded to mass tourism with a spatial organisation that encourages and promotes consumption. But just how different is the Gold Coast in reality?

The LGA covers a territory of 1333.8 km^2, less than a quarter of which is urban in nature. Architectural historian Philip Goad (1997) describes the city's urbanisation as a series of linear strips or bands that run parallel to the coastal edge: the beach strip, the high-rise tower or residential coastal strip, the highway strip, the canal estates, the suburbs, and the semi-rural hinterland (see Fig. 1.2). One of the reasons the Gold Coast is not perceived as a real city is its lack of a discernible centre, much less a formal central business district: 'there is no radial hub, only parallel zones that are separated by their function – the coastal tourist

Fig. 1.2. Looking north to Gold Coast coastal strip – Broadbeach and Surfers Paradise, 2013 (Image courtesy of Gold Coast Tourism)

strip, a belt for the suburban service class, and the "alternative" lifestyles and tourism of the hinterland behind this' (Holmes 2006, p. 112). In contrast to cities with a typical single dominant business centre – a natural concentration of high-rise buildings and administrative functions – it is a multi-precinct city with a distinctive urban form. It is strongly linear with a close alignment to its 57-km coastline, the north–south oriented Pacific Motorway running parallel further inland, bifurcating the city's westward sprawl, and the hinterland mountain ranges (Gold Coast City Council 2005). On the Gold Coast, the functions typical of city centres, such as government, law and cultural institutions are dispersed outside the dominant high-rise concentrations at Surfers Paradise and Broadbeach.

Parts of the Gold Coast may look similar to other cities at first glance, with the appearance of a distinct centre corresponding to the highest density evident on the beach edge. It makes for a surprising image when mapped against the expectations a visitor might bring to a city that has until recently been habitually viewed as a resort town of only half a million people. Rather than offices, however, this mini-Manhattan comprises residences and holiday rentals. Spearritt (2006, p. 61) reports that in 2006 the Gold Coast had 212 apartment blocks over 12 storeys high whereas the nearby capital of Brisbane – a sprawling, low-rise river city – had 'fewer than thirty'. The Gold Coast has the distinction of being home to the tallest residential tower in the southern hemisphere: the 322.5-m Q1 tower, built by the Sunland Group. When it was completed in 2005, Q1 was the tallest residential tower in the world until the completion of the Torch in Dubai in 2011 (CTBUH 2011).

The Gold Coast's development has long been a matter of 'firsts' and 'mosts'. Its design and tenure innovations include the development of Australia's first canal estates, which were approved in 1957 (McRobbie 1991) and contribute to the distinctive physical structure of the city as much as the high-rises. Australia's first gated community and master-planned resort, Sanctuary Cove, was established on the Gold Coast in 1986 (Coiacetto 2009a). The city was one of the pioneers of individually saleable strata-titled apartments, and home to the country's first timeshare developments. Australia's first private university, Bond University, was founded there in 1987. Dreamworld opened in 1981 as the country's first major home-grown theme park and 'Australia's answer to Disneyworld' (*Amusement Park Journal* 1985, p. 17). The Gold Coast is now the self-evident theme park capital of Australia, with a greater concentration of theme parks (17 in number), resorts and tourist-oriented shopping centres (32) than anywhere else in Australia (Holmes 2006) – including Australia's first mechanised water-skiing park, Cable-Ski Water Park (Holmes 2001), and the country's first and largest purpose-built factory outlet shopping centre, Harbour Town, which opened in 1999. It has the greatest retail area (in retail square meters) and the largest number of car parking spaces of any Australian city (Holmes 2001). According to Holmes (2001, p. 182) even though the Gold Coast replicates most of the features of large-city urbanisation, it is more distinguishable as a 'pleisure' (pleasure + leisure) landscape because here 'the salient features of this postmodern 'kitchscape' are assembled in a display more concentrated than anywhere else in Australia'.

Conclusions

The chapters that follow address a series of historical circumstances and factors that have informed the present-day form and character of the Gold Coast. The relationship they together describe, between history and the contemporary city, is not shared with any other Australian city in the same admixture, even if the forces at play on the Gold Coast are more than familiar to those readers with an eye on other urban settings. The popular assessment of the Gold Coast tends to rehearse several of its (relative) oddities: the relationship between tourism and urbanisation; its kitsch, postmodernism and bad taste; and its sunbelt growth. In spite of its growing importance in the national and international realm – as an idiosyncratic city with paradigmatic consequences for the Australian (and western) experience of rapid, developer-led urbanisation – the Gold Coast has largely escaped systematic research as a subject of urban and planning history. The authors whose work follows have together addressed this gap in our knowledge, bringing new rigour to known historical events and their connections within the city's history. They also draw a fresh assessment of established work into conversation with the increasingly fine-grained analyses of the Gold Coast to which the reader can now turn for further material on some of this book's themes.

The purpose of this book is to pose a simple question to which the answers are inevitably complex: what are the historical factors that have conspired, wittingly or otherwise, to produce the Gold Coast as we now know it?

The multi-focal historical lens with which the following pages address this question derives from a sustained investigation on the Gold Coast 'case' by a research community anchored to Griffith University's Urban Research Program and within it the Gold Coast Area Research Team (GoCART). The story they together tell will resonate with other world cities intended to one extent or another to parallel planning, economic, governmental and development histories, helping scholars to better assess the urbanisation and development that occurred on the Gold Coast. *Off the Plan* positions this city as a complex urban field that results from historical forces, both circumstantial and structural, intentional and accidental. The chapters that follow argue the value for the Gold Coast in looking back as it moves relentlessly forwards – in and of itself, but also as a model of rapidly evolving western urbanisation.

Authors' note

This essay revises and expands on Dedekorkut-Howes and Bosman (2015).

Chapter 2

All that glitters: an environmental history 'sketch' of Gold Coast City

Jason Byrne and Donna Houston

Since ancient times, most cities have been established in locations that possess natural attributes that are essential for the survival and wellbeing of their citizens. Such attributes have included harbours, permanent freshwater sources, forests, fertile agricultural land, building materials and defensible topography. More recently, however, some cities have seemingly transcended these biophysical limitations by exploiting resources found in 'hinterlands' that stretch hundreds or even thousands of kilometres from the urban core. Such cities ostensibly defy the biophysical constraints of the environments upon which they depend. Some of these cities, like Las Vegas, exist overtly for pleasure and commerce rather than industry or culture. Davis and Monk (2007) suggest they are underpinned by the production and marketing of distinctive environmental imaginaries of cornucopian abundance. In reality, these 'paradises' manifest ecological degradation, social polarisation and boom-bust growth. Could Australia's Gold Coast be this type of city?

Australia's Gold Coast City exemplifies a style of urban development that can readily be observed in other 'sunbelt cities' including Cancun, the Costa Del Sol, Miami and Waikiki, among others (Perry and Watkins 1977). These places are synonymous with seaside skyscrapers, palm trees, sandy beaches, ritzy hotels, marinas and boutique shopping malls. Moore (2005, p. 205) has argued that 'from its very inception [this city] was not meant to be taken seriously'; it was a place that was imagined into being, where nature was remade according to the dreams of property developers, speculators, entrepreneurs and holiday makers. This chapter seeks to peel back such a superficial characterisation of the Gold Coast to explore the (human) ecologies that scaffold its existence. By understanding some of the complex relationships between humans and the biophysical environments on which they depend, we can begin to take the Gold Coast seriously; we can see how ecological resilience and environmental damage are entangled in the material life of the city.

The purpose of this chapter is not to recreate the pre-European or pre-human environments that preceded the contemporary city, although we do sketch out a brief natural history. Nor does the chapter present a detailed environmental history of the Gold Coast; that would entail a longer discussion of place, time and scale than this short chapter can provide. Instead, we sketch out some 'pivotal' events in the historical relationship between people and their natural environment, and attempt to illuminate how past socio-ecological interactions have configured Gold Coast's contemporary form and function. We seek to better understand how people have previously imagined the city's environment – as a larder, a treasure trove, a paradise or a home – and how in turn this might (re)configure the future viability of Gold Coast City.

What is environmental history and why does it matter?

Environmental history is an interdisciplinary field dedicated to understanding how the interactions between humans and the biophysical environment have changed over time (Dovers 1994, p. 3). As Dovers notes, 'environmental history seeks to discover and explain the past' with specific attention to the meaning of nature, how humans interact with the environment and the socio-cultural processes that configure those interactions. In other words, environmental history seeks to uncover what the biophysical environment was like in the past, and how humans have changed that environment to make it the way it is today. These actions in turn enable or constrain present and future human activities (O'Connor 1997).

According to O'Connor (1997) environmental history seeks to illuminate four facets of environmental issues: (i) relations of power; (ii) changes in technologies of economic production and distribution; (iii) changes in socio-cultural structures and processes; and (iv) the outcomes of environmental contestation. Environmental history is thus attentive to environmental and social movements, the evolution of environmental regulation and to shifting 'patterns of ... settlement and governance' (Dovers in Brown *et al.* 2008, p. 5). Environmental history aims to 'trace the impact of people ... on the land' (Gaynor in Brown *et al.* 2008, p. 1) – and of land on people. It includes the study of responses to issues such as land degradation, water pollution, biodiversity loss, fisheries collapse and climate change, among others (see also Dovers in Brown *et al.* 2008). Environmental history, as Griffiths (2007) contends, gives us insights into the historical-cultural roots of contemporary environmental problems on the Australian continent. He writes, '[o]n such a continent we can never blithely assume the dominance of culture over nature, nor can we believe in the infinite resilience of the land' (Griffiths 2007, n.p.).

Much of environmental history is dedicated to understanding the hybridity of social and ecological relationships over time and space. This is what the geographer Steven Hinchliffe (2007) has called the 'co-production of nature and society'. Environmental history is not the same thing as natural history. Natural history is the study of plants, animals, landforms and earth processes over time – and has an evolutionary perspective (Archer *et al.* 1998). Natural history pre-dates humans. Environmental history on the other hand, seeks to understand the character and scale of transformations that humans have wrought upon the so-called 'natural world', and vice versa. Environmental history is oriented towards 'a deeper understanding' of past decision-making to 'help clarify choices and options' for the present and future (Schott 2004, p. 519). While environmental history requires some understanding of natural history, the task of environmental historians is to bring place-based stories of environmental and social change together (Griffiths 2007). As Griffiths (2007, n.p.) writes:

> *[s]cientists often argue for the need to overcome deficits of knowledge, but rarely ask why we do not act on what we know. Most constraints working against environmental change are cultural: we have to know ourselves as well as the country.*

Environmental historians have focused on cities (e.g. Cronon 1992), but this is an understudied topic in Australia. Environmental history can frame a historical perspective of urban development on the Gold Coast (and elsewhere) against the backdrop of the geographic and ecological conditions that have made urban development possible, and which configure the city's present morphology and future development trajectories (Brown *et al.* 2008). As Nix (1994, p. 199) observes, environmental history 'demands a knowledge of change in form and function, pattern and processes through space and time'. For Brown *et al.* (2008), the key questions include: 'how planning patterns determine land subdivision ... ; how housing and domestic lifestyles shape suburban areas; ... [how] transport patterns influence housing development ... [and how] changing understandings of the environment have impacted ... planning and development' (Brown in Brown *et al.* 2008, p. 12). Many of the chapters in this book address these sorts of questions. We will not replicate their work. Rather, we turn our attention to some 'pivotal moments' that have been formative in the Gold Coast's development. We sketch out the key biophysical aspects of the city and its hinterland, identify formative events in the city's environmental past and point to topics that warrant closer investigation in the future.

A concise biogeography of the Gold Coast

Geographers understand the physiography of a region as a type of palimpsest (McManus 2004), as a canvas that has been reinscribed multiple times. Geographers and environmental historians believe that landscapes catalogue generations of human activity (Marcucci 2000). As Dovers (in Brown *et al.* 2008, p. 4) observes, 'geological provenances determine production potential, vulnerability to erosion, and vegetation alliances' in landscapes, thus shaping urban pasts and futures.

The main physiographic characteristics of the present day Gold Coast have been shaped by many different land-forming processes – some relatively abrupt, such as volcanic activity, and others slow and gradual (e.g. littoral drift). Many of these land-forming process have created the city's current mineral resources, shaped the biota, and ultimately have determined areas suitable for agriculture and other land uses. Although difficult to imagine, the land that is now the balmy subtropical Gold Coast once faced south, not east, and was situated near the current position of Antarctica (~70 degrees south). Hundreds of millions of years ago, it lay at the bottom of an abyssal trench, off the coast of the supercontinent called Gondwana (Graham 2001). That supercontinent comprised the landmasses we now call Antarctica, Australia, Africa, South America and India (Archer *et al.* 1998).

About 180 million years ago, Gondwana began to rupture. As continents fragmented, basalt lavas were extruded from the sea floor; much of that former eroded sedimentary rock and volcanic basalt eventually became the bedrock of the present-day east coast of Australia (Taylor 1949). The sea floor was upthrust in places and fused with the Australian continental landmass. The location of Gondwana meant that ocean currents readily transferred heat from the equator to the poles, so it was lushly vegetated. Remnants of that vegetation (e.g. Antarctic Beech trees) can still be found in the Gold Coast's hinterland. Australia separated from New Zealand ~85 million years ago, and from Antarctica some 45 million years ago.

Fast forward to 20 million years before present: an important land-forming process began, as the east coast of Australia drifted over a 'hot spot' in the Earth's mantle – much like the hot spot driving the formation of the Hawaiian Island chain (Johnson *et al.* 1989, pp. 114–16; Graham 2001; Knesel *et al.* 2008). A key landmark in the Gold Coast hinterland, Mount Warning is a remnant of a massive shield volcano known as the Tweed shield volcano (see Fig. 2.1). That volcano was once almost 2000 m high and spanned the area from near Ballina in the south to Mount Tamborine in the north (~100 km long) and from

Fig. 2.1. Mount Warning (*c.* 1923), an ancient shield volcano, frames the physiographic context for the Gold Coast (State Library of Queensland, image 202277)

off the coast of Byron Bay in the east to an area west of Mount Lindsay (~70 km wide) (Graham 2001).

At the time of splintering from Antarctica, land now the east coast of Australia had a cool temperate climate. Coal deposits show that deciduous trees dominated the landscape, together with ferns and conifers. These slowly gave way to evergreen rainforests around 45 million years ago. Australia already had well-developed marsupial mammals at this time, including the relatives of bandicoots, koalas and marsupial lions. But as the landmass drifted north, the climate became subtropical (and even tropical during past warmer climates) (Archer *et al.* 1998).

Subtropical paleoclimates were punctuated by periods of both warmer and much colder temperatures (e.g. during periods of global glaciation) (Morley 1981). During ice ages, for instance, the temperature differential between the poles and the equator was much higher, generating hurricane-strength south-easterly winds that roared along the Australian coastline. Those winds produced characteristic landforms associated with the modern Gold Coast region. Because sea levels were much lower during the ice ages, exposed sandy sea floors became large sand plains; the strong prevailing winds whipped the sand into large dunes that abutted the rocky coastline. Some of these dunes are still visible today, in the form of sand islands, including North and South Stradbroke Island (Morley 1981). The action of wind and waves also concentrated heavy metals in the sediments washed off the landscape around the Clarence River in New South Wales, which were then consolidated along the present Gold Coast coastline by wind and later littoral drift. We return to this point when we discuss sand mining.

The present-day humid subtropical climate of the Gold Coast is one of the 'golds' that attracts people to the city. The hottest months of the year are in January and February with average temperatures of 29°C and the coolest average temperatures are in June and July with maximums of 21°C. Minimum average temperatures range from 12°C (July) to 22°C (February). The hottest temperatures during the summer months can reach almost 40°C and the coldest (night-time) temperatures approach zero in the winter months (Australian Bureau of Meteorology 2015). Rainfall averages range from a minimum of 44 mm in September to a maximum of 169 mm in February. Total yearly rainfall averages around 1259 mm (at the Gold Coast Seaway: latitude 27.94 degrees south; longitude 153.43 degrees east). Winds are predominantly from the south-east in summer and from the north in spring. The average maximum wind speed is ~25 km/h in summer falling to 13 km/h in winter (mostly south-west), with the highest wind speeds occurring during cyclones or east-coast low pressure systems. Wind speeds during such storms can exceed 120 km/h, with the highest recorded wind gust reaching ~139 km/h. Of course, there are marked regional variations due to topography and distance from the sea. There are also seasonal variations due to El Niño and La Niña variations in sea surface temperature, wind and associated moisture.

Just as there is an interaction effect between climate and landforms, so too is there an effect between landforms and biota (plants and animals). South East Queensland is one of the most biodiverse regions in the world. The wide variability in landforms and the region's location at the intersection of different climatic zones means that many species are at their northern and southern limits, overlapping in this region (Queensland Museum 2007).

Leiper *et al.* (2008) classify the landforms of the Gold Coast into dunes and headlands, tidal wetlands, freshwater wetlands, coastal heath, eucalypt forest, rainforest and mountain areas. Many of these landforms and drainage patterns are tied to the now extinct Tweed shield volcano. The landforms can be characterised as elevated plateaus around the volcano (Springbrook, Beechmont and Tamborine Mountain), steep mountainous terrain to the south (McPherson Range) and west (Darlington and Tamborine Ranges) and a narrow coastal plain punctuated by rocky headlands (Greenmount, Currumbin, Burleigh and Miami) – the latter are the remnant outcrops of ancient lava flows from the shield volcano. The coastal plain comprises sand that was deposited when sea levels were much higher in the past. A radial drainage system reflects the shape of the remnant volcanic caldera. Major rivers include the Tweed, Nerang, Coomera, Albert and Logan Rivers, with larger creeks including Mudgeeraba, Currumbin and Tallebudgera Creeks (Middleton and Roberts 1968).

The biota of the region is closely influenced by geology, topography and drainage systems. More than 4000 plant species exist in the bioregion, comprising 154 native plant communities or 'regional ecosystems'. Approximately 60% of these regional ecosystems are considered endangered, vulnerable or threatened due to land clearing, land and property development and past land use (South East Queensland Catchments n.d.). There are 1672 plant species that have been identified in the Gold Coast area. Of these, 93 species are considered rare, vulnerable or endangered. Moreover, of the 58 regional ecosystem types found in Gold Coast City, 24 of them (~41%) are considered poorly conserved (Gold Coast City Council 2009a). Prior to European invasion, many of the upland plateaus were covered in dense rainforest. The dunes and headlands are characterised by *Pandanus* (screw pine), *Casuarina* (she-oak) and *Banksia* trees – plants that are able to cope with stronger winds, salt spray and nutrient deficient sandy soils. Further inland, on the hind dune, away from the effects of wind and salt, *Eucalyptus*, *Acacia* (wattle), *Casuarina* and *Banksia* species form closed woodlands. Between dunes are wetlands and swamps, characterised by low shrubs (tea-trees), sedges and reeds, and trees such as *Melaleuca* species (paperbarks).

Where the rivers reach the ocean, there are a series of estuaries, such as the Gold Coast Broadwater and Currumbin Estuary. These estuaries were once fringed by mangroves, saltmarshes, she-oaks and paperbarks – depending upon tidal variations and associated levels of salinity. A large area of coastal heath (Wallum) once stretched from the present border with New South Wales all the way to Brisbane and beyond, covering much of the coastal plain. The heath was characterised by wetland species (including sedges, tea-trees and paperbarks) and dryland and woodland species (e.g. *Banksia*, *Casuarina*, *Acacia*). Along the rivers and creeks and near some of the headlands were patches of riparian and littoral rainforest and vine thickets, which included cabbage tree palms, Alexander palms, figs, bottlebrushes, ferns, mosses and lichens. Native grasses and *Eucalyptus* woodland covered the upland areas, between the coastal plain and the mountainous hinterland (Leiper *et al.* 2008).

As can be seen from the preceding broad description of plants, the region is floristically diverse. The combination of widely varied topography and plant communities provides a mosaic of habitats for a bewildering array of wildlife. Over 600 species of native animals have been identified on the Gold Coast. There are 50 species of freshwater fish, 36 species of amphibians, 70 species of reptile, 357 bird species and 91 mammal species. Of these, 53 species have been identified as threatened, vulnerable or endangered, including 3 freshwater fish (6%), 11 amphibian (30%), 9 reptile (13%), 22 bird (6%) and 8 mammal species (9%) (Gold Coast City Council 2009a). Countless more invertebrate species exist and we have very poor information about which species are rare, threatened or endangered. In the broader bioregion there are 60 species of land snails, 600 species of spiders, 30 species of freshwater molluscs, 80 species of dragonflies and damselflies, and 180 species of butterflies (Queensland Museum 2007).

Human occupation and environmental transformations

Environmental impacts are a function of the intensity of an event and the scale, frequency and duration of that event. They are also a function of the vulnerability of an ecosystem to disturbance, which in turn is configured by the life cycles and physiology of individual species – and their interactions with other species. The extent of an environmental impact results from how it affects the structure and function of ecosystems. A large meteor strike (such as the one that extirpated the dinosaurs) will be a cataclysmic global extinction event, due to its high intensity, broad scale and cascading collapses of global ecosystems, even though such events occur very infrequently. A storm or a severe fire will have high impacts too, but the effects are typically localised; recurrence intervals are usually infrequent. This typically gives ecosystems time to recover. Unlike pre-European invasion impacts, modern anthropogenic environmental impacts tend to be high intensity, high frequency, broad scale and long duration, lasting decades or even centuries, causing long-term ecological harm.

The archaeological record suggests that Aboriginals arrived in Australia some 60 000 years before present (Mulvaney and Kamminga 1999). Prior to European invasion, the Aboriginal population in South East Queensland was likely in the tens of thousands (Adam 1994) but absence of archaeological evidence means this can only be inferred. As explained in earlier sections, climatic shifts resulted in very large fluctuations in sea level during the time period of Aboriginal occupation. Past shorelines may have been as far as two kilometres eastwards of the present coastline. When sea levels rose after the last glacial maximum (some 6000 years ago), many coastal Aboriginal sites, such as hamlets, ceremonial stone circles, fish traps, rock art cave dwellings and burial grounds, would have been submerged (Adam 1994).

The existing archaeological evidence suggests that the Gold Coast area has been continuously occupied by Aboriginal peoples for many thousands of years (at least some 5000–8000 years before present) (Walters *et al.* 1987; Walters 1992). The region is the traditional homeland of the Kombumerri, Wangerriburra, Minjunbal, Gugingin and Numinbah peoples, the traditional owners of this part of Australia (Horton 1994). Several notable archaeological sites exist in the Gold Coast area, including bora rings, middens and burial grounds. An Aboriginal cemetery in Broadbeach Waters is at least 1000 years old (it was disturbed first by illegal sand excavation then later by the development of canal estates in the 1960s) (Mulvaney and Kamminga 1999, p. 282).

Aboriginal people thrived on the abundant natural resources offered by the Gold Coast and had semi-permanent settlements. Resources included rich fishing grounds, shellfish beds, timbered flood plains and lushly vegetated highlands. Indeed, we can characterise the natural environment of the region as the second kind of 'gold' (following climate) that made the area so attractive to humans. Aboriginal subsistence practices had relatively limited impact upon the natural environment compared to the damage that has occurred since European invasion. They included the gathering shellfish, fishing (including stone fish traps), cutting trees and scrub to make shelters, fashioning tools from timber and stone, and burning vegetation to attract game. This limited impact is mostly because Aboriginal people had an ethic of taking only what was needed to sustain them, and the low intensity and diffuse character of their impacts gave ecosystems time to adjust to these pressures (e.g. fire regimes) (Best and Barlow 1997).

Aboriginal subsistence patterns followed seasonal variations. From April to July, fish were (and still are) abundant – especially whiting, bream, tarwhine and catfish (Alfredson 1984). Mullet, salmon and tailor were especially plentiful in the cooler months around June and July through to September, spawning in the estuaries (Hall 1984; Graham 2001). There are accounts of Aboriginal people working in partnership with dolphins to catch mullet (Hall 1984). Aboriginal people also hunted dugong, and gathered turtles and crustaceans, such as freshwater crayfish and lobsters, as well as eels. The tubers and rhizomes of bungwall ferns and bracken ferns as well as yams provided a staple source of food on the coastal plain, and bunya pine nuts were a staple food in the hinterland (Mulvaney and Kamminga 1999; Graham 2001). Fruits and nuts included 'wild ginger, midyim berries, native olives, figs, palm hearts and macrozamia nuts' (Graham 2001, p. 203). Large shell middens attest to the abundance of shellfish, including oysters, mussels, cockles, eugaries (common pipi) and whelks. Seasonal variation in diet included fruit bats, goannas, carpet snakes, mud crabs and land snails. Aboriginal people also hunted koalas, kangaroos, pademelon, wallabies and possums, as well as waterfowl (Alfredson 1984; Adam 1994).

It would be naive to suggest that Aboriginal people did not impact the environment of the Gold Coast area. Although they did not extirpate species like Europeans have, the use of fire, to create pastures for game such as kangaroos, shaped to flora of the region. Aboriginal people also shaped the contemporary transportation routes as many European roads simply followed Aboriginal tracks. Aboriginal biogeographies of the Gold Coast, while severely altered by European colonisation, continue to shape the environmental history of the region. Indeed, parts of the Gold Coast area are subject to a native title claim by the Gold Coast Native Title Group, recognising customary and procedural rights derived from continuous connections to Aboriginal country.

European invasion dramatically transformed the area we now call the Gold Coast. The first European settlement occurred in the early 1840s, when timber getters crossed into Queensland from New South Wales. Between 1842 and 1889, the logging camps of the timber getters grew into small hamlets and then into villages and towns (Hajdu 1993). We

Fig. 2.2. Bullock drays hauling red cedar logs near Canungra, *c.* 1920s (Image reproduction courtesy of the Gold Coast City Council Local Studies Library, image number LS–LSP–CD073–IMG0086)

consider four key environmental transformations: cedar cutting, agriculture, mining, and tourism and property development.

Cedar cutting

European colonisers were first attracted to the area we now call the Gold Coast by red cedar trees (*Cedrela toona*), once called 'red gold' (Adam 1994). The timber was highly valued for its termite resistance and durability. Cedar was used for furniture, musical instruments, building construction and ornamentation (e.g. wood panelling), and even for constructing railway carriages and ships (Douglas 1975; Frawley 1990). Early timber cutters stripped vast quantities of cedar from the rainforests and caused significant ecological damage. Because cedar was irregularly interspersed among other rainforest trees, timber cutters initially hand-felled the giant trees, and then dragged the logs into nearby rivers to float them downstream. Some, though not all, logs would be recovered from the estuarine waters and transferred offshore to ships to be transported to domestic and international markets. As the technology changed, and the readily accessible cedar was logged out, bullock drays were used to move large logs to the rivers or to sawmills, later to be replaced in places like Canungra by a tramway (see Fig. 2.2).

The environmental impacts of cedar cutting are diverse. Because we lack historical data about the harm caused by early logging practices, they must be inferred. Impacts were large-scale. They likely included the spread of weeds, soil compaction and erosion, desiccation of soils from wind and sun exposure and the disruption of ecological communities. Some of these impacts would have been short-lived when the logging was limited to isolated trees. But as large-scale clearing occurred, it would have caused severe and long-term harm. For instance Joyce (1966, p. 8) writes that during the life of the Canungra tramway, it 'carried 128 million super feet of timber' to sawmills. The cedar-getters had two lasting impacts on the present city. First, they opened up the hinterland, using the river systems, then roads and rail for transport; second, they provided the impetus for permanent European settlement.

Agriculture

Agrarian pursuits followed logging of the rainforests. The primary agricultural pursuits were farming sugarcane and cotton and dairying, but livestock grazing was common too (Gold Coast City Council 2007). Potatoes, pumpkins and maize were also cultivated (Middleton and Roberts 1968). Some sugarcane plantations still exist in the city's hinterland, but they are becoming less economically viable. Following the opening of the railway to Brisbane, dairying was pursued more intensively. Large areas of land were cleared on the coastal plain and in the foothills for pasture. From the 1950s, other crops were introduced including arrowroot, bananas, avocados, pawpaws (papayas) and macadamia nuts. Agriculture produced large-scale environmental impacts through the broadscale clearing of vegetation, including sediment export to waterways, the spread of weeds and habitat destruction (we can see some of these impacts in Fig. 2.1). The rate and intensity of clearing increased markedly post World War Two, following increased mechanisation and population growth. This, in turn, markedly increased biodiversity loss. Multiple habitat types were affected because clearing occurred across scrublands, woodlands and rainforests.

Mining

In 1878, gold was discovered in the black mineral sands along the shoreline of the Gold Coast, from Coolangatta to the mouth of the Nerang River. Wind and wave action concentrated the gold, together with tin and platinum and heavy minerals – zircon, rutile and ilmenite. At this early time, prospectors were only interested in the gold. The sand seams were estimated at ~20 cm thickness, yielding up to 25 g of gold per week of mining (Morley 1981). However, by the 1920s, mineral sands had been recognised as a new resource. A private company obtained a mining permit from the Coolangatta Shire Council and commenced mining at Tugun in 1928. Mining was labour intensive and remained small scale, relying on horse and cart transport along the sandy beaches. Later transport was via small trucks pulled by a diesel locomotive along tracks on the sand.

Prospecting intensified along the Gold Coast beaches between 1934 and 1941, and the Nerang Shire Council granted mining consent to multiple companies in 1941. The outbreak of World War Two and a burgeoning demand for zircon and rutile (used in aircraft manufacturing and later in weapons systems) saw the intensification of mining on the beaches around Burleigh. Bulldozers, dredges and skid-mounted concentrators were used to mine the beaches and sand dunes (see Fig. 2.3). From 1942 to 1954, all the Gold Coast beaches from The Spit to Burleigh, and from Coolangatta to Tallebudgera Creek were extensively mined for mineral sands. Vegetation was cleared from sand dunes and deep excavations tore up the beaches. Mining extended inland into areas of coastal heath and littoral rainforest. Australia became the world's leading producer or zircon and rutile. By 1950, reserves had been discovered at South Stradbroke Island. With the outbreak of the Korean War, demand for the minerals grew and mining operations intensified, becoming increasingly mechanised.

Up to this time, there had been no environmental conditions imposed on mining permits, but from the early 1950s onwards, the Queensland Department of Mines began to require rehabilitation by seeding mined dunes with grasses (Morley 1981). In many areas,

Fig. 2.3. Conzinc sand dredging on Stradbroke Island, Queensland, 1957 (Photograph by Wolfgang Sievers. National Library of Australia, nla.pic-vn3295796)

such as Broadbeach, once mining was completed the Queensland Government subdivided the land and sold off allotments to property developers. As these seams ran out, mining shifted to South and North Stradbroke Islands. Even the current sites of the Oasis Shopping Centre (Broadbeach) and the Gold Coast Airport (Tugun) were mined during the height of the mineral sands boom. From the mid-1950s onwards, there was a slowly building opposition to mineral sand mining by local residents and tourists. Protests began to escalate in the late 1960s and early 1970s and by the 1980s mining had virtually ceased.

The environmental impacts from mineral sand mining have been extensive. Dune vegetation was cleared, mobilising sand and exposing beaches to extensive erosion during storms. Rehabilitation efforts were rudimentary by today's standards and caused further harm through the introduction of noxious weeds. The 'restoration' of the beaches after mining also changed the profile of the dunes, making them more vulnerable to erosion from large storms. There is widespread evidence of this from photographs during the late 1960s and early 1970s, which show that many beaches lost almost all their sand, and houses, roads and other infrastructure crashed into the sea.

Tourism and property development

From the middle of the twentieth century the city attracted entrepreneurs, who opened a range of tourist attractions such as wildlife parks and marine attractions, as well as shop-

Fig. 2.4. Urban intensification on the coastline, Surfers Paradise *c.* 1970 (National Archives of Australia, image 11415262)

ping malls and up-market hotels. Property development has been a source of great wealth, giving the city its name, because developers saw it as 'the gold coast' where land sales provided easy money (see Fig. 2.4). The development of Surfers Paradise in the 1950s and the beginning of the first canal estates saw extensive environmental degradation. The canal estates, in particular, resulted in the widespread clearing and filling of mangrove wetlands, which reduced biofiltration and destroyed fish nurseries. Closed-ended canals had low oxygen levels and this caused 'dead zones' at the bottom of those canals. The period from the 1970s onwards saw increasing numbers of international tourists, a trend that gained momentum during the 1980s and 1990s. New developments during this time included a casino, theme parks and the opening of a movie production studio. Around this time, land and property developers also began to market the Gold Coast as a 'lifestyle destination', and large-scale residential developments, including canal estates and golf course estates, permanently transformed the landscape of the city (Stimson and Minnery 1998). Tourism was accompanied by increased water consumption and generated waste that required more landfills. Golf courses destroyed wetlands and woodlands and provided little habitat.

More recently, the primary form of environmental impact has been from rapid urbanisation. As Fig. 2.4 illustrates, growth has advanced along the coastline and inland waterways, removing littoral rainforest and filling flood plains, replacing them with houses, high-rise apartments, hotels, roads, parking lots, shopping centres, canal estates and the like. Industrial development though has been limited. Environmental impacts have included coastal erosion, sedimentation of estuaries, surface and groundwater pollution, aquifer drawdown, nutrient enrichment of waterways, weed invasion, heavy metal export, land clearing and light pollution among other problems.

The environmental movement

Kellow and Niemeyer (1999) observe that the Gold Coast, like Queensland generally, has tended to be politically conservative. The distributed population and economic reliance upon primary industries, mining and tourism have been drivers of conservative politics. Although early national parks protected some hinterland habitats, there has been limited environmental activism during much of the city's history. Only in the late 1970s did residents begin to protest the clearing of native vegetation (mainly rainforests) and the mining of mineral sands. The state government has been reliant on resource exploitation since the Queensland colony was established, and there were few government agencies that had any environmental functions until the mid to late 1980s. Indeed, for most of Queensland's history, the state has been either apathetic or hostile towards the environment, for example, resisting attempts to end sand mining on the offshore sand islands, to establish world heritage protection of rainforests, and more recently to manage carbon pollution and address climate change. Incredible as it may seem, the systematic mapping and scientific study of the region's ecosystems did not begin until the early 1990s.

Since the late 1990s, the Gold Coast City Council (GCCC) has begun to engage with environmental issues. For instance, in 1997 the GCCC prepared a state of the environment report, which revealed that many of the taken-for-granted environmental attributes of the city were becoming threatened by poorly planned development (Thomas 1997). Council's subsequent corporate plan (1998) embraced sustainable development as an overarching goal for the city. Not long after, the GCCC prepared a Local Agenda 21 Action Plan to steer the city to a path of more ecologically sustainable development (Anonymous 2000).

Since then, Council has prepared several plans and strategies that support the goal of sustainability, including a nature conservation strategy (1998, rev. 2009), a sustainability advocacy strategy (2006) and a climate change strategy (2009). Perhaps most telling though, in early 2007, Gold Coast Mayor Ron Clarke stated that he wanted to make the Gold Coast a 'zero greenhouse gas emissions city by 2017' (Barnes 2007). The mayor's goal reflected a growing realisation that Gold Coast city is extremely vulnerable to the impacts of climate change – especially to the threats posed by increasing intensity of storm events (cyclones) and rising sea levels (Byrne *et al.* 2009). The former mayor's vision also reflects a changing sentiment among Gold Coast residents and decision-makers, that the city is not just a glamorous tourist destination or lifestyle residential resort. The city's subtropical environment is special and warrants protection. This is echoed by the establishment of community environmental organisations such as the Gold Coast and Hinterland Environment Organisation (GECKO) in the 1990s and, more recently, the Save Our Spit Alliance, fighting plans to build a cruise ship terminal and hotel complex on The Spit or Wave Break Island.

Conclusions

Reading about the past environments that characterised the Gold Coast area at the time of European invasion, it is hard not to feel a profound sense of loss. Wildlife-filled littoral rainforests and mangrove-fringed wetlands have given way to coastal skyscrapers, strip malls, canal estates, theme parks and golf courses. Nonetheless, parts of the city still harbour surprisingly high levels of endemic biodiversity. Environmental history tells us that landscapes are in a state of constant flux. We cannot 'freeze' ecologies in time, nor should we try to do so. But we also need to recognise the value of ecosystem structures and functioning, and must seek to maintain their integrity.

Looking at Chicago's gold coast (Zorbaugh 1929), Spain's Costa del Sol, Mexico's Baja peninsula and Florida's Fort Lauderdale, we can see a type of urban development that is irrevocably dependent upon exploitation of waterside natural environments for hedonistic pleasure, tourism, land and property development, and conspicuous consumption. Particular environmental imaginaries have made such places 'golden' in the eyes of their developers, visitors and residents. The environmental problems facing these and other 'gold coasts' stem from similar historical patterns of urban development, which have concentrated wealth in risky places (prone to earthquakes, tsunamis, hurricanes, flooding and/or landslides) and failed to recognise the value of local ecosystems. Urban environmental histories of gold coasts can illuminate how these places interact with the ecological processes that have shaped them.

From our cursory examination of the environmental history of the Australian Gold Coast we can see how some early patterns of development have locked the city into a form of 'path dependence'. The mining of mineral sands and subsequent development of residential and commercial land uses on the primary dunes have heightened erosion of the coastline, and exposed valuable assets to damage and loss. Local government has been locked into spending ever-increasing sums to 'protect' these assets through sand-bypassing, groynes, rock walls and other interventions. Rather than buying back vulnerable properties and zoning the primary dunes for parks and recreation, the city allows intensification of development on the coast and in flood plains, leaving populations and assets exposed to future harm and the municipality exposed to potential legal action. The building of canal estates on mangrove wetlands ultimately reduced the value of the coastal fishery and created a flood risk. The protection of sugarcane lands in the 1980s and the decision to develop the northern growth corridor of the city on some of the last remaining koala habitat is now threatening the future survival of that species. And as sugar prices have plummeted, the city has been left with low-value cane land, which could have been developed instead. The clearing of native vegetation has threatened many species, reduced the capacity of the city to sequester carbon, and has increased urban temperatures.

The struggle between civic boosters and property developers on the one hand and ordinary residents and environmentalists on the other, which characterises the contemporary Gold Coast, portends a future of environmental conflict. Current environmental contestations include: some residents' efforts to rid their suburbs of flying foxes (fearful that these animals will spread Hendra virus); battles over proposals to develop a cruise ship terminal and hotel-casino complex on public land; efforts to protect local parks threatened by municipal 'asset rationalisation'; protests over the removal of weedy camphor laurel trees (cherished by some residents); conflict over attempts to develop the remaining areas of coastal flood plain; and concerns about bull sharks in residential canals, which threaten drunken swimmers or property owners' pets.

As we noted in the introduction to this chapter, environmental history attempts to illuminate: (i) relations of power; (ii) changes in technologies of economic production and distribution; (iii) changes in socio-cultural structures and processes; and (iv) outcomes of environmental contestation. Limited space has precluded attention to all of these important aspects of the Gold Coast's history. Future research will need to fully investigate many important issues, including: the evolution of coastal planning, the development of a professional environmental workforce, changes in local and state government environmental policy and institutional apparatus, examination of how new technologies have shifted environmental relations (e.g. better knowledge of impacts due to technologies such as remote sensing), and a comprehensive reconstruction of patterns of urban growth and their impacts on habitats, ecosystems, coastal processes, hydrology and environmental awareness. The future of environmental protection and management of Gold Coast City might not yet be 'golden', but we have the opportunity to learn valuable lessons from the past and to take seriously the unique environmental histories of an urbanising coastal plain.

Chapter 3

Holidaying on the Gold Coast

Noel Scott, Sarah Gardiner and Ayşın Dedekorkut-Howes

Since the 1980s, the Gold Coast has consistently ranked as the third most popular destination among Australian cities for domestic travellers (after Melbourne and Sydney) and fourth or fifth most popular destination for international travellers. Tourism has been and remains central to the development of the city of Gold Coast: it is the main economic activity and source of employment within the city. In 2013, tourism sustained more than 30 000 direct jobs in the city, and directly contributed $4.7 billion to the economy (City of Gold Coast 2014a), demonstrating its importance to the Gold Coast.

Tourism has also directly influenced the Coast's urban landscape, with the numerous high-rise buildings along the coastline being iconic features of the city. Development along the coastal strip has been prolific and led to three quite distinct areas: a densely populated, high-rise coastal beach area, surrounded by suburban sprawl and backed by a green semi-rural hinterland containing a small population – the 'green behind the gold' (Potts *et al.* 2013, p. 323). Most of the hotels and resorts are located in the northern precincts of the city at Southport, Surfers Paradise and Broadbeach, while the southern end of the Gold Coast is characterised by mostly older accommodation stock (Dredge and Jamal 2013). The hinterland has a distinct character, containing Queensland first national park (Frost 2004) and small-scale, dispersed tourism developments, such as health retreats, chalets and lodges, and bed and breakfast accommodation, as well as local art and craft, food and wine and nature-based tourism experiences.

This chapter seeks to understand the role of tourism in the development of this city by exploring how the northern Gold Coast (around Southport and Surfers Paradise) was able to out-compete two historical competitor regions (first Sandgate, then Coolangatta) but now faces competition at a global scale. The historical expansion of the Gold Coast as a site of tourism began late in the nineteenth century. At that time, the coastal resort of Sandgate, now part of metropolitan Brisbane, was the main competitor for Southport, and both resorts developed facilities and attractions modelled on the well-known and popular English resorts of the time, such as Brighton and Blackpool. Eventually Southport became the preeminent calm water resort when an early governor of Queensland established a holiday house there.

In the first half of the twentieth century, following changes in swimming habits and development of Australian beach culture, the focus of tourist activity in the northern Gold Coast shifted to Surfers Paradise with its surf beaches. During this period, Surfers Paradise faced competition from Coolangatta on the southern end of the Gold Coast. In the

1950s, Surfers Paradise adopted a more sophisticated style of tourism, arguably modelled on Miami, Florida and other American beach destinations, attractive to visitors from southern states. Most recently, the northern Gold Coast has experienced rapid growth in the numbers of visitors from Japan, Korea, China and other Asian countries due to the economic growth of these countries and availability of air services. These new markets again require the Gold Coast to adapt its product offering to meet needs and wants of visitors from different cultures.

This chapter therefore considers the complexities and interdependence of Gold Coast tourism with other economic sectors, ranging from local to global scales. It then examines the changing characteristics of tourism market demand and traces the way tourism products, attractions and services on the Gold Coast have evolved and shaped lines of future development. It concludes with a discussion of current and future implications of these relationships in destination management and among the diverse professional groups involved in creating and maintaining the image and qualities of the Gold Coast as a tourist landscape (see Chapter 10).

Historical development

As outlined in Chapter 2, the region that would become the Gold Coast tourism region began as a series of coastal dunes ~40 km in length. Behind this coastal strip are plains some 10 km wide that have been developed into residential housing estates and an extensive canal system of waterfront homes. This urban area is adjoined by a mountainous hinterland. The plain narrows in the south where the McPherson Range meets the sea at Coolangatta. This hinterland is the remains of the caldera of a 20-million-years-old shield volcano (WCMC/WCU 1993) and is the source of the Logan, Albert, Coomera, Nerang and Tweed Rivers as well as Tallebudgera and Currumbin Creeks. In some areas, such as Tamborine, Springbrook and Beechmont, the remains of the volcanic plain form a plateau with rich soil, and covered with temperate rainforest and sclerophyll forest. The region was rich in cedar and other desirable timbers, while the plateaus, valleys and coastal plain provided fertile agricultural land.

These farming lands were taken up predominantly by English people who developed cotton and sugar plantations from the 1860s. These settlers would have been well aware of seaside resorts in England, such as Blackpool, Bournemouth and Brighton. Sea bathing was a popular pastime associated with health and pleasure and, by the time Nerang Creek Heads was surveyed and renamed Southport (in 1875), seaside towns in England were popular (Brighton had received royal patronage) and, with the coming of the railway, were places where high society from London and working class from manufacturing towns would spend holidays (Gilbert 1949). Indeed, the Gold Coast's Southport is named after a seaside resort near Blackpool (Gilbert 1939). Features of English resorts, found in towns such as Brighton, included piers with entertainment, a promenade, churches, a School of Arts, hotels and seaside bathing. Boarding schools near the seaside were popular as they were thought to encourage healthy development.

In the 1880s, Sandgate on Moreton Bay near Brisbane (also named after a English seaside resort in Kent) boasted calm and clean beaches that provided a popular weekend destination, with droves of people visiting from Brisbane to escape the heat (Gregory and McLay 2010). There were several hotels and boarding houses, a pier, enclosed sea bathing area, and a band that played on summer evenings repeating the features associated with English resort towns. A railway line to Brisbane opened in 1882, increasing visitor numbers, especially on weekends. Thus, Sandgate modelled its infrastructure and services on an established pattern that residents in Brisbane would have been familiar with and attracted to. Similarly, the later developing tourist town of Southport repeated each of these attractions.

In comparison to Sandgate, travel from Brisbane to Nerang Creek Heads (now Southport) in the 1870s was typically via a Cobb and Co coach to Nerang, then by steamer to the river head (Southport). (See Chapter 4 for more detailed exploration of the evolution of the Gold Coast's connectivity to Brisbane.) One such steamer, the 'Maid of Sker', is now on display in a park in Nerang. Thus, Southport was more difficult for tourists to access and Sandgate had the advantage of proximity to Brisbane. In 1875, when the Southport Township was surveyed, the Nerang River entered the sea in a sheltered bay open to the sea, and the area now known as The Spit, north of Main Beach, was not as pronounced a feature as it is today. Construction of a bridge over the Nerang River was begun in 1876 to provide access to the ocean beaches such as Broadbeach and Burleigh Heads, but access was restricted by the swampy land behind the coastal dunes. Visitors to Southport could also cross the Nerang River by ferry then travel south in coaches along the hard sand on the beach to the Tweed River. At this time, Southport was a small and isolated settlement.

The Governor's residence

Southport's fortunes improved when the then Governor of the Queensland colony, Governor Musgrave, bought a home (called 'Summer Place') along the Nerang River near Southport in 1885. Today, this is the site of The Southport School, a private boys' school. Governor Musgrave was formerly Governor of Jamaica and enjoyed being able to spend time at the ocean. He administered the colony of Queensland for up to three months of the year from this residence. Consequently, those on government business had to travel to Southport and the area then known as the South Coast (in relation to Brisbane) became a fashionable resort for the wealthy and influential who enjoyed the calm waters and comfortable climate (Allom Lovell Architects and The Office of City Architect and Heritage 2010). After Musgrave's death in office in 1888, his successor was General Sir Henry Wylie Norman. A former Governor of India, he moved his summer residence to Toowoomba, which was more reminiscent of the Indian hill stations he had known from that earlier post.

However, a trend had begun for the families of graziers and Brisbane gentry to visit the Southport seaside and, accordingly, Southport became the summer watering hole of wealthy squatters and sheep farmers from the Darling Downs. By this time Southport had numerous hotels and boarding houses as well as a pier and enclosed sea bathing area. There was also an organised Easter boating regatta (Longhurst 2001). The 1879 Southport Easter Regatta attracted several steamers full of visitors, including the government steamer with Cabinet ministers aboard (Allom Lovell Architects and The Office of City Architect and Heritage 2010). A School of Arts was proposed for Southport in 1880 (Blackman 2013).

Southport also developed a reputation as a place for wealthier Brisbanites to visit. The fortunes of Southport improved further with opening of a railway line on 25 January 1889 (Anonymous 1889) that further boosted visitor numbers to the South Coast (Allom Lovell Architects and The Office of City Architect and Heritage 2010). This was the beginning of what might today be called 'mass tourism', whereby visitor numbers to the destination increase quickly but often with some decrease in the attractiveness of the destination for the more up-market visitors (Macnaught 1982; Weaver 2012). Seaside parks and a promenade were developed along the foreshore to service the growing number of visitors. Tourist accommodation was concentrated along the frontal coastal strip of Southport Township near the railway station (Pigram 1977) located in Railway Street and only 50 m from the

Broadwater (Gold Coast City Council 2009b). These tourism developments were somewhat discomforting for the privileged residents of this small resort town (Bishop 1998; Holthouse 1982). Daytrippers and weekend visitors were considered to include many 'drunken larrikins' and 'shameless hussies' who disrupted an established pattern of life (Holthouse 1982). In 1898, there were two trains daily from Brisbane to Southport during the Easter vacation period to accommodate the large numbers of holidaymakers (Longhurst 2001). Southport had become a seaside resort town similar in many ways to its namesake in England.

Coolangatta, regional competitor

The extension of the railway to Coolangatta in 1903 to allow transport of agricultural goods also brought public transport to a rival tourist township on the Queensland border (see Chapter 4). This railway boosted tourism right along the coast by improving access to a series of beaches, such as Burleigh and Tugun, as well as Coolangatta and Tweed Heads. It also meant that the South East Queensland population had 'a whole range of new beaches to choose from. Coolangatta, free from many of the conservative attitudes of the Southport community, [and] would soon become the resort most favoured by young people' (Keane 1958, p. 74). By 1914 there had been considerable tourism growth at Coolangatta and there were three hotels and eight boarding houses, although 'the permanent population was only 300, one of the highest population concentrations on the Gold Coast strip' (Vader and Lang 1980, p. 25). At this time 'accommodation establishments [of Coolangatta] were more downmarket than the grander establishments further north around Southport and the tourist clientele attracted to the area as more distinctively working class' (Russell and Faulkner 1998, p. 103).

By the 1930s Coolangatta became the most popular of a string of camping areas along the foreshore, partly because it was where the railway came closest to the coast. These campers included workers from the Ipswich railway workshops who enjoyed concessional ticket prices (Russell and Faulkner 1998). As a result, Coolangatta began to develop into a resort town in the early twentieth century, providing a more egalitarian environment and surf beaches that perhaps better matched the Australian working class social and cultural fashions of those times. After World War Two and until around 1960, Coolangatta was popular for beach events such as the 1955 Sun Girl Quest at Kirra. It had a national reputation as a fun place for families and young singles. Beach picnic entertainment coordinated by metropolitan radio stations and a variety of structured beach activities, mainly at Greenmount, were popular. Jazzland was the South Coast's undisputed headquarters of ballroom dancing (Russell and Faulkner 1998). However, after the 1960s Coolangatta stagnated as a tourist resort.

Cars and the Miami model

While Southport and Coolangatta were developing and competing as tourist centres, another location on the Gold Coast, destined to supplant them, emerged. In 1888, Johann Meyer built the Main Beach Hotel on the southern side of the Nerang River to accommodate the influx of people brought in by his ferry from Southport. The Nerang River at Southport was an obstacle to southwards travel but, in 1887, Meyer began a ferry service to allow better access for stagecoaches, which would then travel south to the Tweed Heads region along the beach. Meyer's family provided transport from the Southport hotels to Main Beach. In 1889, the Elston Post Office was established at Meyer's Main Beach Hotel, soon thereafter lending its name to the burgeoning settlement. There were real estate developments at Main Beach in the 1920s and later at Elston after a bridge to Southport was built in 1925. During World War One, the development of Elston slowed, but it was to be revived by other developments at Miami, Florida, half a world away.

As discussed more fully later in this book, there are interesting parallels between the development of Miami, Florida in the United States and the Gold Coast as tourism destinations. The two locations are similar in that they both consist of a narrow coastal dune system and were tourist cities founded on beach-based experiences of 'sun and sand'. They also developed at roughly the same time: seven years after the railway came to Southport, a railway was built to Miami. A two-mile (three-kilometre) wooden bridge from the mainland to the coastal dunes was built to Miami Beach in 1913 to service the increasing visitor numbers. Similar to the Gold Coast, the bridge in Miami led to a building boom with homes, apartments, businesses, public buildings and hotels constructed nearby. The Miami tourism boom began in 1921 and continued to 1926 when a hurricane destroyed a significant proportion of what was built. The bust was followed by the Great Depression of 1929 (Ballinger 1936). The Miami property boom was news around the world.

A similar development pattern is found in the Elston–Surfers Paradise area (Mayere *et al.* 2010). The extension of the South Coast Road to Burleigh Heads began in 1922 and revolutionised the South Coast, prompting numerous seaside developments such as Miami Shores in 1923–24 (Blackman 2013). The name Miami Shores reflected the great interest in all things American among Australians in the 1920s, when Hollywood dominated popular Australian culture. At this time, access to Elston was initially by means of ferry from Southport or from the towns along the Coolangatta railway line, such as Mudgeeraba and Tugun. Longhurst (1991) suggests that excitement about the success of Miami was a likely impetus for constructing the Jubilee Bridge across the Nerang River at Southport in 1925. An entrepreneurial business man, Jim Cavill, was quick to anticipate and capitalise on this development, opening a 16-bedroom hotel at the intersection of the South Coast Road and the coach track which ran from Meyers Ferry to the beach (now Cavill Mall) in 1925. The Miami Hotel further south also opened that same year. Road bridges were constructed over the Tallebudgera and Currumbin Creeks in 1926. In the same year, the Palm Beach Hotel was erected and soon became a convenient stopping place for passing motor traffic. The motor car was beginning to become a mass phenomenon and Australians looked to developments in the United States to see its effects.

As O'Hare and Burke discuss in Chapter 4, the Pacific Motorway between Brisbane and the South Coast was complete by 1935. Bridges constructed over the Coomera (completed in 1930) and the Logan Rivers (completed in 1932) meant that the coastal resorts were now only a few hours away for Brisbane motorists over a two-lane bituminised road. Southport increasingly developed as a service centre for the local region. The 1930s were something of a boom time for the South Coast and Southport as a popular weekend destination for a diverse group – from families and workers to wealthy city businessmen and rural graziers (Watt 1999). In 1933, Elston was renamed Surfers Paradise and its hotel even offered the novelty of its own in-house zoo. The car and railway provided the means to visit the South Coast. Visitation was increased by Australians' growing love of the beach and beach culture.

Shaping the culture of the Gold Coast

Already in the twentieth century's early decades an Australian beach culture had started to emerge. The burgeoning popularity of surf swimming, along with the necessity of surf life saving, was evident. Surfing – the art of riding a board across the face of a breaking wave – arrived in Australia before World War One (Booth 1994). The Greenmount Surf Life Saving Club was Australia's first such club and began surf patrols as early as 1908. By 1919, surf life saving was practised at Main Beach and the club was granted affiliation with the Royal Life Saving Society of Queensland in March 1928. Gibson (2001) argues that at a time when the Australian nation was developing its identity, beach culture differentiated Gold Coasters from their colonial masters and also demonstrated the egalitarian values of a new post-war country. This association of the region with the beach was cemented in the history of the place with name changes from Elston to the more glamorous Surfers Paradise and from the South Coast Town Council to the Gold Coast Town Council in 1958.

The Gold Coast was used as a rest and recreation site for Australian and American troops during the Pacific War (1941–45) (Longhurst 1991). Officers stayed at Southport and Surfers Paradise in former guest houses and rooms in the Surfers Paradise Hotel and enlisted men stayed at Coolangatta, Greenmount and Kirra in barracks, tents, rooms in hotels and flats (Jenkins 2013). This led to some social change. Swimming trunks were regulation US Army issue and this created a precedent for less-revealing swimming costumes to be abandoned. The policing of men's bathers was formally relaxed in 1945, abandoning rules that had been in place since the 1930s. Dancing also became less restricted and was eventually allowed on Sundays, with the local government by-law prohibiting these practices suspended in 1943 (Longhurst 1991). These shifts in acceptable behaviour (and others) had a lasting effect on the Gold Coast, shaping the Gold Coast's culture in the post-war era.

Post-war boom

After World War Two, the government ended building restrictions imposed as part of the war time economic regime and, as a result, 'weekender' holiday houses became popular on the Gold Coast (Watt 1999). From the 1900s until the 1950s, the Gold Coast had been 'Brisbane's traditional seaside resort' (McRobbie 1984, p. 81) and tourism development reflected this. With few exceptions, the accommodation was not fancy or flash, but just an affordable place for the people of Brisbane to escape to (Davidson and Spearritt 2000). Camping was also popular and many of the holidaymakers participated in communal games and festivities on the beaches (Condon 2003). The late 1950s began with a new style of accommodation, the development of motels and high-rise hotel and apartment blocks, again mirroring developments in popular American tourist destinations, such as Hawaii and Miami. Rickard (2013) identifies three key buildings constructed during the 1950s that heralded the establishment of a new type of architecture on the Gold Coast and established the trajectory the city has followed for the following six decades: Lennons Broadbeach Hotel (1955), the Chevron Hotel (1957) and Kinkabool (1959). Googie and pop-styled motels were built along the Gold Coast Highway in the 1950s and 1960s. Such confidence and exuberance helped establish the defining hallmark of the city skyline.

The new hotels and apartment blocks brought a taste of sophistication to the Gold Coast and the place image began to change somewhat (Bosman and Dredge 2011). Interstate visitors from Sydney and Melbourne became more attracted to the areas, and in 1956 regular air services from southern capitals began to use an emergency landing strip at Coolangatta. The Chevron Hotel in Surfers Paradise became a favourite with tourism promoters, and its image representing a vision of the Gold Coast is found on advertising posters in the 1960s and 1970s. Surf life saving fashion parades with scantily dressed female models and outlandish Gold Coast hotel entertainment and business events received heavy media coverage (Rickard 2013). The city had become a household name throughout Australia, synonymous with neon signs, motels, beach beauties and a somewhat irreverent and slightly sinful lifestyle. The social and political conservatism of Queensland was openly defied, with Bernie Elsey hosting pyjama parties at the Beachcomber Hotel from 1957, which gained their popularity mostly because they provided an opportunity for partygoers to wear their nightwear outside of the bedroom and flout Queensland's liquor laws.

In 1949, a local entrepreneur, Paula Stafford, began making two-piece bathing suits – the bikini – which had been paraded in Paris a few years earlier. It was soon commonplace to see women in bikinis along the Gold Coast beaches, a practice that was not accepted on other beaches in Australia at that time. This anticipated the emergence of surfie culture in the early 1960s, which attracted a new generation of youngsters to the Gold Coast's beaches and board racks. A local surfing culture developed on the Gold Coast based on a mix of rock 'n' roll music from the US, beach parties and teenage revolt. Movies such as 'Gidget Goes Hawaiian' in 1961 and surf pop singer, Patricia Thompson, pioneered a new outdoors model for the popular girl stereotype. Both showed how the young in Australia could get together and have fun at the beach. Surfing and surfing music caused a revolution in teenage habits (Drew 1994). The image of the Gold Coast as the home of Australia's surf culture was reinforced when the first Australian surf championships in Queensland were held at Southport and Coolangatta beaches in 1947. The Gold Coast emerged as the preeminent surf culture destination in Australia and its association with 'surf, sun and fun' fuelled Australians' appetite to holiday there.

Australia's love affair with the Gold Coast flourished during the 1960s, 1970s and 1980s. Increases in car ownership and increasing numbers of interstate visitors resulted in rapid changes on the Gold Coast to accommodate the burgeoning tourism industry. During this time, there were a series of investment booms on the Gold Coast. Surfers Paradise offered boutique shopping, entertainment, restaurants (such as Margot Kelly's Hibiscus Room, opened in 1955) and a cosmopolitan crowd from the southern states who tended not to visit the Queensland capital, and other parts of the Gold Coast were unable to compete. This is given as a reason for the decline in popularity of Coolangatta in the 1960s, when 'trendy youthful thrill seekers were gravitating northward to the more risqué Surfers Paradise' (Russell and Faulkner 1998). Another reason for the decline of Coolangatta was the closure of the railway line from Nerang to Tweed Heads/Coolangatta in 1961. This resulted in tens of thousands of cars descending on the Gold Coast from Brisbane every weekend.

Theme parks

Allom and Jones (1997, p. 362) suggest that theme parks on the Gold Coast 'exist as a natural extension of the themed environments of shopping centres, resorts, and gated communities which characterise much of the Gold Coast'. While such developments would be eclipsed by the later theme parks of Village Roadshow, as early as 1966 McRobbie (1966, p. 133) could observe:

> *The Gold Coast's major tourist attractions are remarkable in that put together, the total investment involved would probably not exceed the amount spent on one multi-storey building in Surfers Paradise. Yet the Gold Coast would go on thriving even if multi-storey buildings went out of existence. But where would the Coast be without its man-developed tourist attractions?*

He notes that the early promoters of the Gold Coast were people with show business associations and tells how Jim Cavill used show business promotion and publicity tactics.

'Most Gold Coast attractions have one thing in common – they all started off in a small way then gradually grew, usually after considerable hardship and financial risk by the proprietor' (McRobbie 1966, p. 133). Cavill's 'Surfers Paradise Hotel was not a pub but a whole civic centre' which 'was a meeting place for almost every organisation in Surfers Paradise' (McRobbie 1966, p. 19), a centre of social life, entertainment, accommodation; artists used it as an art gallery; schools held their annual balls there. He created a backyard zoo that had leopards, orang-utans and exotic birds.

As a national tourism destination since the mid 1950s, the Gold Coast also boasted a variety of man-made tourist attractions, including wildlife parks, zoos, ski gardens and chairlifts. Wildlife parks and zoos with animal shows, such as the zoo at Jim Cavill's Surfers Paradise Hotel, Jack Evans' Porpoise Pool at Snapper Rocks, Tweed Heads and Currumbin Bird Sanctuary, were among the popular early attractions. Prideaux's (2004, p. 31) resort development spectrum model predicts that the third phase of resort development, relating to national-scale tourism, involves the construction of international hotel chains and other developments, including large theme parks. By the fourth phase, international tourism, 'the focus of attention will shift from the beach to nonbeach activities, such as theme parks and up-market shopping'. The Gold Coast followed this model and convincingly took up the mantle of Australia's 'theme park capital', an extension of its title as the country's 'tourist capital' (Symes 1994). Its parks vary in size and sophistication and embrace a gamut of themes, ranging from wildlife sanctuaries to the 'colossal Disney-style mega-structures' of Dreamworld (opened in 1981), Sea World and Movie World (Symes 1994, p. 30).

Sea World was the country's first theme park. Many credit its founder, Keith Williams, as father of the theme parks (McRobbie 2000) and the person who initiated the emergence of the Gold Coast as the theme park capital of Australia (Russell and Faulkner 1999). The earlier generation of attractions on the Gold Coast could not compare with Sea World in terms of scale or international appeal. Williams was a long time entrepreneur on the Gold Coast and had in 1956 developed the Surfers Paradise Ski Gardens (see Fig. 3.1). In 1971 he moved his investment to The Spit with the new name of Ski Land (see Fig. 3.2) where a rival attraction, Marineland (which started as the Seaquarium in 1966) was located. After a disastrous first year on The Spit, Williams renamed Ski Land Sea World, incorporating performing dolphins to its existing water-ski shows. The venture was a major success and he eventually absorbed Marineland.

John Longhurst developed Dreamworld as 'Australia's answer to Disneyland' (*Amusement Park Journal* 1985, p. 17). Holmes (2001, p. 182) describes Dreamworld as:

> *a multi-themed world of worlds modelled on the US Disney parks [which boasts 11 themed worlds of rides, shows and attractions including] wild log rides down rapids; cruises along a man-made canal in a paddle-wheeler; bushranger shows; an 'interactive' tiger exhibit; as well as chairlift rides through 'Koala Country' and 'Gold Rush Country', following which one can view other worlds projected onto 180° screens.*

Dreamworld is the largest theme park not only in Australia but also in the southern hemisphere (eTourism Holidays 2013).

While the first theme parks on the Gold Coast were personal enterprises, the products of the dreams of individual investors and developers (McRobbie 2000), they were eventually sold to out-of-state or international investors who started developing additional theme parks in the city. Village Roadshow, distributor of Warners Brothers movies in Australia, partnered with the studio to develop Movie World in 1991. Film studios were constructed

Fig. 3.1. The Aquabelles, a star attraction at the Surfers Paradise Ski Gardens on the Nerang River, *c.* 1958 (Photograph by Alexander McRobbie. Image reproduction courtesy of the Gold Coast City Council Local Studies Library, image number LS-LSP-CD452-IMG0002)

on adjacent land. Studio builders chose the Gold Coast over Sydney and Melbourne because it provided them with the opportunity to build a theme park alongside the studio complex (Ward and O'Regan 2009). Village Roadshow, Australia's largest theme park operator (Anton Clave 2007), currently operates five theme parks in the Gold Coast: Sea World, Warner Bros. Movie World, Wet'n'Wild Water World, Australian Outback Spectacular (an evening dinner show opened in 2006) and Paradise Country (an 'Aussie' farm tour with an authentic farm experience reflecting Australian bush culture) (Village Roadshow Limited n.d.). Ardent Leisure operates Dreamworld and White Water World (Ward and O'Regan 2009).

Holmes (2001, p. 182) reports that of nearly one million international tourists who visited the Gold Coast in 1994, just over 570 000 visited one or more theme parks. In addition to domestic and international tourists, parks are visited by a significant number of locals as well. Merrilees *et al.* (2007) report that local demand for the Gold Coast theme parks represents about a third of total visits. It is, of course, difficult to give the definitive number of theme parks on the Gold Coast without defining 'theme park' first. Some authors (Symes 1994; Lawton 2005) include urban wildlife parks such as Currumbin Wildlife Sanctuary, while others (Weaver 2005) view wildlife parks and amusement parks as 'allies'

Fig. 3.2. Keith Williams' Ski Land attraction on The Spit, eventually to be called Sea World, *c.* late 1970s (Image reproduction courtesy of the Gold Coast City Council Local Studies Library, image number LS-LSP-CD015-IMG0069)

of theme parks. Some of the parks mentioned in the literature, such as the Skirmish World (an outdoor war game park) and Cable-ski Water Park (Australia's first mechanised water-skiing park) (Holmes 2001), no longer exist – subject as they are to market dynamics. In addition to the major parks already noted, Holmes (2001) also mentions Frozenworld (a giant cool room in which one can make snow figures, go tobogganing, ice skating and the like while outside the humidity may be 90%). The Gold Coast Tourism website (Gold Coast Tourism 2013) lists 43 attractions under the collective banner of amusement and theme parks; however, this number seems to include a wide variety of attractions ranging from nature parks, rainforest skywalks and museums to spas. Theme parks actually number around 10 to 15, depending on whether wildlife parks are included or not. eTourism Holidays (2013) count almost a dozen family entertainment parks in the number.

The growth of the Asian market

The Gold Coast has long been subject to economic cycles of boom and bust, which have had a direct effect on the profile of its visitors. This is particularly the case for its Asian tourism numbers. In September 1987, the Japanese Ministry of Transport announced that overseas trips by Japanese would double from five to ten million in five years (Polunin 1989). This government-led endorsement of international travel focused attention on the sector and led to a Japanese international investment boom that peaked in 1989–90. Japanese investors were attracted to tourism by a range of economic factors, including the wealth generated by a revaluation of the yen, the concept of a vertically integrated travel sector with Japanese travellers staying in Japanese hotels and playing golf on Japanese golf courses, as well as banks keen to lend for property. Gold Coast developers built several world-class integrated golf resorts in the region to attract Japanese visitors who had a keen interest in golf tourism. The status of golf club membership and ownership of these golf courses among Japanese visitors promoted golf tourism on the Gold Coast (Hajdu 2005). The pre-sale of expensive Gold Coast golf club memberships was central to this business. The Japanese bubble economy created a landscape of golf course estates, as well as luxury hotels, apartments and resorts at a time when the Gold Coast had only a small five-star resort market. Hajdu (2005) notes that Japanese developers were involved in many landmark projects, such as Ephraim Island, Rivage Royale, Daikio Palm Meadows and Sanctuary Cove, a trend in the city's development history that continues to today (see Chapter 5).

The Japanese stock market crash of 1990 and following asset devaluation led to a massive contraction in overseas investment. The number of Japanese overseas travellers to Australia continued to grow strongly until around 1996. In the 1990s, several other 'tiger' country economies were growing strongly including Korea, Singapore, Taiwan, Indonesia, Malaysia and Thailand. As these countries developed an affluent middle class, outbound tourism grew and Australia was well positioned geographically to capitalise on this growth. The Gold Coast was promoted as a must-see destination, despite cultural issues, including its high levels of sun exposure and, for some travellers, a fear of water (Scott *et al.* 2014). For these visitors, Australia offered a close English-speaking Western destination that had unique animals, a good natural environment and a good climate. Asian countries experienced an economic crisis in 1997 and some countries, such as Indonesia and Thailand, have not yet fully recovered. Prior to the Asian economic crisis in 1997, Japan represented 46% of all international visitors to the Gold Coast – a number that by 2012/13 had dropped to 10% (Faulkner and Tideswell 2002; Tourism Research Australia 2011).

In the past decade several new trends in visitor travel behaviour have had effects on Gold Coast tourism. The domestic market has been affected by increasing overseas travel by Australians, due in part to the strength of the Australian dollar against other currencies and the deregulation of air travel in Australia in 1990, opening the doors for low-cost carriers to offer discounted airfares in the Australian market (Australian Government 2008). In the year ending September 2013, Gold Coast received 3.64 million domestic overnight visitors spending around 14.4 million visitor nights. During the same period, there were 812 000 international visitors spending 7.6 million visitor nights. Trends in these figures show only small changes in percentage terms with international numbers growing slowly and domestic visitors essentially static.

These figures mask the growth in Asian, mostly Chinese, visitors following a now familiar pattern of an increasing middle class experimenting with travel overseas. This growth contrasts with a decline in visitors from the United States and Europe due to recessions in these countries. The introduction of low-cost airline routes such as those from Malaysia (Air Asia) and Singapore (Scoot) has increased visitation by our northern neighbours. Gold Coast has also been affected by increased competition from other domestic and overseas destinations, which are becoming more innovative and aggressive in the way that they market and develop their tourism offerings.

The future of tourism on the Gold Coast

The Gold Coast began as an English-styled, calm water resort centred on Southport, attractive to the wealthier of those who lived in Queensland's capital towards the end of the nineteenth century, but becoming more egalitarian with camping and seaside houses at a series of coastal villages stretching south to Coolangatta. In the 1920s and 1930s it began to emulate a model derived from Miami in particular and an image of Florida and the American west coast in general, driven by investment in the north coast strip around Surfers Paradise. In the 1950s, post-war affluence, the car and then plane brought increasing numbers of visitors from southern states with Surfers Paradise now positioned as a stylish beach destination. Development of the tourist city was further catalysed in the 1950s to 1980s by property-led investment booms (and busts) and an increasing resident population living in apartments, canal estates and, further from the coast, in residential housing developments. The beach remained the core attraction but, increasingly, theme parks were created to occupy the family market. The growth of Japan, the 'tiger' economies and, most recently, China has led to an increasingly Asian visitor mix.

Over some 130 years, the Gold Coast has remained essentially a tourist city but with a steadily increasing market catchment area. Initially it has drawn its visitors from Brisbane and South East Queensland. Improvements in transportation and infrastructure have linked the Gold Coast first to markets in southern capital cities and later to cities around the globe. Interestingly, it was travellers from the more remote western countries that arrived first, with our closer Asian visitors able to travel only after their economies had developed. As these transformations occurred, the Gold Coast has adapted but remained positioned as a paradise by the beach. Prideaux (2004) has suggested that resort development occurs through opening up a series of new and increasingly distant markets enabled by transportation improvements and this provides a useful first approximation of the Gold Coast's situation. Each new market has requirements for different facilities, with international travellers expecting the highest levels of services and facilities as they have the greatest choice amongst competing destinations.

At a finer level of analysis we may see increasing differentiation amongst visitors to the Gold Coast. The domestic market fragments into schoolies, surfers, marathon runners, casino gamblers, convention visitors and V8 spectators whose interests orbit the core beach positioning and occasionally intersect it. Additionally, there is a significant and growing residential population for whom the Gold Coast is also a 'slice of paradise' (Potts *et al.* 2013), and the complex and changing portfolio of overseas origin countries. Across these differences, perhaps the uniting theme is that the Gold Coast represents 'a dream', similar to postmodern cities like Las Vegas and Dubai. Balancing the needs of these different market segments is difficult, perhaps impossible. Instead it may be better to do as those on the Gold Coast have done before them: create 'the dream' and let others follow.

A 1997 study by the Queensland Tourist and Travel Corporation examining the general attitudes and perceptions of the domestic market regarding the Gold Coast found that the destination delivers fun and excitement leaving visitors with positive experiences, but is also often regarded as too 'touristy' (Queensland Tourist and Travel Corporation 1997). It is likely and perhaps inevitable that the Gold Coast has always evoked a mixture of positive and negative perceptions. The Gold Coast has always walked a line between family fun and sin, between a down-to-earth, quintessential Australian beach holiday and six-star opulence and luxury destination. The natural assets of the Gold Coast – its beaches, hinterland and sunny weather – are an enduring lure for visitors. Yet, it's the development of built environment – its theme parks, attractions, hotels and transport infrastructure – and culture – the lifestyle and colourful characters – that have differentiated it from other tourist hot spots around the world.

The past and future of the Gold Coast is as a tourist city. Yet, planners cannot rely on the success of the past to govern the city's tourism future. The tourism industry needs to continue to be experimental, innovative and cutting edge to remain at the forefront of new ideas and experiences. This entrepreneurial spirit measured with planned, sustainable development will ensure that holidaying on the Gold Coast continues to be aspirational for future generations of Australian and international visitors and a major tourist destination in the Asia-Pacific region.

Chapter 4

Transport: from cream cans and campers to city centres and commuters

Daniel O'Hare and Matthew Burke

This chapter explores the history of transport provision on the Gold Coast. As a city that experienced most of its growth in the golden age of the motor car, the Coast is synonymous with the motoring way of life. But its transport planning history is more complex. Transport accessibility and transport policy – or lack of it – have played a major role in shaping the Gold Coast over time. Several of the most important centres and suburbs established their dominance in a period when transport was mainly by water. Later, the Coast's collection of towns, resorts and early suburbs developed around a rail corridor that was removed, then replaced decades later on an inferior alignment. In the period between the two Gold Coast railways, the city was shaped by cars and roads so that today it is a sprawling car-dependent city. Despite attempts to re-image the city with light rail investment, the Gold Coast has been closely associated with cars, from Mayor Bruce Small's Meter Maids of the 1960s, through the motel strip of the Gold Coast Highway, to the Indy-Car and A1 Grand Prix car races of recent decades.

In this city of over half a million people, 88% of all daily trips are today made by car, while only 3% are by public transport. Fewer than 2% of trips are by bicycle, and only 7% are by walking (City of Gold Coast 2013b). The figures are all the more startling for a city in which tourism and lifestyle-oriented activities are economic pillars. Beach tourists like to walk or cycle, yet these modes have been poorly addressed here until recently. This chapter describes how the Gold Coast reached this level of car-dependency, via a chronological exploration of the relationship between transport decisions and the settlement pattern over the past century and a half. The chapter concludes by considering future prospects for how the Gold Coast might be shaped by current transport policy documents of the Gold Coast City Council and the Queensland Government.

Continuation of Aboriginal pathways in today's transport routes and destinations

The first people to make transport routes in the area now known as the Gold Coast were the local and visiting Aboriginal groups using rich natural resources shaped by the region's mild subtropical climate. This area is believed to have been the most densely settled on the continent before the arrival of European settlers. The local Kombumerri and Minjungbal people have continued to live in the area during almost two centuries of European settlement. Steele's (1984) *Aboriginal Pathways of South East Queensland and North East New South Wales* plots a large number of the many food sources and ceremonial sites of these people in the Gold Coast, but provides little or no information on transport routes in the area.

Whereas major contemporary roads have been shown to follow the routes of Aboriginal pathways in Brisbane, Sydney and many other Australian places, such routes are not clearly identified by Steele in the case of the Gold Coast. Some routes on the early maps that may have pre-dated European settlement include a track through dense bush to link the Tweed River and Coolangatta beach, as well as other routes close to the beach. Another track was recorded crossing the McPherson Range from the Tweed estuary (Steele 1984). The number and spread of important Aboriginal sites (such as fishing areas, middens and bora rings) suggest that such pathways would have been numerous; however, no clear links appear to have been made between Aboriginal pathways and the major elements of today's road system. The beaches themselves were used as roads by both the local Indigenous people and the early European settlers.

The extensive waterways of the region were clearly used as transport routes by Indigenous groups. Early photographs record Aboriginal people using outrigger canoes in the surf in the late nineteenth century (Jones 1988). Scar trees record the making of canoes: for example, a 1980s photo by Michael Aird from the Gold Coast City Library 'Picture Gold Coast' collection shows a long scar on a tree at Nerang, indicating 'bark removal by aboriginal peoples for the purpose of canoe building or for shields' (see Fig. 4.1).

Water transport in the nineteenth century

Land-based transport was extremely difficult in this region in the early decades of European settlement, due to the many waterways, the extensive coastal wetlands, the dense vegetation and rugged topography of the mountainous hinterland, and the periods of extremely wet weather associated with the subtropical summers. Ships plied the east coast between Sydney, Newcastle, Port Macquarie and the new penal settlement at Brisbane from its inception in 1824. At the southern end of today's Gold Coast, the names given to the prominent natural landmarks of Point Danger and Mount Warning by Captain Cook in 1770 were effectively signposts for hazards to shipping.

Cedar was being shipped to Sydney and Brisbane from the Tweed Valley by the 1840s, establishing Tweed Heads as an important port. The growth of Tweed Heads was assisted by ships having to await the high tide to negotiate the shallow bar at the mouth of the river. Cedar cutting moved into the Nerang and Tallebudgera Valleys by 1846, with access by the rivers and creeks. Farmers quickly followed the timber getters into the valleys in the 1850s, and this accelerated with the passing of the *Crown Lands Alienation Act* in 1868 (Longhurst 1996).

The water transport era laid down important aspects of the urban structure of today's extensive Gold Coast city area. The development of the initial South Coast settlements was limited to places easily accessible by water, and small towns were established as places for transferring produce and people between water transport and the limited local land transport. Several of the Gold Coast's inland centres and suburbs, including Nerang and Mudgeeraba, have grown from towns that were established at the navigable limits for water transport on the coastal rivers and creeks.

The beaches with the best water access were the first resort areas developed. These were Southport, Burleigh Heads and Coolangatta–Tweed Heads (Arundell 2011).

Fig. 4.1. 'Canoe tree' showing signs of bark removal over 100 years ago by Aboriginal peoples, Nerang State Forest, 1986 (Photograph by Michael Aird. Image reproduction courtesy of the Gold Coast City Council Local Studies Library, image number LS-LSP-CD057-IMG0012)

Tweed Heads was originally larger than Coolangatta due to the importance of the wharves for the shipping of timber, seafood and agricultural produce. The Tweed Heads wharves were a place of transhipment between coastal shipping and both land and water transport of goods from the Tweed Valley. The growth of beach holidays, particularly after completion of the South Coast Railway, quickly resulted in Coolangatta growing to equal prominence (Arundell 2011, p. 35). The name of Wharf Street, the main street of Tweed Heads, is almost the only reminder of the town's early significance for freight and passenger transport, as the wharves are long gone and even the waterfront itself has been largely removed from the street due to reclamation of estuarine waters for property development by Tweed Shire Council in the early 1970s.

Although the era of water transport on the Gold Coast has long passed, there has been lobbying in the early twenty-first century to reintroduce it in a new form, via urban ferries similar to Brisbane's CityCat system.

The early roads

Most of the early roads in the area were bush tracks connecting the timber and agricultural industries to marine transport via wharves. One of these can still be traced in the Tallebudgera area, with its route now occupied by parts of the Pacific Motorway and the Old Coach Road. This hilly route, linking two valleys, developed because the sand bar at the mouth of the Tallebudgera Creek was declared too shallow for safe and reliable shipping, so cross-country transport of timber and farm produce to the Little Tallebudgera Creek and Nerang River was necessary (Longhurst 1996).

As European settlement and economic activity expanded into areas away from the navigable waterways, the South Coast became part of the inter-city and interstate horse-drawn stagecoach networks of Cobb and Co and other private carriers of passengers and freight. Cobb and Co introduced its southern service from Brisbane in 1873. This was extended to Tallebudgera by 1883, and over the border ranges to Murwillumbah by 1886 (Longhurst 1996). Builders of roads for early coaches and motor cars sought well-drained land away from the coast, and far enough inland to ford the rivers and creeks. It was only a century later that these inland areas experienced significant urban and suburban development as the more attractive coastal land began to be more fully developed.

The beach itself was a serviceable and well-used road for horse-drawn vehicles, and continued to play this role for early motorists (Arundell 2011; Longhurst 1996). Longhurst (1996, p. 65) shows an early horse-drawn tourist coach using the 'convenient highway' provided by the hard inter-tidal sand of the beach, on the run linking the three original coastal resort areas of Southport, Burleigh Heads and Coolangatta (see Fig. 4.2). With the coastal resorts having been surveyed in the early 1870s, their growing popularity led to the operation of a daily coach service along the beaches from Coolangatta to Southport by 1888. Hotelier Otto Vetter's coach transported passengers and mail between these resort areas,

Fig. 4.2. Horse-drawn carriages on the beach at Palm Beach, 1900 (Image reproduction courtesy of the Gold Coast City Council Local Studies Library, image number LS-LSP-CD099-IMG0116)

enabling passengers to transfer to the Murwillumbah Steamer at the southern end, and the South Brisbane train at the northern end (Longhurst 1996). The horse-drawn coach forded the Currumbin and Tallebudgera Creeks, turning inland along today's Cavill Avenue to cross the Nerang River to Ferry Road in Southport via Meyer's Ferry. The popularity and convenience of the 'beach highway' supported the viability of the Burleigh Heads Hotel as a stop for refreshments and accommodation and to feed and change the horses (Longhurst 1996, p. 66).

When the road system became more established from around the turn of the twentieth century, the many rivers and creeks remained as barriers, so ferries provided the essential links for several decades before the construction of bridges. The river crossings were places where motorists would need to wait, and some commercial activity developed to service the passing trade. Street names, such as Ferry Road, Southport, remind us of this earlier transport era. Although superseded by two successive bridges further downstream in 1925 and 1966, this ferry link assisted Surfers Paradise to take over from Southport as the primary resort town when Jim Cavill established his Surfers Paradise Hotel at the then Elston in 1928.

Study of early motoring guides suggests that crossing points – by ford or ferry – had surprisingly little significant long-term impact on the overall settlement pattern, for example, see Fig. 4.3, published in the late 1920s in the *Official Motor Guide to Northern NSW with Through Routes to and from Brisbane* (New South Wales Government Tourist Bureau and NRMA n.d., p. 199). This limited effect can be attributed to key aspects of the settlement pattern being well established before road transport reached significance, so that the settlement pattern was more affected by both the early water transport and the later construction of the first South Coast Railway. The city has been shaped much more by the major wave of road-based and car-based transport that occurred after the mid-twentieth century, rather than the less significant first wave of road transport. In turn, the dominance of the motor car in the past half-century or more has meant that an integrated approach to land-use planning and transport planning has been largely absent until the turn of the twenty-first century.

Before the 1950s, car and bus travel to the Gold Coast was not competitive with the railways for several reasons, including low car ownership, poor roads, low speed limits and the petrol rationing that continued into the early post-World War Two period. In the 1920s to 1930s, car

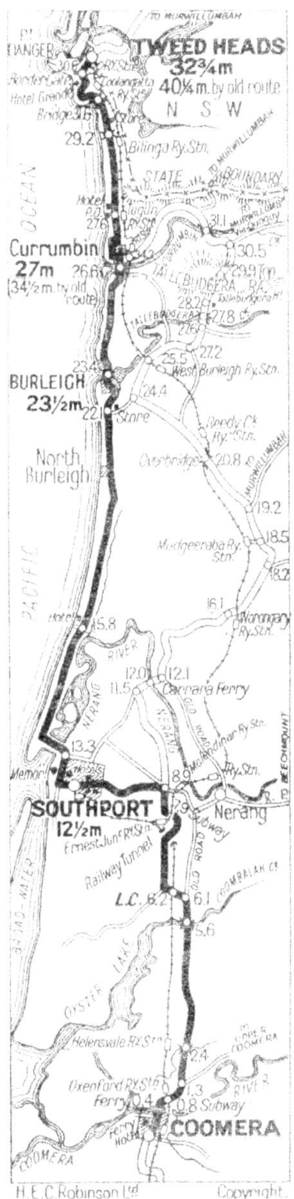

Fig. 4.3. Coomera to Tweed Heads motoring map, also showing the South Coast Railway line, late 1920s (New South Wales Government Tourist Bureau and NRMA n.d., map 117. Map section reproduced with permission of Universal Publishers Pty Ltd, Copyright Universal Publishers Pty Ltd DD 11/14)

travel from Brisbane to Southport took 4.5 to 5 h, with delays for ferries at river crossings (Arundell 2011).

The South Coast Railway 1893–1964

Planning for the first South Coast Railway was underway by 1890, influenced by the growth of towns, agricultural expansion, the spread of Queensland Railways into other regions of the state, and changes in marine transport towards larger vessels unsuited to the hazardous conditions of the shallow rivers and creeks of the Gold Coast area. Rural districts in the productive Coomera, Nerang, Mudgeeraba and Tallebudgera valleys saw rail transport as essential to their economic development. At the same time, absentee property speculators and tourism businesses were lobbying for a coastal route to bring more holidaymakers from Brisbane to the beach playgrounds in the popular coastal resorts at Southport, Burleigh Heads and Coolangatta. According to Longhurst (1996), the lobbying from the rival inland and coastal interests was intense, with the Brisbane-based railway officials reportedly in favour of a coastal route.

Just as it shaped the initial settlement pattern, the underlying physical landscape played a significant role in achieving a compromise between rural and coastal interests in the choice of a rail route. A coastal railway would have required larger and more expensive bridges. Although downplayed in the historical literature, the selection of a predominantly inland route was no doubt influenced by the political weight of the established rural communities and the revenue opportunities afforded by freighting rural produce to market. The chosen route captured these benefits as well as providing links to the key coastal resorts and stimulating tourism development and passenger growth there.

The line was built in stages, with the Southport line opening in 1893 and the extension to the border at Tweed Heads in 1903. The railway routes south via the two branches to Southport and Tweed Heads are shown in Fig. 4.3. The arrival of the railway saw Coolangatta boom, overtaking both Tweed Heads and Tallebudgera in population (Longhurst 1996). Passengers for Burleigh Heads had to travel four kilometres by road from the transfer station at West Burleigh, and Palm Beach passengers transferred at Elanora Station for their one kilometre road journey. Stations at Southport and Coolangatta, and the coach link to Burleigh Heads, reinforced the accessibility of the three early coastal settlements and further spurred their development. It was not until around the 1920s that road links along the coast, linking the railway access points, were sufficient to support tourism development at the places in between, such as Broadbeach, Miami and Mermaid Beach (Arundell 2011).

The Queensland Government built the Tweed Heads station and over 200 m of line into New South Wales as part of the Border Railways Agreement, under which the New South Wales Government was expected to construct a line to Murwillumbah on the New South Wales North Coast Line (Arundell 2011, p. 35). Connection to the port at Tweed Heads was a major consideration for shipping of produce. The missing link to Murwillumbah was never constructed, of course, because the New South Wales Government feared loss of economic benefits to Brisbane and the nearby markets in Queensland.

As well as passengers, the train carried a wide range of freight, as detailed by Arundell (2011, pp. 57–58): timber, from Nerang and the Tweed, for the Southport sawmill; pigs and cattle from the Tweed, transferring from river to train at Tweed Heads wharf; milk and cream for Kingston and other butter factories; sugarcane from Stapylton, Pimpama and Helensvale to the Benowa Mill for crushing; fresh fish from Southport and Tweed Heads to the Fish Board at South Brisbane; mineral beach sands from Southport, Tweed, Currumbin and Tugun stations, for glass making and cement works in South Brisbane (up to 300 tonnes per day of sand was carried in the 1950s); fruit and vegetables, including potatoes; building materials for the construction of the Gold Coast towns and infrastructure such as the Little Nerang Dam; mail; and movies and other goods for the towns and tourism industry.

Freight transport by rail was significant, peaking in the 1950s with freight loads of up to 1100 tonnes per train being despatched from Southport Station at this time (Arundell 2011). Passenger numbers grew rapidly from the 1920s, until the 1950s when the car (and private buses) began to dominate.

Having 'effectively superseded Cobb and Co's coaches and also transport on water between Brisbane and the Coast' (Arundell 2011, p. 37), the railway retained its competitiveness against road travel until the 1950s because of constraints to car travel. Bridge construction took several decades. The Albert River bridge at Yatala opened in 1925, the Coomera River bridge in 1930, and a Logan River toll bridge opened in 1931. The highway from Brisbane to Southport only became a fully sealed two-way road by the 1940s. Before the bridges, ferries over the Logan and Coomera Rivers carried only two vehicles, causing long delays for motorists. The Jubilee Bridge over the Broadwater opened in 1925 and was replaced in 1966. Further south, fords over the Tallebudgera and Currumbin Creeks were replaced by bridges in 1926. The New England Motor Co. and other private bus companies began to compete with the railway for tourists, providing accessibility along the beaches and making development of the intervening beaches more viable. Car ownership was still the province of the wealthy at this time, and contemporary tourist advertisements for hotels and guest houses at Coolangatta and Tweed Heads boasted of being only a few minutes' walk from both railway station and beach (QGITB 1927).

Despite this, the small settlement sizes meant no passenger tramcar network was established, such as was found in all the state capital cities and many regional cities in Australia, from the late 1800s up until the 1970s. No streetcar suburbs, which were dominant settlement types in Sydney and Melbourne, were built on the Gold Coast. As such, the local councils (Gold Coast City and Albert Shire) played no meaningful role in public transport operations, seemingly doing little more than the occasional approval of bus stops. This lack of funding public transport operations by local government continued until the 2000s.

With the steady improvement in road conditions, accompanied by the rapid growth in car ownership as Australia's long post-war boom got underway in the 1950s, car traffic mushroomed and rail patronage began to fall. As the townships were small, rail operations were unprofitable. The state government announced in the early 1960s that the South Coast Railway, together with dozens of other minor lines throughout the state, was to be closed. The Tweed line closed in 1961, followed by the closure of the Southport line in 1964. While some saw it as an opportunity to develop the land (McRobbie 1966), the closure was unpopular with some of the public. Arundell (2011) reports that road traffic congestion was already significant and that it worsened markedly after the rail closure. Agitation for re-opening continued long after closure. It was to be a long wait for the next train.

The golden age of Gold Coast motoring: 1950s to today

The explosive growth of the Gold Coast began only in the 1960s. Mass market tourism started at this time and the population swelled to around 55 000 inhabitants (Burchill 2005, p. 31). Australia had just ended petrol rationing, a domestic automobile manufacturing sector under tariff walls was enabling affordable motoring, and the focus of the nation's transport planners was on reshaping cities to the car. On the Gold Coast attention was

Fig. 4.4. From the 1960s, cars have dominated Gold Coast streets (D O'Hare)

firmly on developing a modern highway system and facilitating private automobile transport (Fig. 4.4). In 1965 the Queensland Main Roads Department was commissioned to undertake the *Gold Coast Travel Study* (Queensland Main Roads Department 1966). This planning exercise was exemplary of the 'predict and provide' modelling studies conducted in all the Australian state capital cities at this time, often using American consultants. As was common in these studies, the plan produced for the area ignored public transport entirely. It focused solely on gathering data on traffic conditions in the City of Gold Coast and in the neighbouring Albert Shire, to assist with the development of the *Gold Coast Area Major Road Plan*, which set out the staged development of a freeway spine for the coast at a then projected cost of some $13 million. A set of vehicle counts, travel speed surveys and population projections were used to model and test the viability of a new freeway inland from the major settlements, finding the road was necessary. Much of the road network of today's city conforms with these initial plans.

During the 1960s, the city's urban form also became more automobile dominated. Designed according to what architect Jan Gehl calls the 60 km/h (35 m/h) 'design speed' (Gehl and Gemzoe 2004), the nature of buildings and structures changed to accommodate the faster speeds of motorcar travel. With car-o-tels and oversized street signage, a whole new city imagery based on the car and a relaxed coastal lifestyle was emerging. As Allom and Jones (1997, p. 361) note:

> *The motor car itself as a symbol of social freedom, fantasy and seduction became part of, and sat perfectly with the developing image of the Gold Coast itself. Motels, drive-in picture shows, banks and fast-food outlets were a natural expression at the Gold Coast, unlike other cities where these facilities were forced into existing urban fabric ...*

There was no meaningful attempt to shape land-use development to anything but car transportation – except for boating. The latter was via the development of large canal estates, which were a significant innovation on the Gold Coast. The first canals were planned by Karl Langer, apparently under the influence of the principles used in Radburn, New Jersey. But whereas Radburn was designed for segregated travel on either a motor vehicle street network or a separate pedestrian network, the canal estates pioneered on the Gold Coast ignored pedestrians and created networks solely for cars and boats instead. A corollary of canal development is that it creates excessive separation and distance between land uses, more than even the low-density residential subdivisions elsewhere in the city at that time, meaning that servicing these areas with public transport ever since has been highly impractical.

Storage for the motor vehicles became more important. Tourist operators began to cater for tourists by providing large open air car parks in front of their establishments, including at Sea World on The Spit. Car-based shopping malls proliferated, including Pacific Fair at Broadbeach. Regulating car parking, including at the most popular beaches, became a necessity. The introduction of parking meters to Surfers Paradise streets led to local entrepreneurs paying Meter Maids in bikinis to fill expired meters.

While the eras of water and rail transport had favoured the development of selected inland towns (particularly Nerang and Mudgeeraba) and the most accessible coastal resort areas (i.e. Southport, Burleigh Heads and Coolangatta), improvements in roads created a broader accessibility that led to the joining up of towns through the 'filling in' of the areas between. From the 1920s to the 1970s, the new roads and increasing car ownership enabled tourism and residential development to create a narrow linear city extending for 30 km along the coast. In many areas, this new linear city extended less than a kilometre inland. With a grid subdivision pattern predating the car era, this linear edge to today's city would later come to be seen as supportive of public transport development. This strip supports the Gold Coast's most well patronised bus route now, and can be expected to make a lengthy light rail extension viable.

By the time the first 'master-planned communities' were being constructed, at Helensvale from the 1960s and Robina in the 1980s, the car was entirely dominant in transport and land-use planning, with little attention paid to mobility and accessibility for the majority of the population who are too young, too old, too ill or too poor to have their own individual use of a car. These 'new towns' were composed of low-density suburbs, with disconnected street patterns and a strict road hierarchy that made public transport inefficient and the pedestrian experience impractical and unpleasant. Connectivity was deliberately blocked by golf courses, waterways and major roads, with few shared paths and no dedicated on-road cycling infrastructure. All this made walking to destinations too hard.

In some smaller master-planned communities, developed at the start of the current century – notably the New Urbanism-influenced Varsity Lakes and (less notably) Emerald Lakes at Carrara – greater efforts were made to deliver more transit-oriented and pedestrian-oriented precincts, with concentration of denser mixed-use local centres and connected local streets. However, the effectiveness of these places in reversing car dependency is greatly limited by their placement within a dispersed and disconnected overall city structure.

A long wait for the train: reintroduction of the Gold Coast railway in the 1990s

In 1983, within 20 years of closing the South Coast Railway, the Queensland Government commenced feasibility studies and planning for a new railway line to the Gold Coast (Queensland Rail n.d.). This was to be, indeed, a new railway line as the original rail corridor had been alienated for construction of sections of the Pacific Motorway down the western side of the coastal strip in the 1980s, and more urban sections of the alignment had been sold off for property development in Southport, Coolangatta and Tweed Heads. The site of Southport Station continued in a transport role as the Southport Transit Centre, servicing local and inter-city buses. The former rail yards were occupied with cheaply developed 1970s commercial properties. Railway Street, Southport, was stranded 11 km from the nearest heavy rail station, an anachronistic reminder of a time when trains went to the centre rather than the edge of this city. The last ghost of the Southport line can be discerned from above: satellite images show a curved line of buildings, on the former railway alignment, cutting across the gridded street pattern (Fig. 4.5).

In the Queensland Parliament in 1988, Premier Bjelke-Petersen announced that a new Gold Coast Railway was to be built (Queensland Rail n.d.), but no funds were committed and no date set for its construction or opening. The federal government opened a funding window in the 1990s through its *Building Better Cities* program, to enable the $280 million project to be brought forward, with the new line reaching as far as Robina by December 1997 (Commonwealth Department of Housing and Regional Development 1995). Under this program 43 km of new railway line with five stations (Ormeau, Coomera, Helensvale, Nerang and Robina) would connect the Gold Coast to express services on the Beenleigh line into Brisbane and then on to Brisbane Airport. The line was extended an additional 4 km to Varsity Lakes in 2007–09 under the Queensland Government's (2005) *South East Queensland Infrastructure Plan and Program 2005–2026* (SEQIPP). Under later updates of SEQIPP, completion of the railway southward to a planned terminus at Gold Coast Airport continued to slip beyond the 20 years covered by the *Plan* (Queensland Government 2009a) and may take many decades.

There was significant potential to use the new railway line to provide some structure to and help reorient the city, especially in the development and reinforcement of town centres and urban precincts around the stations. But little attention was given to this and many of the land use decisions were nonsensical. Disappointing outcomes in this respect reflect the Queensland Rail orientation towards developing a commuter line for Gold Coast residents working in Brisbane, rather than providing for intra-urban travel within the Gold Coast. The lack of integration of stations with the Gold Coast's existing and newly developing centres remains evident today. The isolated Ormeau Station sits adjacent to a very low-density semi-rural subdivision. A major centre is planned next to Coomera Station, but there are challenges related to difficult topography and linkages to contemporary suburban development in the station area. Helensvale Station is separated from its car-oriented suburb by the Gold Coast Highway, and is hemmed in by the Pacific Motorway a few hundred metres to the west and Ramsar-listed Coombabah wetlands immediately to the east. Gold Coast City Council has had some success in requiring Westfield's Helensvale centre,

Fig. 4.5. Traces of the closed South Coast Railway can be seen in the name of Railway Street, Southport, and a line of infill buildings cutting across the Southport grid (Satellite image from Google Maps, with annotations by Isara Khanjanasthiti)

opened in 2005, to include a partial street structure with clear pedestrian connections to the station and to a new community centre at the original Helensvale shopping centre. Connections beyond these first few hundred metres are, however, very poor for those without a car. Nerang Station is located on the flood plain, beyond comfortable walking distance of the original Nerang town centre 1.5 km west, beyond the Nerang River and a massive cutting containing the contemporarily upgraded eight-lane Pacific Motorway.

Perhaps the worst outcomes were at Robina. The Town Centre regional shopping centre was developed a good kilometre from the rail station, beyond reasonable walking distance, despite being constructed at the same time as the rail line. Where important facilities are located near the station, such as Robina Hospital and Robina State High School, the streets have not been designed to be walkable for users of the train and bus interchange at the station. Investigation of the reasons for the failure to integrate Robina's station and town centre has revealed that Queensland Rail had a park-and-ride mindset, which is far from the highest and best use for a rail precinct. Station location was influenced primarily by the effect on trip times; construction of the railway viaduct on the flood plain was minimised to reduce costs; and there were perceived difficulties in coordinating public and private sector development priorities and timelines. Robina's developers were concerned that bringing the station closer to the shopping centre might impact on the opening date and operation of the shopping centre (O'Hare 2008). The shopping centre is only a small element of an intended 200 ha major town centre. Expectations regarding speed of development of the land around the station have not been met due to cyclical changes in economic conditions and a structural decline in the demand for suburban office locations for banks and other service industries, particularly when there are negligible state government office jobs on the Gold Coast that might spur such development.

With extension of the railway line further south to Varsity Lakes in 2009, the Queensland Government sought to correct the problem of isolated stations. They bought 17 ha of vacant land adjacent to the station and prepared plans for Varsity Station Village, a transit-oriented development district-level centre (Queensland Government 2009b). These plans have not yet been realised, initially because of the 2008 property market downturn. In the longer term, development of this land will be in direct competition with vacant town centre land adjacent to Robina Station, only 4.5 km away. Varsity Station is also constrained by being adjacent by the Pacific Motorway immediately to its west, which prevents direct connection to two large private high schools and 400 medium density dwellings just across the highway.

Two waves of railway and consistent road building have combined to consolidate basic elements of the settlement pattern and major movement routes. This overall pattern persists, with strong north–south routes in the inland and along the coastal tourism strip, and little emphasis on east–west routes. From a more optimistic perspective, however, the linear coastal development accelerated by the growth of car use after World War Two has created a pattern that supports the city's best-patronised bus route and offers support for the eventual extension of the light rail system.

Which century is this timetable? 1940s travelling times for twenty-first-century commuters

The South Brisbane to Southport train took 1 h 40 min in the 1940s, and 1 h 42 min in 1962 (Arundell 2011, p. 51). It is an indictment of the continuing low priority given to public transport that a similar commuter trip from Southport to South Brisbane in 2014, requiring changing from bus to train at Nerang, could still take 1 h 41 min (TransLink 2014). The lack of integration between modes is critical, as is the lack of meaningful bus priority on the most congested road links. Indeed, the first stage of the new light rail system does not connect with the heavy rail line, with stage one aimed at local intra-Gold Coast travel rather than commuters to Brisbane (Mepham 2013).

Travel times by public transport to the southern end of the Gold Coast have fared little better. In the 1940s, the ~100 km train trip from South Brisbane to Coolangatta took 2 h 40 min (Arundell 2011). The 'new' Gold Coast railway only extends ~85 km south of Brisbane, terminating at Varsity Lakes. Passengers transfer here to a bus, which, ironically, follows the former South Coast Railway alignment along a section of Pacific Motorway built in the rail reservation in the 1980s. Today's commuter trip from Coolangatta to South Brisbane, transferring from bus to train at Varsity Lakes, shaves only between 22 and 38 min off the 1940s trip. In light traffic, this trip can be made by car in just over an hour, though the competitiveness of public transport is gaining steadily as car congestion increases at peak times.

In the late 1940s, when rail patronage on the South Coast Railway was at its peak, coastal buses on the 30 km trip from Southport Railway Station to Coolangatta took 'about an hour' (Arundell 2011, p. 30). The same bus trip in mid-2014, through a more urbanised coastal environment, took around 1 hr 15 min. With a transfer to light rail at Broadbeach South, a similar trip now takes about 1 hr 22 min (TransLink 2014). Better timetabling and bus/light rail priority are urgent needs.

Shaping a borderless city with a cross-border railway line, airport and highway

Three significant transport infrastructure projects have assisted the development of an urban settlement pattern in which the Gold Coast's urban footprint is not contained or spatially defined by the Queensland–New South Wales border which constitutes the city's southern political boundary. These three projects were: the South Coast Railway's final stage, which served the contiguous 'twin towns' of Coolangatta and Tweed Heads from 1903–1961; the Gold Coast Airport, constructed progressively after World War Two at Coolangatta; and the Tugun bypass on the Pacific Motorway, built in the first decade of the twenty-first century. The three projects represent a level of interstate cooperation in planning and infrastructure development that remains rare in Australia (O'Hare 2011; New South Wales Government 2012).

These three transport infrastructure projects have shaped the city in significant ways in addition to their overall effect in facilitating 'the 200 km city' (Spearritt 2009) of continuous coastal urban and suburban development extending into a 'border shadow zone' (New South Wales Government 2012, p. 5) in the adjoining state of New South Wales. Whether examined on Google Maps or on the ground, the visibility of the state border is very low. Yet this contiguous urban development has been truly 'off the plan' on planning scheme maps until very recent times: a case of 'out of state, out of mind'. Gold Coast Planning Scheme maps and Tweed Shire Council's Local Environmental Plan maps, before their early 2000s updates, show 'the other side' of Boundary Street completely blank, making it appear identical to a beachfront esplanade. The mapping of the *South East Queensland Regional Plan 2009–2031* (Queensland Government 2009a) continues the depiction of a 'terra nullius' south of the border, while the *Far North Coast Regional Strategy 2006–2031* (State of New South Wales 2006) recognises that the twin towns of Tweed Heads and Coolangatta are a future major centre, while also recognising the economic and social importance of the major centres of Robina and Southport to residents south of the border.

As discussed earlier, Tweed Heads and the Tweed Valley cemented their close relationship to Coolangatta, Gold Coast and Brisbane, with the construction of the South Coast Railway across the border into Tweed Heads in 1903 under the Border Railways Agreement with New South Wales.

At the height of the Gold Coast's 'golden era of the motor car', the two states again cooperated in the early 2000s, to build a major new road across the border, the Tugun bypass on the Pacific Motorway. Once again, the cooperation was uneven, with the New South Wales Government refusing to contribute financially despite the majority of the seven-kilometre route being in New South Wales; Queensland contributed $423 million and the federal government contributed $120 million (Queensland Government n.d.). This road was built concurrently with an expansion of Gold Coast Airport, whereby the highway was constructed in a tunnel under the extended runway. Opened in 2008, this road was built to ease traffic congestion in the southern beachside suburbs of Tugun, Bilinga and Kirra. An effect of the Tugun bypass, in combination with constant upgrades to the Pacific Motorway (by construction of additional lanes) has been to stimulate coastal suburban development south of the border, expanding existing towns and creating new ones such as Casuarina Beach and Salt within little more than an hour's drive of Brisbane, just over 100 km away. This increased accessibility for the New South Wales Far North Coast has, in turn, created more congestion on the Pacific Motorway as it traverses the Gold Coast north to Brisbane, or alternatively to the park and ride facilities of the most southerly Gold Coast railway stations at Robina and Varsity Lakes.

From a small locally oriented airport for inbound Australian tourists, Coolangatta Airport has been expanded into an international airport servicing not only inbound tourists from Australia and overseas, but also an increasing amount of outbound travel by businesses and residents of the Gold Coast and North Coast New South Wales. In parallel with growth of the City of Gold Coast into Australia's sixth largest city, the Gold Coast Airport has become Australia's fourth-busiest international airport (GCAPL 2011, p. 5).

Right from its commencement in 1936 as three emergency landing strips on the Sydney–Brisbane flight path, and initially known as Bilinga Airport, the airport's development and layout have paid virtually no attention to the border location – most notably with the runway straddling the border. Regular commercial flights commenced in 1939 and the name Coolangatta Airport came into use in subsequent decades. By the early 1950s, 12 000 passengers annually were passing through the airport (GCAPL 2011, p. 26). Continuous growth in inbound tourist numbers contributed to the growth of the Gold Coast as a major tourist destination, with over five million passengers passing through the airport annually by 2010 and over 16 million annual passenger movements forecast by 2031 (GCAPL 2011, p. 17). International airport status was granted in the 1980s and the

Fig. 4.6. Gold Coast Airport signs showing terminals ahead and Southern Cross University to the left (D O'Hare)

first international charter flights commenced in 1990. Regular air services to New Zealand commenced in 1999 and the airport's international status was upgraded to 'permanent' in 2000 (GCAPL 2011, p. 29).

Coolangatta Airport was privatised in 1998 and rebranded as Gold Coast Airport the following year, reflecting the growing status of both city and airport. Privatisation has meant that the airport lessee and operator is also a land developer, resulting in an acceleration in the development of non-airport uses on the now privately controlled Commonwealth site. Adding to its uniqueness in being located just 300 m from a surfing beach, the airport has acquired a university campus (Fig. 4.6). Southern Cross University opened its Coolangatta campus on a three-hectare site on airport land in 2010, and by 2014 ~2000 students and 130 staff had occupied the first two multi-storey university buildings (Southern Cross University n.d.). This expansion by a university with its main campus in the inland northern New South Wales regional city of Lismore, 100 km away, recognises the growth of the Gold Coast to become a city with a population nearing 20 times that of Lismore. Courses available at the campus relate to Gold Coast industries, including health, business, tourism, social sciences and education.

The growth of Gold Coast Airport and its Southern Cross University campus can be expected to increase the expressed demand for either the Gold Coast (heavy) Rail or Gold Coast light rail to be extended south to the airport more quickly than the post-2031 date indicated in current planning (City of Gold Coast 2013b). An expediting of the light rail link, in particular, would enable the southern Gold Coast to make a greater contribution to the realisation of the 'Gold Coast research triangle' identified in the Council's latest economic strategy (City of Gold Coast 2013a, p. 11; see also Chapter 11).

Gold Coast light rail: promising beginnings

The Gold Coast light rail brought the first trams to the city in July 2014. The scheme was first proposed in the 1998 *Gold Coast City Transport Plan*, in response to increasing traffic congestion (Mepham 2013). After an initial feasibility study in 2004 and further detailed planning from 2006, the Queensland Government endorsed the project in 2008 and Gold Coast City Council committed to a $120 million contribution towards the cost of the first stage. In 2009 the federal government committed $365 million and the state government $464 million, bringing total funding to almost one billion dollars. The GoldLinQ consortium was selected in May 2011 to construct and operate the first stage under a public-private partnership (Mepham 2013, p. 13).

The first stage, 13 km with 16 stations, travels through the heart of the city from the Gold Coast Health and Knowledge Precinct with stations at the new hospital and Griffith University, through Southport's business centre (see Fig. 4.7) and the tourism centres of Surfers Paradise and Broadbeach, finishing adjacent to Pacific Fair shopping centre. This route includes the Gold Coast Convention Centre and the major tourism infrastructure, but stage one does not connect with the heavy rail line to Brisbane and travel to Gold Coast Airport requires changing to a bus. Only when future stages are constructed – extending to connect with heavy rail at Helensvale and south, to the Gold Coast Airport – will these limitations be overcome.

Given patronage on stage one of more than 18 500 passengers per day, there is encouraging political, academic and media support for extending the Gold Coast light rail on the four lines depicted in the *City Transport Strategy 2031* (City of Gold Coast 2013b). With no funding attached to the proposal, a more popular (and cheaper) option to connect the light

Fig. 4.7. Gold Coast light rail at Southport Station (M Burke)

rail to heavy rail along the Smith Street Motorway, running east–west, emerged. The *Gold Coast Bulletin* began lobbying for the system to be extended immediately after stage one opened. Other parties have been more quietly assembling their case for moving quickly towards implementing other key routes, such as linking from the coastal line via Bond University to Robina Station on the heavy rail line and to Gold Coast Airport (Bitzios Consulting 2013).

Active transport for Australia's least active urban residents

Unfortunately, the low levels of walking and cycling in the city will also be a significant challenge to overcome. Too great a proportion of the city's cyclists are adult males, with children, women and seniors notably absent compared to European or Asian cities where cycling is common. The city's flat topography and good weather should be conducive to 'active' non-motorised travel. But there are other barriers. Only in recent decades has attention been given to creating a meaningful network of bicycle routes and shared paths. Council is now very pro-active through its active transport strategy but 50 years of disinvestment could take a similar time period to reverse. Green bridges for walking and cycling to connect the canals and islands will be needed, in significant numbers. A signature shared path along the coastline – the Oceanway – is world class and achieves extremely high usage. But it deviates through narrow high trafficked streets in key areas where it should clearly stay along the shoreline. The Gold Coast also suffers the same out-dated speed limits of 50 km/h that are common in local streets across Australia, and which threaten vulnerable road users and dissuade everyday cyclists.

Conclusion: future planning, future prospects

The transport future looks much brighter for the city, thanks to increased attention to planning in recent decades. The best example of its strengths in planning is stage one of the light rail system, which was one of the few federally-funded projects during the funding window of the Rudd and Gillard administrations, and which has since slammed shut. The light rail was 'shovel ready', with the route planned, sensitivities negotiated and a sound business case prepared, when stage one was recommended by Infrastructure Australia, the Commonwealth's advisory body on infrastructure. By contrast, Canberra's very similar light rail scheme was knocked back due to a paucity of sound transport and land-use planning.

The Gold Coast is blessed by having more coordinated and relatively consistent transport and land-use planning from 1998, which culminated in 2013 with its *City Transport Strategy 2031*. The challenges, as in any growing city, are considerable. There will be major issues in funding new transport infrastructure, given declines in already low fuel excise, low corporate taxes and debt challenges across all levels of government in Australia. Corridors for new arterial road expansion in the built-up area are non-existent, essentially forcing a focus on public transport, walking and cycling capacity in coming years. The irony is that, after 50 years as Australia's most car-dominated city, the Gold Coast's structure is ideal to support a long line-haul public transport corridor along the route that the full light rail scheme is planned. This will link up its many land uses (an airport, universities, tourist centres, shopping centres, business centres and hospitals) like pearls on a string and may prove one of the most cost-effective routes in the nation. The heavy rail line also has significant capacity to support a set of more urban activity centres connected by quality public transport. The potential for a rapid change in mode share is therefore substantial, particularly if the population starts to walk and cycle more. This will make the city both more sustainable and more resilient, as well as more tourist friendly.

Acknowledgements

The authors have separately undertaken a series of interviews with key actors in planning and development of the Gold Coast, conducted in the period 2009–13. Though this paper does not draw directly on this material, our thanks go to the interviewees for their insights, which influenced and informed parts of the work. The Urban Research Program receives research funding from Gold Coast City Council and the Queensland Department of Transport and Main Roads. The views expressed are entirely the authors' and do not represent any institution; the authors take responsibility for any errors and omissions.

Chapter 5

The Gold Coast: innovation incubator for the real estate development industry?

Eddo Coiacetto, Sacha Reid and Andrew Leach

Property development is a volatile industry, reliant upon market demands and environmental conditions. Subject to significant cyclical economic trends, it relies on a high degree of strategisation to retain competitive advantage. It requires constant innovation to the extent that it needs products and services that are explicitly novel both to meet emerging market demands and to foster new markets. While innovation does not always benefit those who engage in property development, it has over time resulted in welcome housing and finance products, greater consumer choice and lower or more resource efficient production costs, not to mention lower prices. Hargroves and Smith (2005) astutely contend that innovation underpins an economically sustainable real estate development industry. The following pages explore innovations in real estate development on the Gold Coast, testing the accuracy of the sense pervading the city's local history that the Gold Coast sustained a higher concentration of innovations than other cities in Australia and in the region.

Real estate development and innovation

The real estate and development industry is difficult to study. In part this is because of the secrecy necessary to secure economic advantage (Healey and Barrett 1990), but also for the more mundane reasons that such data as fiscal output are not usually made publicly accessible, development entities constantly enter and leave the industry, especially through development cycles, and it is not always easy or possible to precisely identify an individual leading development in a corporate setting (Coiacetto 2009b). Many kinds of businesses, organisations and individuals undertake development on either a once-off or an ongoing basis, and there are no registration or certification requirements as to who can enter and participate in this industry.

In market-based economies, real estate development is subject to a high degree of risk, operating as it does in an imperfect market situation where property values are difficult to establish and maintain, demand and supply conditions can be difficult to predict, and where buyer and seller psychology have an effect on prices (Adams 1994; compare Neilson 1976). Land assembly can be complex and characterised by secretive dealings and negotiations to prevent developers' intentions from being fully known (Dodson *et al.* 2006). The process involves risk and uncertainty around such matters as funding, interest rates, building and development approvals, construction timeframes and costs, and site conditions. Projects can involve long lead times but, once commenced, often require irreversible commitments of significant resources. The opportunities offered by site availability or market conditions can, nonetheless, be fleeting, requiring those involved in real estate development to regularly make decisions with a high degree of uncertainty and in the absence of all the information that might otherwise alleviate their risk (Whitehead 1987; see also Daly 1982).

The importance of local information and local contacts to reduce risk and uncertainty has meant that development has historically been largely a local industry: a developer, an individual usually, operating within a given local area with good local knowledge and contacts. The developer typically borrowed from banks or financial institutions on short-term, above-average interest rate loans subject to frequent reviews and site inspections (Logan 1993). However, new ways to finance development in recent decades permitted the growth of much larger corporate developers operating at national and even international scales, albeit maintaining a strong local presence (Logan 1993). Australia has seen the emergence of publicly listed firms Lend Lease, Delfin (since absorbed into Lend Lease), Mirvac and Stockland, and the arrival of international corporations like ING and Seiksui House. Developers adopt different strategies with respect to matters like the geographical scope of operations, their exposure to risk, innovativeness, decision-making processes and reliance on local knowledge (Coiacetto 2001). There is also considerable variation in developer sub-market targeting and associated strategies: for example, some specialise on narrow development sub-markets, some target a range of markets in the one location while others are more opportunistic (Coiacetto 2007).

Novelty is central to the development industry. Damanpour (1991, p. 376) defines innovation as the 'adoption of an idea or behaviour, whether a system, policy, program, device, process, product or service, that is new to the adopting organisation'. Innovations range along a continuum from disruptive and radical through to incremental (Dewer and Dutton 1986). Radical innovations produce fundamental changes to organisational structures or activities that result in clear adjustments from previous norms or practices. However, as Garcia and Calantone (2002) acknowledge, radical innovations that actually change or revolutionise the world are rare. Incremental innovations, representing a lesser degree of adjustment from existing practices, are in fact much more common (Kleinschmidt and Cooper 1991). Herbig and Golden (1993, p. 77) suggest that 'the predominant attitude in innovative communities is one not only of acceptance of entrepreneurship but admiration'. Entrepreneurs are risk-takers who are able to innovate to gain competitive advantage. Therefore, innovation is reliant upon a range of stakeholders collaborating to provide innovative outcomes that are new to an industry, market or company. In real estate development, it has long been important for individuals and corporations to differentiate themselves to secure a competitive edge – but then with the proviso that any innovator can bring with them an individual or group of individuals who are willing to step outside of industry norms to try something new, with all the risks this entails.

Industrial economics seems to suggest that competitive industries with many small players tend to be more innovative than those dominated by a concentration of large-scale entities (Shepherd 1997). Real estate complicates this image, however, since larger-scale firms can be highly innovative (Coiacetto 2006) and any measure of industrial concentration in real estate development is clouded by geographical scale and the nature of what is 'local' for commercial purposes. Real estate is spatially fixed, so any developer can exercise some degree of spatial monopoly. Showpiece developers, in addition, can be motivated by

Fig. 5.1. The Oracle by DBI Design, Broadbeach, completed 2011 (Photograph by Jason Thien 2010, https://creativecommons.org/licenses/by/2.0/)

status and the desire to somehow stand out, occasionally having sufficient access to funds to comfortably neglect market research, risk and detriment of return. Usually showpiece developers are motivated to produce developments that are atypically innovative – and tend to be iconic in character, or found in special locations like waterfront settings and significant tourist destinations (Coiacetto 2001).

On the whole, however, real estate development depends upon consumer trends and demand and Ball (1999, p. 12) is typical of a view holding that 'consumers are notoriously conservative in their tastes in house styles'. Projected property values and tradability can shape a consumer's decision about the style of his or her housing, with greater deviation from any given norm risking appeal to a niche market with consequent risks to the consumer and volatility for the developer regarding the length of time a property remains on the market, given fiscal costs. These factors influence the degree of innovation and practices within the development industry.

Development on the Gold Coast

A highly varied physical geography has informed diverse opportunities for property development along the Gold Coast. Urban development follows the coast in a strip from Coolangatta to the mouth of the Nerang River and then along the western edge of the lower reaches of the Broadwater, as well as on some of the small low islands within the lower reaches of the Broadwater. The two Stradbroke Islands are relatively undeveloped while, as others in this volume have noted, urbanisation follows more or less parallel strips to the coast itself: the beach strip, a high-rise tower/residential coastal strip, the highway strip, the canal estates, the suburbs and the semi-rural hinterland (Goad 1997).

A salient feature of this urbanisation, worth repeating in this context, is the variability of the intensity of development, with some sites prone to redevelopment and others not. In the coastal strip, especially, one finds recently constructed high-rise towers, on sites that may have been developed three times, overlooking buildings from earlier phases of development: low-rise flats from the 1970s, 1960s motels and 1950s fibro shacks and single family homes. The most intensively developed area is in the central coast starting from the mouth of the Nerang River at Southport and south through Surfers Paradise to Broadbeach.

While development is important in shaping Australian cities, in no other Australian city is development so linked in the public imagination as Queensland's Gold Coast. Moreover, the reality appears to match the imagination. The name itself, formally adopted in 1959 as the City of the Gold Coast, was promoted by developers (Moore 2005), building on a tradition extending back to the supplanting of the settlement of Elston by the name of the city's first successful subdivision, the Surfers Paradise Estate, which in 1917 seeded the Gold Coast's most iconic district (Moore 2005). The most widely read accounts of the Coast's history, growth and culture focus on the contribution of development and developers (Kilmartin 1966; McRobbie 1966; Moore 2005; Hajdu 2005). While many cities have had histories written from the perspective of property development, one could imagine a robust history of the Gold Coast written solely as if it were a history of development and its characters: individuals like Stanley Korman who 'strode like a giant across the Gold Coast scene' (McRobbie 1966, p. 43), alongside such local heroes (celebrated and disgraced alike) as Bruce Small, Bernie Elsey, Christopher Skase and, more recently, Michael Gore, Alan Bond, Jim Raptis and Soheil Abedian. There is great significance in Small's canal estates of Paradise City (now Isle of Capri) and Miami Keys being known by the name of their developer rather than that of their planner, Karl Langer, just as Langer is eclipsed by Korman as author of Paradise Island.

McRobbie's (1966) *Gold Coast Story* is an early document in the city's development history, and in many respects seeks to capture its innovations at the moment of their occurrence. He recounts a series of Australian firsts (or nearly firsts) that did much to set up the easy equivalence of the Gold Coast's urbanisation history with that of its development culture. As early as 1952, McRobbie recalls, a 'Chinese syndicate' built the first serviced apartment in the town (as it then was) (McRobbie 1966, p. 23). He cites the Surfers Paradise Motel, built in 1955 by Greg Graham and Bill Reichelt (later called the El Dorado), was only one of three in Australia (presumably accounting, too, for the Tarzana Trav-o-tel in Coolangatta, built in 1949, and Elsey's Sky Rider Motel, from 1952); he recalls the construction of Lennons Broadbeach Hotel, which opened for business in December 1955 as the Coast's first world-class hotels, complete with in-house entertainment; and he recounts the cooperation between authorities of the Albert River Shire and Gold Coast to approve works on a canal estate, Florida Gardens, which 'was considered almost unbelievable in those days' (McRobbie 1966, p. 32). Techniques for developing 'normal estates' through site levelling and preparation were also at the end of the 1950s, and on Chevron (Goat) Island Stanley Korman pioneered the transfer of full-grown trees to the Chevron Hotel. The construction in 1966 of a 10-storey apartment block called The Sands made the Gold Coast a pioneer of individually saleable strata titled apartments.

During the 1950s and 1960s, progress and success were measured by the magnitude of change, by the extent of the re-shaping/re-moulding of the land. A local newspaper proudly reported the transformations evidenced in the Gold Coast area: 'FROM ABORIGINAL

[sic] corroboree ground and bora ring to a rapidly developing Gold Coast residential area – that is the success story of [the Gold Coast]' (Anonymous 1968). And in an earlier article: 'All around Surfers Paradise today, there is ample evidence of foul swampy areas being eliminated and producing excellent land suitable for subdivision' (Anonymous 1958). As Arthur Richards put it in the *Courier Mail* in 1954 (McRobbie 1984, p. 81): 'The large, rambling, essentially Queensland holiday home is dying out as a commercial proposition, and the sophisticated apartment and service-flat are coming in. They are the sort of thing you see on a larger scale in Honolulu.' The new and modern 'American' serviced apartment proved so popular that many other holiday accommodation types were left vacant for much of the year.

A building boom of the late 1970s and early 1980s saw the widespread inclusion of spas and heated swimming pools, electronic security systems and such postmodern features as atria and view-maximising glass exteriors (Jones 1986). The expansion of the Japanese tourist market into the late 1980s also set a new and high standard for the quality of development and luxury on the Coast and in Australia, with easy access to amenity and high standards of comfort. Developer Michael Gore introduced an Australian novelty in 1986 by way of the Sanctuary Cove development, which was the country's first gated community and master-planned resort. It set the scene for much of the development that would follow in later decades. Such high-rise projects as Atlantis in northern Surfers Paradise explored the 'vertical' gated community (Fig. 5.5). In a signal that the city's development culture would continue striving for novelties and extremes, when the Q1 apartment tower (see Fig. 5.2), built by Soheil Abedian's Sunland Group, was completed in Surfers Paradise in 2005, it was the world's tallest residential building – a title since acquired by other buildings in Dubai and New York – and the southern hemisphere's tallest building. In 2011, the completion of the $700 million Surfers Paradise Hilton Hotel and Residences introduced a new style of premier living with residents having access to all the advantages of a five-star hotel, such as concierge, valet and room service.

While the history of the Gold Coast might have been written as a history of development, its episodes are populated with the exploits of individual actors. The mechanisms and imperatives of this history exceed the scale of the individuals who applied them to specific situations. Historical accounts of Gold Coast development tend to present the early developers as small, entrepreneurial, risk-taking and even heroic businessmen. Russell and Faulkner (2004, p. 567) recall the wave of development in Coolangatta following the construction of its first purpose-built accommodations, the Greenmount Guest House (see Fig. 5.3), which was 'built by a colourful Irish entrepreneur, Paddy Fagan'. Fagan recognised Coolangatta's potential as a destination for visitors following the extension of the railway from Brisbane – and had even built stations along the length of the new rail line.

Writing in 1986 and the era of Christopher Skase, Michael Jones (1986, p. 8) lamented the disappearance of the Gold Coast visionaries and their predictable trajectories from promise to collapse:

> *Much of the charm of the Gold Coast came from the small entrepreneurs such as Bernie Elsey, Bruce Small, Stanley Korman and other small operators who took risks and often failed. The 1980s is seeing a new type of capitalism. Investments are on a far greater scale, often involving several hundred million dollars in the one development. Sophisticated market research and complex American entertainment technology mean that the small operator is now less important. There is risk that big capitalism is as bureaucratic and boring as big government and the Coast may lose some of its charm.*

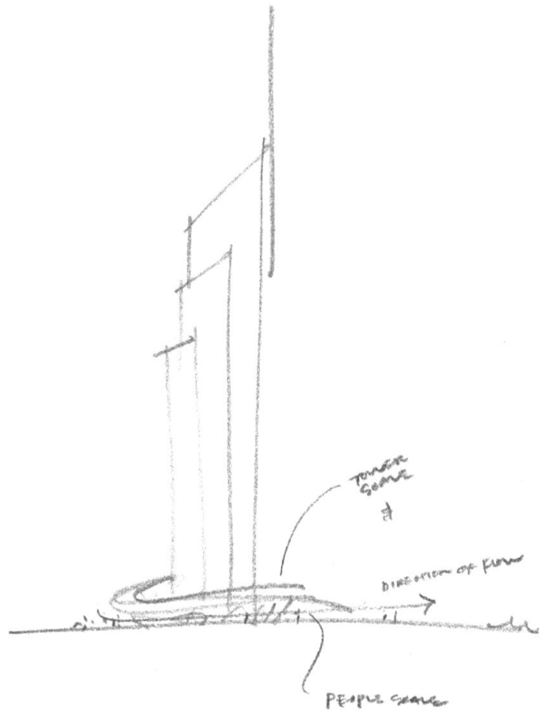

Fig. 5.2. Design sketch, Q1, by Sunland Design Group with Buchan Group (tower) and Innovarchi (podium) (Image courtesy of Innovarchi)

This regret at the excessive scale of later development and commercialisation echoes commentaries by other witnesses of the Gold Coast's rapid urbanisation (McRobbie 1966; Mullins, 1984). This nostalgia notwithstanding, the city's popular histories actually show that the Gold Coast since the 1950s has been subject to large-scale investments in both apartment buildings and estates (especially canal estates – see Kilmartin 1966; Jones 1986; McRobbie 1966).

Migrating from Melbourne in the 1950s, Bruce Small developed 1000 ha of land, pioneering canal estates on the back of its American successes in southern Florida. His efforts laid the foundations of the present day Isle of Capri, Sorrento, Benowa and Cypress Gardens. Small understood that the success of the city as a whole and the success of individual enterprises were inextricably linked – one must see his initiative to combat the introduction of paid parking with the introduction of Meter Maids, as well as his successful bid for the mayoralty in 1967, as part of a continuum that began with acting on the promise of the city's undeveloped marshland (Jones 1986). A result of the efforts of another migrant from Melbourne, the first stage of the Chevron Hotel was completed in 1958 at a cost of more than £2.75 million. In 1960, its developer, Stanley Korman, flew in 200 interstate guests to promote the hotel and the investment opportunities bound up in its construction – not a cheap feat at the time. Kilmartin (1966) notes that the activity of many smaller developers relied upon the success of large developers and the momentum fostered by their efforts.

Forbes and Spearritt (2003, p. 1) note that 'Australians, for generations, have demanded the right to buy (or even be given) land and to proclaim their right to develop

Fig. 5.3. Greenmount Guest House by Burling Brown and Partners, Coolangatta, completed 1981 (Drawing courtesy of Burling Brown and Partners)

it for the highest possible economic return'. This has been manifest in many Australian families increasing their property holdings beyond the family home, to include holiday homes and investment properties. The *Home Units Building Act 1965* (McRobbie 1966) opened the way for strata titling, which allowed Australians to own a unique part of the 'sun, surf and sand' dream that developers and marketeers sold. Abolition of death taxes (in Queensland, especially), cash grants, and interest rate and tax concessions have all facilitated the Australian dream of home ownership and stimulated the production of home units, many for investment. This legislative change created a taxation system that favoured property investment, positioning the Gold Coast and Queensland as an appealing subtropical tax haven where investors can reduce their tax payment (Jones 1986). Strata titling enabled the selling of units to 'mum and dad' investors, further opening up demand for developers to create holiday units on the Gold Coast. The introduction of timeshares likewise allowed an apartment building to be broken into thousands of small tradeable shares that required intensive direct marketing to sell. First introduced in Australia in 1983, by 1984 the Gold Coast had eight out of Australia's 20 timeshare developments (McRobbie 1984).

There were 6220 approvals for low-rise flats from 1963–1970, 8369 approvals from 1971–1977, 6742 approved during the period 1978–1980 and 10 885 from 1981–1983, primarily clustered around Surfers Paradise. At the peak of the property boom on the Gold Coast in 1981, almost 2500 high-rise units were sold and over 3500 were under construction. These highly leveraged investments were exposed to fluctuating interest rates and the Gold Coast also experienced several 'property busts' in these years that affected prospects for investors and developers alike. In 1984, a major crash occurred with property sales dropping to virtually zero and prices for high-rise dwellings declined 50–60% (Jones 1986).

The opening up of the Gold Coast to international tourists in the 1980s and 1990s through international air travel and infrastructure provided further avenues for investment. At this time the Australian Government instigated changes to foreign investment regulation, allowing for greater foreign direct property investments (Rimmer 1994). The role of timeshare, strata titling and marketing the Coast's development products elsewhere over this time (and since) demonstrates that Gold Coast real estate products have often been directed towards external investment rather than for the local consumption of owner-occupiers. Investment property marketing helps boost consumption beyond what the rental market currently wants and the Coast spawned a phenomenon known as two-tier marketing: different prices for local and remote buyers, sometimes resulting in overpricing of more than 30% (McDonald 1999).

It does seem that from early days, the Gold Coast has been a mecca for flamboyant, showpiece developers. The many Japanese investors of the late 1980s boom were motivated by the high status afforded to property and to golf club membership in contemporary Japanese culture and a desire to produce landmark developments of the very highest quality (and sometimes attracted by the comparatively laid-back Australian lifestyle) (Hajdu 2005). Backed by ready funding, the Coast attracted an array of players from both development and non-development backgrounds, including pop stars, fashion designers and plastic components manufacturer Nifsan, one of the last Japanese developers still creating landmarks on the Coast. The construction of the first six-star Versace Hotel in Australia, a joint venture between the Versace Group and Sunland Group, provides a nationally famous example of a more contemporary showpiece development on the Gold Coast, as does Nifsan's quirky Emerald Lakes project (see Fig. 5.4). The race to build the world's tallest residential tower places Sunland Group firmly in this set of developers for whom the economic imperative was only part of the story of their investment.

Indeed, over time, the scale of projects on the Gold Coast has grown, as it has elsewhere. By the 1980s some of the proposed estates were for areas amounting to hundreds of

Fig. 5.4. Two views of Emerald Lakes by Nifsan Development, (a) architectural style and (b) urban design detail, Carrara, early 2000 (C Bosman)

hectares and hundreds of millions of dollars: Gaven Forest, a $400 million large-lot satellite city for a population of 25 000; Hope Island, which on 200 ha proposed to be the Coast's first international standard fully self-contained themed resort; and Robina, a $1.2 billion proposal for a 1600 ha satellite city to house a population of 60 000 (McRobbie 1984).

Whether the impact of the Gold Coast's development industry is more pronounced than it is in other Australian cities is a matter of perception and difficult, therefore, to assert with any confidence. What kind of balance does the city sustain between national developers and smaller (or individual) entrepreneurs? Unlike other industries, measuring concentration in development is methodologically problematic and extremely rare, while geographically comparative measures are seemingly non-existent (Coiacetto 2009b). However, it does seem that the same large national developers that are dominant elsewhere in Australia and the Asia-Pacific region are now dominant here: Stockland, Delfin-Lend Lease, Mirvac and Nifsan, along with the regionally-focused Brisbane firms, Heritage-Pacific and Devine. Whether one can reconcile the role of such individuals as Elsey, Small and Korman with the scale of their projects, it seems fair to suggest that the Gold Coast has never been – or has not for many decades been – a realm of small gestures. '[The] scale and complexity of the tourism industry on the Coast now make it more difficult for an individual acting alone to initiate a turning point in the direction of development' (Russell and Faulkner 2004, p. 574). The grand development gestures of the 1960s, 1970s and 1980s have ceased being identified with the visions of individuals and have since become a matter of corporate imagination – in their public presentation if not in reality.

Fig. 5.5. Atlantis by The Heather Thiedeke Group, Paradise Waters, completed 1982 (Photograph by Richard Stringer)

In this regard, the Gold Coast has been at the forefront of promotion and marketing, especially in its cultivation of the city's image for interstate or overseas markets. From the 1950s, media personalities and signature events helped to sell developments or – amounting to the same thing – promote the city itself as a destination for visits or investment (McRobbie 1966). These events included widely reported 'pyjama parties', staged international air hostess quests, lottery prizes, and newspaper and television competition prizes of new homes. Developers in the 1960s spent millions in the 'boom' period of orthodox advertising, but were active, too, in promoting stunts that caught the imagination of the nation and attracted their own publicity. Chartering flights to bring prospective land buyers up from Melbourne and Sydney – replete with champagne lunches and in-flight bikini fashion parades – not only offered a novel way to inspect a real estate development (McRobbie 1966), but fostered a media image around these efforts themselves. This continued in later years, as in Frank Sinatra's famous opening of Sanctuary Cove.

A more recent development product has emerged in the form of active adult (age-segregated) lifestyle communities (AALCs), targeting owners above the age of 55. Widespread in the United States, they nonetheless have their problems. AALCs are age-segregated, master-planned communities designed specifically for active adults between the ages of 55–74. They are usually niche market developments, targeted at financially secure, healthy and active baby boomer cohorts or WOOAPies (well-off older active persons). AALCs began to emerge in the Australian and New Zealand market in the early 2000s. AALCs offer owners the opportunity to reside within a community of likeminded individuals with similar backgrounds, interests and aspirations. In AALCs resident age restrictions are enforced by property title deed and covenants, and children are prohibited from residing in the community for any length of time. There are no investors or renters in AALCs, resulting in a relatively homogenous socio-economic and demographic composition. AALCs are explicitly exclusive, at the high end of the property market. Halcyon Waters (2005–13) (see Fig. 5.6) is one

Fig. 5.6. Halcyon Waters by Halcyon, Hope Island, mid 2000s (C Bosman)

such master-planned lifestyle residential resort, designed specifically for baby boomers. Built on ~14 ha, it is situated within 100 ha of protected wetland and offers detached two or three-bedroom, mostly single-storied houses on 250–350 m^2 blocks.

The Gold Coast and real estate innovation

In what sense do these episodes add up to a history of innovation? Some developers, like Korman, a lover of all things American, built monuments to themselves. Others imported ideas to the Coast that had taken hold elsewhere, but especially from the United States, which culturally and economically shared a great deal with Australian society since the end of World War Two. Canal estates and home units – along with the value of 'lavishness' – are certainly the most iconic of these local innovations. Japanese investors of the 1980s sampled ideas from the western seaboard of mainland America (and especially the highly mediatised California) and Hawai'i to evolve an image that represented everything prestigious and desirable about the affluent, cosmopolitan lifestyles they saw in these situations in the later decades of the twentieth century. They translated these, in particular, in rolled out instant golf-estate landscapes and such instant landmarks as the mauve Belle Maison in Broadbeach (Hajdu 2005). But the Coast also has smaller-scale, less showy environmentally contextualised initiatives, like the Couran Cove tourist resort on South Stradbroke Island (see Fig. 5.7) and the Currumbin residential eco-village at the margins of the coastal urban strip. Facilitated by accommodating financial supporters, these showpiece developments boasted practical innovations in planning and building technology that other developers were quick to investigate.

Fig. 5.7. Couran Cove Resort by Daryl Jackson, South Stradbroke Island, completed 1998 (Photograph by D Sandison, courtesy of Jackson Architects)

The entrepreneurial character of developers on the Gold Coast has gone a long way towards shaping the image and identity of the city. As McRobbie (1988, p. 19) observed more than a generation ago: 'Surfers Paradise is the story of free enterprise … bold and innovative risk-taking which involved true entrepreneurial flair'. Mullins (1984) noted that it was the leaders of the city's inextricably linked public and private sectors who 'had entrepreneurial skills, close and important links to major investors and the maverick politics needed to create the investment climate necessary to attract the hallmark projects' (in Prideaux 2004, p. 46). This alliance is exemplified 'in the actions of the Gold Coast City Council in the 1960s and 1970s when Bruce Small (a developer-politician) was mayor and a state politician' (Mullins 1990, pp. 40–41). A pro-development attitude of local and state government certainly facilitated the Gold Coast's rapid growth (Mullins 1990; Morris 2004; Prideaux 2004). Russell and Faulkner (2004, p. 572) show that the Coast went 'beyond the situation of a lax regulatory environment to a point where entrepreneurs co-opted the regulators by infiltrating the political structures (state and local) to which the planners were accountable'. Development approvals were gained or obtained, regardless of holistic infrastructure concerns or requirements (Burchill 2005; Dedekorkut-Howes and Bosman 2015).

These environments for property development introduced new kinds of real estate product to the Gold Coast – and to Australia as a whole. Not radical innovations in and of themselves, many of these developments were new and innovative in the Australian context. These include product innovations as in the creation of gated communities and canal style developments; process innovations in the preparation of environmentally sensitive wetland sites for canal style developments; and administrative and organisational innovations in the sector allowing many companies to expand and contract during times of volatility to cope with market conditions. Marketing of developments was a central innovation that many Gold Coast developers and marketeers pioneered. Institutionally, the introduction of strata titling and timeshare developments changed the availability and options for consumers. Together, these innovations, along with the entrepreneurial and innovative spirit of developers on the Gold Coast, have reshaped the city again and again over the course of its history.

Chapter 6

Changing landscapes: Gold Coast residents and the impacts of rapid urban development

Caryl Bosman

With a population of half a million people, the Gold Coast is already far larger than some of the state capitals and it remains one of the fastest growing cities in Australia. Its population continues to grow, with many migrants from the eastern states of Australia and elsewhere in Queensland having previously visited the Gold Coast as vacationers. There are significant differences between the migration cohorts of the decades between 1950 and 1990, and the current influx. The early years swelled the city's entrepreneurial, professional and business cohort. Growth today reflects a steady stream of baby boomers moving to the Gold Coast to retire – the 'sandrush' as Brendan Gleeson (2007) calls it – along with people aged 20–25 who seek part-time work, mainly in the tourist and hospitality industries. These two population groupings constitute the largest sectors of the Gold Coast City population growth pie.

Who are the residents of the Gold Coast? This chapter addresses this question in order to highlight links between demographic cohorts and real estate, planning and development. In doing so I present a demographic account of the Gold Coast, describing the forces that shaped the city's permanent, semi-permanent and short-term populations at key moments in its history. I consider the Gold Coast through the lens of its long-term residents, their quality of life, needs and requirements, rather than through its transient tourist population. I discuss the long-term consequences of rapid urban change to the residential population and the effects of planning policies that are predominantly orientated towards tourist populations. I conclude by emphasising, as others have done before me, the importance of acknowledging local residents in urban planning and decision-making processes.

The outcomes of rapid population growth and urban change on the Gold Coast have effectively produced two different forms of urbanisation: resident and tourist. This has not always been the case. During the early years of its urbanisation (from the 1950s to the 1980s) the Gold Coast was perceived and experienced as a family-friendly, safe environment in which to live and holiday. The current resident landscapes of the Gold Coast paint a very different picture. Like many other tourist cities, the residential landscapes are physically, socially and aesthetically different from the city's tourist landscapes. This segregation has had significant effects on residents' experience of home and place. As others have found, the failure by planners and urban designers to take into account local everyday significance and values can result in the alienation of residential subjects 'from each other and from their own place' (Cartier and Lew 2005, n.p.). The result is a 'risky' place that holds little meaning for local people and that can consequently fail to capture and hold the interest of tourists, placing the city into peril as local everyday activity nodes move elsewhere.

The potential to 'lock out' local people from a place – be it a result of social or economic factors – is perhaps the greatest impact tourists have in touristed cities. I argue that the values and meanings maintained by local people are pivotal in ensuring viable places that are economically, socially and ecologically sustainable. The key message of this chapter is that experiences of home and place are affected by the pace and extent of change. The narratives conveyed here remind us of the importance of pro-active planning practices that focus on both people and home-places, residential places that engender and harness positive urban narratives, not just over a single life-course but for future generations.

Change, risk and home

In order to understand the histories of the Gold Coast it is necessary to understand processes of change. Change is historical and the relationships between change and adaptation are not always equitable. Change is socio-spatial (Ellison and Burrows 2007); it is a layering process that has both positive and negative outcomes. Yet the negative aspects and risks of both the threat and actuality of transformation are most often promulgated over its positive effects. Change is linked to rationalities of risk through discourses of choice and loss: of community, of local identity, of the 'good life'. To combat these losses, this instability and insecurity, discourses on risk are produced with the aim to secure 'safe' and 'pleasant' environments and ultimately the health, wealth and wellbeing of the individual, the collective and the population. This is achieved primarily through active, responsible choice. However it might be defined, risk and change impact on notions of home.

There is a substantial body of literature on the home (Williams and McIntyre 2001; Easthope 2004; Hart and Ben-Yoseph 2005; Blunt and Dowling 2006; Cloutier-Fisher and Harvey 2009). Most authors agree that home cannot be tied down to a single definition. It is frequently understood emotionally, historically and often tied into political, social, cultural, economic, environmental and spiritual beliefs and concerns. It is linked, too, to memories and tied into different temporal and spatial experiences. Home may be related to ontological security or to a bounded location or be rooted in place. It may also be 'nomadic' (Hart and Ben-Yoseph 2005), fixed in neither time nor place. Home in this instance is transferrable and applicable to any time and any place depending on the home-maker. In addition, home may be experienced at different scales: the planet, the country/nation, the state/region, the city, the street, the allotment number, the house or the room; or it may be indexed in a piece of furniture.

Stories of rapid urban change

To understand how Gold Coast residents have come to regard their home on the Gold Coast – or indeed the Gold Coast as home – I draw upon 16 interviews and oral histories conducted with Gold Coast residents. These stories offer insights into everyday life experiences of change and specifically how residents' homes have been affected by these changes. All participants were born between 1946 and 1963 (i.e. baby boomers). The majority of participants moved to the Gold Coast between 1960 and the mid-1980s, and others had grown up on the Coast. A snowball method was used to identify potential participants: after the initial participant (who was known to the interviewer personally) each subsequent participant was suggested by the previous interviewee. This method ensured that there was a large pool of potential participants within the research parameters. Interviews were semi-structured and allowed for active conversation throughout whereby the interviewee took on the role of a storyteller and the interviewer as occasional prompter. Interviews were explored using NVivo software and coded and analysed following Miles and Huberman's (1994) key tactics in qualitative analysis.

Planners, urban designers and developers – place makers – often overlook local everyday attachments to place and perceive place meaning in accordance with pre-conceived notions and pre-determined outcomes. As a consequence urban landscapes potentially become de-localised as property prices and place-making development reflect tourist industry ideals and economies. John Urry (1995, p. 166) observes that the:

> *[s]pace of a neighbourhood, town or region may become overwhelmed by visitors so that locals no longer feel it is their space/place any more. So many visitors pass through, visually appropriating the space and leading locals to feel that they have 'lost their space'.*

Local residents are potentially alienated from the city and delegated to its margins due to financial, temporal and spatial pressures. Cities like the Gold Coast then risk becoming characterised by neoliberal globalisation, social polarisation, spatial inequality and local marginalisation. It is important to note that meaningful places are not meaningful for everyone, and the reason place holds value is different for different people. Mary McLeod (1997, p. 186) writes that difference 'is experienced differently, at different times, in different cultures, by different people. The point is not just to recognise difference, but all kinds of difference'.

Growth from the 1960s to the 1990s

The Gold Coast has grown from a few settlements, which in 1933 had a population of 6600 (Hofmeister 1988). By 1947 the population had increased to 8568 and by 1961 it had grown to 33 716 people (including Tweed). Until the 1950s the Gold Coast had been an affordable family holiday destination for many Brisbane residents, and in the late 1950s the holiday experience began to evolve rapidly into a tourist and residential experience (Davidson and Spearritt 2000). This rapid population growth had a significant social impact and by 1959 the Federal member for McPherson, Mr C.E. Barnes, in an opening address for the new Surfers Paradise Post Office, reminded attendees of the need to 'preserve decent moral standards' in the light of change and progress (Anonymous 1959).

By 1971 the Gold Coast population numbered 76 862 and five years later it was over 100 000 (Mullins 1979). This rapid growth did not abate, with the largest migration increase of the mid to late 1980s, which saw an increase of 250%. Stimson *et al.* (1996) report that Gold Coast migration flows for the period from 1986 to 1991 were characterised by a relatively balanced age distribution. The largest sector of the population was under 15 years of age. The next largest was over 65 years of age, followed by the 15–24-year-old cohort, with the 25–44-year-old group being the smallest. Significantly, many of these new Gold Coast residents had degree-level qualifications, high incomes and were born in Australia. By the early 1990s close to half the Gold Coast population had migrated from New South Wales and Victoria (Stimson *et al.* 1996). Between 1991 and 1996 the city registered the largest population growth (74 200 people) among all local government areas in Australia, with an average annual growth rate of 4.8% (ABS 1997).

The main reasons for migration to the Gold Coast included: job opportunities, cheap housing, mild climate, amenity and lifestyle (Maher and Stimson 1994). Brendan Gleeson (2007, n.p.) writes that 'the new national penchant for surf, sand and sun has been made possible, not to say compulsory, by rising prosperity, technological change (telecommunication) and the discovery that ocean views are vital to happiness'. Employment opportunities were critical to this migration-driven growth and these were fuelled by shifts in the real estate and development industries. Population growth also propagates professional and entrepreneurial job opportunities. Arnie, for example, was drawn to the Gold Coast in the 1980s for its employment prospects: 'the money down here was a lot ... I made three times as much here as I was back home. So, yeah, we stayed here.'

Many migrants who arrived on the Gold Coast in the 1980s were young professionals who had the ability and the intent to purchase a detached house. In some cases migrants bought prime Gold Coast residential real estate for a fraction of the sale price of their previous property in Sydney or Melbourne. Amanda explained: 'younger families, like us, could buy homes far more easily much cheaper than where we were.' Noel, too, saw housing opportunities as an important pull factor:

> *Basically, a lot of people come up here, I guess for the money part of it, that they could actually sell their house down in Sydney, come up here, buy a waterfront home and still have money to spend and whether they retire or not. And there are a lot of opportunities up here.*

Prior to 1991, 91% of migrants were either purchasing or owned their house. This, in part, reflected the high level of employment with just over half the population earning above-average national annual household incomes. There was little housing churn during this period with most migrants retaining their residential address.

Employment and housing opportunities fed the growth machine, which resulted in significant physical and social changes to the landscapes of the Gold Coast. Talking about the change to his home-place, Mike reflected:

> *My first girlfriend lived in a fibro house ... where there's like this high-rise now and next door there was just sand dunes ... and it's just so different. ... Surfers [where he lived] went through this change and there was like – I don't know – souvenir shops, T-shirt shops ... just crappy sort of real estate; sorts of timeshare shops and it all sort of changed as they were marketing towards the tourists more and the locals sort of didn't feel a part of that.*

The change from a small-town, family-friendly home-place of the 1960s to a tourist destination with all the trappings tells a story of the Gold Coast City's real estate and development booms of the 1980s.

After 1991 the Gold Coast experienced an economic depression that resulted in high levels of unemployment, a steep decrease in house ownership and an increase in property rentals. At this time, house ownership on the Gold Coast fell in comparison with other Australian cities. This was influenced by below-average national household income figures for the city and a marked decline in persons earning above the average national income. This corresponds to a drop in professional and managerial occupations among migrants and a significant increase in retired migrants, which almost doubled as a proportion of total migrants, from 17.7 to 34.1% (Stimson *et al.* 1996).

The subtropical climate and relaxed beach lifestyle are among the incentives that attracted many migrants from the southern states (and New Zealand) where the weather is typically colder and wetter, and the pace of life faster and more frenetic. Many migrants had, like Robyn, holidayed on the Gold Coast as children and had fond memories of a particular place: 'Oh Burleigh [said in a happy/nostalgic tone] … the beach and the rocks and the rock pools which is probably why I live here now.' The Gold Coast offers many migrants the opportunity to live 'the good life' all year round. Ann, talking about the Gold Coast's appeal says: 'I think it's a great place to live. I think, even if you're unemployed, why not sit on the beach and be unemployed as opposed to sitting in a dark alleyway in Melbourne and homeless and freezing?' And Arnie expresses the good life as:

> *… let's just say the weather. I've never been out of work while I've been working. If you want something, it's handy, like there's service stations, shopping centres, when you have a boat, … I can just go around the corner, chuck it into the Broadwater, and off you go.*

Although post-1991 job opportunities were not as abundant as they had been in earlier years and housing affordability started to emerge as a major issue, the Gold Coast's climate, amenity and lifestyle nonetheless continued to attract migrants from interstate and abroad.

Growth after 2000

The 2011 census put the Gold Coast's population at 557 822 (ABS 2013b). Between 2001 and 2006 it grew by 64 656 persons with a 2006 population of 433 979. The largest increase in numbers during this period was among 35–49-year-olds followed by 50–59-year-olds and 60–69-year-olds. Between 2006 and 2011 the Gold Coast–Tweed region topped the list in population growth in major cities in Australia with 2.8%. In 2012 one-third of these people were over 55 years old and this cohort is forecast to increase by 68% in 2021. This means the residential profile of many suburbs will see a significantly higher proportion of residents aged over 55, which will have social and economic implications. A relatively low population aged less than 15 years, which is below both national and state averages, exacerbates the skewed age profile of the city. But despite the common perception of the Gold Coast as a retirement hot spot, the actual proportion of the population aged 65 and over has not changed much since 1981. In 1981, 26% of the Gold Coast's population was aged 55 years or more (Mullins 1984). In 2006 this had increased to 26%, and to 27.5% by 2011. It is currently (in 2014) less than 2% higher than the national average.

The Gold Coast also has an increasingly multicultural profile and is becoming a major destination for international immigrants. The percentage of residents born overseas increased from 27.6% in 2006 (Dedekorkut-Howes and Bosman 2011) to 33.2% in 2011, which is much higher than the national and state averages.

Employment statistics for the Gold Coast show a marked change from those recorded in the 1980s, with high levels of unemployment and part-time, causal, low-paid jobs now dominating the field. In 2006, only 19.7% of population indicated they were in the top percentile of income and 17.9% were low-income households. House ownership statistics have also changed significantly. In the early 1990s, 91% of the population owned or were in the process of purchasing their own house. By 2006 this figure had dropped to 56.6%, with 31.9% of the population now renting. The financial gap between Gold Coast residents who can afford to purchase a house and those who cannot is expanding, as it is elsewhere in Australia. Many would-be house owners – a cohort of younger, middle income residents – cannot afford the accommodation of their choice, either because of lifestyle choice or actual house prises (ABC News 2007b). Housing affordability on the Gold Coast is among the worst in the country, with median house prices and rent being among the highest on record.

'Affordable housing' relates to those households who fall within the lowest 40% of the income scale and spend more than 30% of their total income on mortgage or rental payments. These households are defined as being in 'housing stress' and are the subjects of affordable housing discourses. In the development industry, affordable housing is often used as a specific market sector branding, denoting a cheaper range of housing products within a targeted price bracket. It is important to note that low cost housing is not necessarily 'affordable'. The term 'housing affordability' is understood to denote the relationships between household income, household needs and housing costs. According to the Gold Coast City Council (2005) in 2004–05 affordable housing statistics suggest that 35% of all households – either renting or paying off a mortgage – are suffering housing stress. This number was higher than the Queensland state average and also the Australian national average. Statistics suggest that the Gold Coast has a higher number of units and town houses than the Australian and the Queensland average, with most of these dwellings recorded as rented properties.

Continued population growth during the 2000s, coupled with changes in economic and housing landscapes, resulted in radical changes to the physical and social landscapes of the Gold Coast. The city's focus on the tourism and development industries (the economic basis of the city), together with inadequate planning regulations, meant that residential landscapes were marginalised and many of the family-friendly homes of earlier decades were transformed into money-making ventures. Arnie explains:

> *... it's business orientated instead of family orientated sort of stuff as it was when we came to the Gold Coast [the 1980s] ... where now [2014] it's not. It's chuck a night club in there, and then the night clubs bring the drug addicts and drug addicts bring the police and the bashings.*

Amanda, too, talks about the loss of public recreational facilities: 'I guess, you know, it's a sign of the times, too. We've lost squash courts and tennis courts, those kinds of things. I think we've even lost some bowling alleys. Most of the things we need to keep the kids occupied and busy and entertained, whatever.' The outcome of these changes meant that some residents experienced a sense of estrangement and loss.

The current perception and experience of the Gold Coast City by some residents is that the city is now segregated into the tourist precinct (Surfers Paradise, in particular) and the suburban sprawl of the residential precinct. Anne told me:

> *I think there's two sides of the Gold Coast. I think you have that strip that the tourists see and then it's almost like you walk through a curtain to where the locals live. I don't think many locals spend much time in Surfers Paradise. I think this is a totally different Gold Coast.*

The transformation of the coastal strip was seen as inevitable by some residents who experienced the effects, and as inherently part of the Gold Coast's life-stage. Residents' acceptance of change to their home-places was not, however, without effect, especially to their sense or feeling of community.

Mike explains his experience of the change from small town to tourist city:

> *... it was just like you walked through Surfers and you just knew everyone like shop owners whatever and everything. Now there is that – Surfers is perceived as, as amongst my crew, as a no-go zone, it's just too expensive, too dangerous, transport is a hassle, all these things you know. So they don't go there anymore – I don't know whether you would call it the globalisation of Surfers ... it's lost its original sort of surf village identity.*

Bruce agrees that the social dynamics of the city have changed as the population has grown and the urban fabric has been transformed. He says: 'So it's become more anonymous. The second thing is the influx of people, transient people coming and going means a fair amount of social dislocation and a lack of community, a lack of that 'we' feeling.' As other residents have also noted, there has been a decline in a sense of community and the degree of neighbourly interaction within the city over the last four decades.

The loss of community perceived by some residents was not expressed with regret by all. Shelley told me: 'I think, in a way I feel sad, but I think I'm of a generation that's into progress as well ... sometimes I just feel progress has to happen.' Population growth and change is woven into many residents' experiences of the Gold Coast so that some have come to accept these factors as being intrinsic to the city. The 'loss' of community experienced by residents was mostly attributed by interviewees to generational differences, and many accepted it as a mark of the times. Amanda explains the change in community relations she observed:

> *Usually that's when you have a couple working. They've just got their busy lives and we just haven't got that new neighbourhood connection so much in many areas that we've got a little bit used to. When we first came it was very strong ... but there's not quite that connection ... So that's another thing. More people, more turnover at least.*

The perceived loss of community by some residents, attributed mainly to 'more people, more turnover', is heightened by the increase (apparent or actual) of crime. Noel, reflecting on his early days on the Coast (1980s) said: 'it was great and it was a really relaxed atmosphere. You could just walk down the beach and you didn't hear about bashing and things like that.' Most of the residents interviewed have similar memories. Mike told me:

> *The other thing that sticks out is that you could leave your bike there and it didn't get stolen. You leave your towel and stuff and it didn't get ripped off and all that. You know security was a lot, I don't know, you were more blasé about leaving stuff around – and now you just wouldn't, you just wouldn't do it.*

The concerns residents expressed around crime are inevitable, and are recognised in most urban growth histories. An increase in population, and in particular a transient population, coupled with trends in popular media to report violence and criminal activities can dichotomise the past as safe and the present as a hot bed of criminal activity. Arnie told me:

> *Crime rate was down. You very rarely heard about drugs and bashings and muggings and shootings. It was pretty much none of that. And if there was, it was only here and there. Nothing like you see on the telly now, where every day multiple stabbings and robberies and that sort of stuff.*

Bruce moved to the Gold Coast in the 1980s as a young professional. He told me that 'the growth of the Gold Coast has meant that an area, which [in the 1980s] was almost unable to sustain one or two criminal lawyers, now has approximately 40.'

Conclusion

This chapter tells us something about the lived experience of change and rapid urbanisation for which the Gold Coast is famous. High population growth and migration have naturally played a major part in this history. The phenomenal population growth, during 1980s in particular, can be attributed to three key pull factors: employment opportunities, climate and lifestyle, and affordable housing. As the histories of the Gold Coast illustrate, property booms and neoliberal markets have largely contributed to urban and population growth with very little long-term planning being evident. The city's economy has consequently focused on tourism and related industries to the detriment of some residents, with regards to housing affordability, adequate infrastructure, population segregation (tourist and resident), suburban sprawl, loss of community and increase in crime. But, as Bruce asserts, 'the real bulk of the economy is in fact generated not by visitors but by people who live here servicing those visitors and working here, and building up their own businesses and identities'. Arnie described it thus: 'Stupid tourism? If I can use that word, where they're looking at short-term gain but not thinking about the long-term happiness of the people that have lived here all their lives.'

The value of built form on the Gold Coast has generally weighed heavily in favour of economic value rather than social and environmental value. The necessity to stay up-to-date and maintain growth and tourist trends has meant that iconic buildings and places have been obliterated, places many residents associated with as their 'home'. As a consequence of these changes some residents feel ostracised and have established their homes elsewhere with the intention never to return to the places of their formative years. Robyn was a resident of the Gold Cost since the 1970s and holidayed on the Coast with her parents every year for 17 years before she moved here to live, but she felt compelled to leave. And the reasons she gives: 'Oh just so busy, so many people, so much traffic. I just don't like the traffic. I don't like all the high-rises and I don't like having to drive through Surfers. I just don't like any of that.' As others have found, it is not that Robyn and others who share their views are against change and development; it is the type and form of development that has threatened their home-places. If place makers addressed the meaning and value of place for local residents then Robyn (and others like her) might return to the Gold Coast and fulfil her parting wish: 'I don't want to be able to see a change – I would like to be able to feel it: "Ohh isn't this nice" not "jeez another building".'

The growth of cities is historic and growth is synonymous with change and transformation of the city fabric – built, social and environmental. The Gold Coast's growth patterns and their effects are hardly unique. Because the Gold Coast is a young city, opportunities arise for early and significant innovations and interventions to create a viable city that adapts to change and does not follow historically recognised paths: crime, pollution, intensive energy use, etc. Not all residents are alienated and embittered by everyday experiences of rapid urban growth and change. For many, the connection to home and place is far deeper and more complex than a simple attachment to physical, ecological and social contexts of their city. This is not, however, to suggest that past planning and development practices constituted best practice to be replicated in the future. The type and form of development and the planning, or lack thereof, has had serious implications on a resident population. My findings imply that some long-standing Gold Coast residents accept urban growth, and the changes this produces, as a characteristic of the city and as part of their home-place. Amanda observes: 'it's obvious now that it's growing so big since we've been here, the traffic is worse, everything is worse due to the extra population but you can't stop the city growing. I think it's kind of inevitable, really.' The important point is not urban growth and change per se; it is the type and form of development that affects many residents' sense of home-place. Noel says: 'Well, you can't help but love it, the Gold Coast. Despite what people say and all the things that happen, I don't think I'd rather live anywhere else.'

Chapter 7

Thirty years of Gold Coast architecture

Andrew Leach

The decision to establish the Gold Coast Architecture Awards in 1984 responded to a timely confluence of motivations and circumstances affecting the Gold Coast city-region and its architects. The previous decade had seen tremendous growth in the permanent and temporary populations of the south-east corner of Queensland, and its coastal cities in particular, provoking a substantial high-rise building boom centred on Main Beach, Surfers Paradise and Broadbeach. The number of architects active on the Gold Coast more than doubled in this time. The professional landscape transformed from one in which architects were in sustained competition with designer-builders to realise single family dwellings and low-rise tourism accommodation to one dominated by the design and construction of high-rises, which even when realised in the manner of a shoot-from-the-hip approach to property development necessitated the architect's expertise. The Gold Coast's architects nonetheless needed to position themselves publicly in a moment when the effects of their practice were themselves becoming more decisively public: not simply for designing bespoke houses and monumental moments in a city that had clearly taken off – and would, it rightly seemed, continue to do so – but also for the sheer volume of projects that was shaping the morphology of the city and marking out the lines of its future development.

In designing apartment towers, resorts, shopping malls, casinos and theme parks, architects were redrawing the city's skyline, which consequently changed year to year. And while setting out to prove something to the city's population and those who saw scope for investment opportunities along its golden beaches, the Gold Coast Division of what was until recently the Royal Australian Institute of Architects (RAIA) also took on the task of reversing the image maintained elsewhere in Australia of the Gold Coast as a kind of cultural dead spot. The Gold Coast Architecture Awards were self-styled from Southport to Coolangatta as the Architectural Oscars and they conducted battle on two fronts: to demonstrate the value of the work of architects on the Gold Coast to this adolescent city (Burton 2009), and to prove the worth of the Gold Coast to a national architectural culture that had weighed it in the balances and found it curious but wanting. Gold Coast architects were making a city in a culture of experimentation in which anything was possible.

In this objective, the Gold Coast had to contend with some baggage. A generation earlier, coinciding with the City of Gold Coast receiving its charter, the RAIA journal *Architecture in Australia* had in 1959 published a monographic issue on the Coast. This was one of the first moments in which Australian architecture had turned in a serious way to this city-region – which had grown from next to nothing to way too much, as it were, from isolated

Fig. 7.1. Street-level urban amenity on the ground floor of Aria by Sunland Design Group with Buchan Group, Broadbeach, 2001–03 (A Leach)

instances of speculative subdivisional development and an industry based on sugar and timber to become the Australian capital of recreation. The journal took the temperature of Australian architecture's touchiness to the Gold Coast's troubling idiosyncrasies:

> *When sensitive individuals begin to speak of lovely coastlines still unspoilt by man and begin to fear that development may equal despoliation, one indeed must wonder about the condition of our civilisation. The present regional picture of the Gold Coast seems to underline all those anxieties and fears. (Architecture in Australia 1959)*

It goes on:

> *Without hesitation and with much splendid foresight [the Constituted Authority] should tackle and solve the burning problems of roadways, townscapes, localities, waterways and parks: the gold of the Coast otherwise will turn to dross in less than a generation's time.*

This turned out to be no isolated expression of reticence. For many years the relation between individual architectural achievements and the stakes held therein of the entire city were at the forefront of Australia's reception of Gold Coast architecture.

Peter Kollar (1959, p. 58) made his own assessment known in this same issue of *Architecture in Australia*, being that the 'grave mistakes that abound on the Gold Coast from a regional planning point of view must be clear to anybody looking upon the spectacle from unbiased eyes'. But these are only mistakes if one assumes that the maturity of a new city can be planned meticulously from its foundations, and if one allows that the kind of unexpected growth as sustained by the Gold Coast in the decades leading up to Queensland's centennial year of 1959 (and continuing beyond) could be absorbed effortlessly into forward thinking of an exceptional prescience. Robin Boyd (1960, p. 69) called the Gold Coast a 'poor man's Miami,' pointing to its abundance of poor taste and the concomitant relaxation of the culture that produced it – the curious mix of Australian society and American style that he thought to demonstrate in its extremity those tendencies to which Australia would in time become subject. Culturally speaking, the Gold Coast was Boyd's canary in the mine of post-war Australian culture, and for this reason the scorn and derision it sustained was inevitably tempered with an anxiety over where and how its symptoms might normalise elsewhere in the skin-deep ugliness he saw covering the cities of his country.

Twenty-five years later, on the eve of the inaugural Gold Coast Architecture Awards, Sydneysider Neville Gruzman, an advocate for improved public space and amenity in his own city, suggested that the Gold Coast would best be served by a convoy of architects as concerned as he, driving north in bulldozers and nudging Surfers Paradise into the sea. The Gold Coast press and the Division's members gave this suggestion the attention it demanded, translating a call for a fresh start into a touchstone for a determined effort to lift the local game so as to prove Gruzman and his cobelligerents wrong. Indeed, invited to comment on the occasion of the tenth and twentieth Gold Coast Architecture Awards, Gruzman conceded that much had already been done to attend to those of the city's failings that had prompted his suggestion of 1984, even if there remained some distance to go in improving the city's urban design as it continued to grow and grow. Even if Gruzman was not without company, it was a patronising view. Malcolm Cummings held this mirror up to the city's critics: 'It's interesting how architects would come up to the Gold Coast and criticise the buildings. There are a lot of buildings in Sydney you could say could be bulldozed into the sea' (Licence 2013).

If the Gold Coast Division of the RAIA had been established as a way to bring together the small number of architects working on the Gold Coast in 'a structured way', to quote founding member Bill Heather, it also offered a chance to push back against the negative perceptions of the city and its architecture that had been fostered throughout Australia. In a speech to the twentieth anniversary dinner of the Gold Coast Architecture Awards in 2003, reprinted in *20/20 Vision* (RAIA 2003), Heather recalled that when he arrived to set up an office of Melbourne firm Buchan, Laird & Bawden in 1972, there were a mere dozen architects on the Coast, 'thinly spread between Coolangatta to Southport'. He recites a list: Col Merrin and Owen Ryan in Coolangatta, Robert Cummings (emeritus professor of architecture at the University of Queensland), Russ Gibbons at Mermaid Beach, Noel Edser and Bevan Whittington (Design Collaborative) on Chevron Island, George Dunlop and David Raby (working together with Heather at Buchan, Laird & Bawden in Surfers Paradise), Malcolm Cummings (also then at Surfers Paradise), Andris Stenders, Ron Burling and John Mobbs (all at the Southport office of Clarke, Gazzard and Partners), as well as Les Nyerges, an architect with the Gold Coast City Council.

As a member of the Institute's National Membership Committee, Heather was in regular contact with Chapter President David Phillips, who encouraged the small group, then comprising the Gold Coast Area Committee, to consider the example that had been set by the geographically vast North Queensland Division and to establish a Gold Coast Division – even using the North Queensland articles of association as the basis for the Gold Coast's documents, which were adapted, as Heather recalled 'to suit our needs'. While it would expand with time, the Pimpana River was taken as the initial northern border, with the state line defining the Division's southern boundary and the western border taking in the Tamborine Mountain.

Looking back on the atmosphere of this moment, John Mobbs had this to say:

It wasn't as serious and heavy as it was in the cities, and I think there was a bit of jealousy because they weren't having the same fun that we were having up here. Clients were more ready to accept more innovative solutions to projects. Also, a lot happened here in a very short time. (Licence 2013)

Competition for work was fierce, but the Huntington Club offered a venue for the small group of Gold Coast architects to meet on a regular basis as an Area Committee, a practice carried forward as the Gold Coast Division was established. As Cummings had it:

The Huntington Club provided a marvellously talented international chef, though we couldn't figure how he came to be stuck at the Huntington. And a wonderful cellar. It really was a marvellous cellar! We had some very good nights. There are some great stories, though none of them are about architecture. There was never much discussion about architecture. (Licence 2013)

Cummings was the first chair of the Gold Coast Division, serving from 1974 in a committee including Bill Heather and John Mobbs. He was succeeded by Heather (1979–82), who was in turn followed by Peter Clarke (1982–84), Don Williamson (1984–86), Alan Griffith (1986–88), Alan Hayes (1988–90), Deborah Carlile (1990–92) and Mark Trotter (1992–94). During Trotter's tenancy as chair a reorganisation of the Queensland Chapter of the RAIA reconfigured the Division into the Gold Coast and Northern Rivers Region, which went on to be chaired by Bill Giles (1994–98), Greg Forgan-Smith (1998–2002), Brett Saville (2002–2006), Finn Jones (2006–12), Amy Degenhart (2012–14) and, currently, Greg Ewart.

The Division's numbers ballooned from the middle of the 1970s as a sustained development boom and a significant rise in population saw 160 new towers of 10 floors or more built across a 12-year period (as a slightly unbalanced point of comparison, the number of buildings of 12 storeys and above would reach 216 by 2004). Economic conditions were favourable for the scale and pace of this development, especially in light of a decision by the Queensland Government to waive death duties that saw an extraordinarily high and rather sudden investment in rental and vacation property from the southern states. '[Each] new project,' recalled Heather, 'seemed to result in more local offices being set up by metropolitan or interstate firms, and once they were here, and their projects completed, these architects inevitably went into practice for themselves' (Licence 2013). Such firms as Burling Brown and the Davis Heather Group (later Heather Thiedeke) were 'producing interesting high-rise apartments,' and Conrad & Gargett and Bill Job & Associates maintained 'strong local offices'. Heather noted: 'The profession was in good shape, and architectural design was making a difference to the look of the city.'

With a degree of hindsight, Greg Forgan-Smith summed up the situation in this way:

We're a leisure city ... and the people who migrated here were a different type of person ... There was always an attitude here that if you wanted to try something, do it. In

Fig. 7.2. Saint Kevin's Catholic Primary School by The Davis Heather Group, Benowa, 1977–79 (Photograph by Richard Stringer)

architecture we've got some horrible examples and we've got some fantastic examples, but if you're not going to experiment you're not going to get anywhere. (Licence 2013)

A 'portfolio of experiments' (as Philip Follent has put it, pers. comm.), the Gold Coast at once offered a challenge to good taste and a model for the architect's optimism (see Figs 7.3 and 7.4). If this was true of Gold Coast architecture more broadly – and especially in the residential tower – then it was particularly so in the work the profession itself put forward for the Gold Coast Architecture Awards. The program was born out of the simple if strategic desire to demonstrate the best work of the Gold Coast's architecture profession. However, it would come to define the character of the Division (10 years old at the awards' outset) and its defence of a form of originality and variety it held to be its own. In this it offers a rare instance from the 1980s of architects and developers sharing the page. It would define, too, its relationships with Queensland, Australia and those cities, regions and countries against which it could legitimately define itself, which across its history would span from Miami to Honolulu to Dubai.

In a talk to the 1978 Queensland RAIA Chapter Convention 'Insite/Outsight', Bill Heather emphasised the distinctiveness of Gold Coast architecture within the state's professional and cultural landscape. Speaking, he said, as 'a provincial observer from that area you regard as a kind of "architectural purgatory"', he thought Brisbane architecture could use 'a dose of the sunshine and sensuality associated with the Coast'. Reflecting on the relationship of the new Gold Coast Division to the Queensland Chapter ('we are small cheese to you city slickers'), he observed:

Fig. 7.3. Southport Business Park by Fulton Gilmour Trotter, Southport, completed 1991 (A Leach)

Fig. 7.4. Surfers Paradise Bus Station by Cummings and Burns, Surfers Paradise, completed 1992 (A Leach)

Fig. 7.5. Billabong Factory and Showroom by Cummings and Burns, Burleigh Heads, completed 1992 (A Leach)

> *We are more prone to ask 'what do we get out of the Institute' and be less satisfied with the usual reply of 'whatever you put into it'. Nonetheless, we are making progress towards that essential axiom at the heart of the matter – the Institute is you fellow architects – not a building or a thing or an institution, but members and their relationship to each other. (Heather 1978)*

He continued:

> *There is good reason why Brisbane is the branch office capital of Australia and why its architects suffer from a kind of 'architectural colonialism': even if some of the empires are staffed by natives recruited in the colony, sluggish as they may be. The two main problems confronting the Institute here today are inertia and complacency. Inertia because there is a great resistance to change and lack of momentum in the way things are done. Complacency because there is a lack of outward vision about what could be done. We are in the right place at the right time, but our sights are set too low and no one cares. We are at the threshold of the most challenging period of this state's growth.*

Heather asserted that Queensland as a whole, and Brisbane in particular, had let pass the opportunity to realise a moment akin to that faced by Chicago in the 1880s, but that the Gold Coast was not, for better or worse, prepared to do so. 'Impatience and ambition should be the order of the day – a restructuring of our activities should attempt to tap the vitality of the small cell rather than let the inertia of the large organism choke the system.' Inviting his audience to 'substitute personal action for collective inertia,' he offered the

Gold Coast as an example to the state. If Queensland architecture were only prepared to loosen ties, shed vests and trade lethargy for an optimism prepared to absorb mistakes as it moved insistently forward, 'we on the Gold Coast will offer you encouragement periodically and example where necessary'.

The Gold Coast was hardly invisible to the rest of the state and, indeed, Gold Coast projects had from time to time done well in the Queensland Architecture Awards. Hayes and Scott's Miller House in Southport – with its gold-coloured front door – had been named Queensland House of the Year in 1965, and the early 1970s saw The Anchorage apartment block (Clarke, Gazzard and Partners at Budds Beach) receive an award at state level. Before the Queensland Chapter took up the model of the Gold Coast Architecture Awards for a state-wide regional awards program, projects submitted to both the Gold Coast and Queensland awards in the same year had no certainty that strong performance on the Gold Coast would lead to state recognition – or that failure to secure awards at divisional level would undermine success in Brisbane. Simply speaking, the Gold Coast Architecture Awards were judged on criteria that shifted from year to year, responding to the evolving opportunities and problems faced by Gold Coast architects as they went about their work. And until their regularisation within a statewide regional awards cycle, the Gold Coast Architecture Awards rewarded that work, in particular, that took the city with it.

The role of publicist Ken Newton and journalist Brian Mossop in promoting the awards cannot be overstated. Nor can their part in the achievement of the ambitions. With Newton's guidance, especially, the Gold Coast Division affected a meaningful engagement with the public, and the *Gold Coast Bulletin* (where Mossop was on staff) maintained its long-standing interest in issues around architecture, development and the city – for many years being represented on the state-appointed jury by its editor or other senior staff, and often by Mossop himself. Newton and Mossop saw the need to shape the way the public understood and valued architecture, and sought to shift the public perception of the architect's contribution to the Gold Coast for the better. The Division produced a guide to engaging an architect's services as a direct marketing effort, but its public presence was most directly felt in the clear and impassioned communiqués issued by Newton's media office on behalf of the Gold Coast Division of the RAIA. Newton and Mossop's many years of service to Gold Coast architecture decisively shaped the public appreciation of architectural and urban issues in the city and its region, and their contribution is fittingly captured in the naming of the Peoples Choice Award in their honour. The awards took what the architects were doing and built up its popular image among the Gold Coast public, while affording the local profession a chance to take a very public stance on the kind of architectural work that deserved the recognition and praise that the public, thanks to Newton and Mossop, were now prepared to give it. This clearly raised the stakes for the Gold Coast architecture fraternity, since with opportunities for innovation and experimentation came, too, the possibility of a highly visible endorsement or a silent reprimand from an architect's peers.

The definition of 'good architecture' is notoriously difficult to pin down – and for good reason. For the Gold Coast Architecture Awards, the benchmarks are set each year by a jury comprising architects from within and beyond the region, and members of both the building industry and an engaged public. For the first decade, spanning from the inception of the awards to their incorporation into a state awards program feeding the Queensland Architecture Awards, decisions were taken by a jury of three, ordinarily comprising two members of the Gold Coast Division and a third juror drawn from outside the region. In these first years, the Gold Coast Division appointed each jury and the decisions it took

Fig. 7.6. Skilled Park by Populous (formerly HOK Sport Architecture), Robina, completed 2008 (Photograph by Scott Burrows, courtesy of Populous and Scott Burrows)

did not affect a project's capacity to be entered into the state-level competition (which fed, naturally enough, into the national architecture awards).

The inaugural awards saw Balwant Saini (a professor at the University of Queensland's Department of Architecture) and Rita Adviev (an architecturally trained, Melbourne-based building industry consultant) take the decisions. Ian Douglas (Melbourne) and Dudley Wilde (Immediate Past President of the Queensland Chapter of the RAIA) helped judge the 1985 awards; 1986 saw Neville Quarry (Sydney) and David Nutter (Queensland Institute of Technology) join Don Williamson in the jury; Michael Keniger (University of Queensland) and Daryl Jackson (Sydney) in 1987; Sunshine Coast architect Geoffrey Pie and Western Australian Louise St John Kennedy in 1988; Lionel Glendinning (Sydney) and Brisbane-based Robin Spencer in 1989; Bernard Joyce (Joyce Nankivell) of Melbourne and Sunshine Coaster Lindsay Clare in 1990; and Ken Down (another Sunshine Coaster) joining Jeffrey Howlett (Western Australia) for the 1991 awards. Entries were publicly exhibited, and by the 1990s the public was invited to weigh in through a popular vote to parallel the decisions of jurors.

The jury was responsible for visiting each submission and holding a discussion in which projects were held up for examination against criteria that were, in part, treated as natural, but which year by year revealed the preoccupations of the jury. What makes a work of architecture good? Why does one project deserve an award over the others? Or the judges' commendation? The answers were many and varied: detailing, response to context, response to brief, budgetary responsibility, economic impact, attention to environmental impact, expression of the landscape, expression of lifestyle, expression of the city, and on it went. Is good Gold Coast architecture especially good if it would also be considered good elsewhere (where elsewhere, more often than not, meant Brisbane)? Taken year by year, the relationship between the values given away in the jury summations and premiated projects is not difficult to map, but the overall picture is of a series of juries understanding the role of the awards as being to move the city forward by rendering public the best examples of architectural practice. The awards did not track fashion (although they did this, too) so much as they plotted new ideas – ostensibly focusing on the future rather than the present, and on the capacity of the profession in its entirety as revealed in the work submitted for review.

Within a decade of their establishment the Gold Coast awards would set the standard for the Australian Institute of Architects Queensland Chapter. In 1992, the Queensland Chapter adopted the Gold Coast's model for the state awards program and rolled it out across all the Queensland regions. This was hailed as a great coup for Gold Coast, which had demonstrated the value of rewarding work at a regional level, but it became quickly apparent that there was little room left for regional distinctions. The enthusiastic group that had seen the Gold Coast Architecture Awards established, and worked to secure their local importance, was obliged to give way to policies, procedures and judgement criteria intended to make the awards process manageable across the entire state. This left little room (as many had cause to recall) for variety, originality, spontaneity or the kind of specificity demanded by the Gold Coast. Jury appointments, for one, were now made by the Queensland Chapter, with the State Awards Director initially taking responsibility for the juries assessing the Gold Coast (which, importantly, involved the regular involvement of a lay juror – often representing the *Bulletin*, as noted earlier), and increasingly playing an active part in assessing that same work, with progression to the Queensland and National Architecture Awards clearly in mind.

These changes occurred as the Gold Coast Division was re-structured into a Region – more directly accountable to the Queensland Chapter – that also quickly accommodated the Northern Rivers region in New South Wales within what had been increasingly recognised as a coherent cross-border architectural culture. Fulton Trotter Gilmour Moss had an office in Tweed Heads and were acutely aware of the strong logic that ignored the state border in favour of a regional architectural culture. The establishment of a Gold Coast and Northern Rivers Region hence logically built on an initiative led by Mark Trotter during his tenure as chair of the Gold Coast Division. The Gold Coast itself was undergoing change at the same time, substantially increasing its municipal geography and population in the 1995 amalgamation with Albert River Shire. This necessitated a fresh approach to city planning and management that had direct implications for the role of architects both in private practice and in relation to the significantly enlarged and conspicuously less laissez-faire city council. All of this affected the momentum of work and debate on the Gold Coast, and introduced new accountabilities in both procedure and the values shaping architectural quality. The energy, speed and the qualities Heather had espoused in 1978 could no longer set the tone in what had become an inexorable tendency towards greater regulation, both in local architects' relationship with their Institute and in the city as an environment for architectural experimentation.

The city grew enormously in these middle years and so did the numbers of architects practising on the Gold Coast. Those still actively engaged and advocating for Gold Coast architects and architecture found themselves regularly feeling hamstrung in their ability to shape the direction of the Gold Coast and Northern Rivers Region – to retain the character of the group that had established the Institute's presence on the Gold Coast in the early years. As the number and profile of architects and practices was growing and changing, so too was the city. The regional focus shifted away from the direct public engagement fostered by Newton and Mossop to engagement with the Gold Coast City Council and Tweed Shire Council – with their various stakeholders and an increasingly dominant planning profession. The regional group, of their own accord, took an active role in encouraging the City of Gold Coast Council to establish an urban design advisory board for the city, which when established opened the way for the appointment of a city architect and the establishment of a council-driven awards cycle to reward the best instances of urban design (Holden 2013).

As the guest of honour at the Gold Coast and Northern Rivers thirtieth annual regional awards (2013), His Excellency Michael Bryce – an architect and Gold Coast native – chastised the 'literati' and their scorn of 'the decorative nature of the Gold Coast's early 'motel' architecture ... eminently suited [as it was] to the strong sunlight and pastel surfaces – a playfulness that in its kitsch somehow was truthful to its role as a resort town.' Yet the Gold Coast had become aware of its own heritage, and even influenced, he noted, by the character it sought to distil from it. Recalling the Canberra centenary and the loose comparison it offered with the evening's celebrations, he observed that 'while Canberra began as a conservative home for bureaucrats, it now wants to be fun'; and 'while Surfers began as a fun place, it now wants to be taken seriously'. The challenge, we well surmise, is to take Gold Coast architecture seriously on its own terms, and in this the job of documenting its history and that history's key actors and events is paramount.

With DBI's Soul marking one kind of end to a phase of high-rise building emerging from the grim depths of the global financial crisis – and with it, a kind of terminus – the Gold Coast remains at the cusp of realising a series of projects of decisive importance for the city. Preparations for the 2018 Commonwealth Games are enlivening the city's sports infrastructure and further development of the Broadwater Parklands will boost public amenity. The realisation of the Jewel in the Crown development (Oppenheim and DBI for RDG) will open up new possibilities for multiple building high-rise projects in the zone between southern Surfers Paradise and Broadbeach. The rapid transit corridor from Broadbeach to Parklands has reinforced these possibilities since the light rail units first opened their doors in the middle of 2014, just as the urban consolidation on the Parklands Health and Knowledge Precinct (Griffith University and Gold Coast University Hospital), around Varsity Lakes (including Bond University and its new building for the Soheil Abedian School of Architecture by CRAB), at Helensvale (including a new library by Lahz Nimmo and Complete Urban) and elsewhere suggest moments from which the Gold Coast will continue to assert itself by means of its architecture – and continuing, therefore, to offer local practitioners and firms from outside the city, state and nation a fertile venue for experimentation.

A note on sources

Many of the observations synthesised above reflect a discussion held during a lunch meeting of the past and present chairs of the Gold Coast Division and Gold Coast and Northern Rivers Region of the (Royal) Australian Institute of Architects (Surfers Paradise Hilton, 16 November 2012) – a reprise of the Friday lunches dating to the early days of the Gold Coast's architecture fraternity. Present were Amy Degenhart (then chair) along with Deborah Carlile, Malcolm Cummings, Greg Forgan-Smith, Alan Griffith, Alan Hayes, Bill Heather, Finn Jones, Nathan Quartermaine, Brett Saville and Mark Trotter, as well as Sarah Batchelor, Andrew Leach, Brian Mossop, Ken Newton and Jeff Licence, who documented the discussion for the short film *Drawn Here* (Tiger Monkey, online at youtube.com). Balancing the recollections tabled in this meeting, the Gold Coast Architecture Awards Archive – compiled and maintained over many years by Ken Newton and now (temporarily) held at Griffith University – includes a large clippings archive from regional newspapers with ties to the Gold Coast and a substantial number of press releases. In more recent years absorbed into AIA records and activities through Gold Coast participation in

Queensland's regional awards cycle, coverage, jury comments and project descriptions are readily available online through the AIA Awards Gallery. Full documentation of the Gold Coast Architecture Awards is published in *GC30+* (Leach *et al.* 2015).

Chapter 8

The politics of paradise: intergovernmental relations and the Gold Coast

Michael Howes

Good relations with your neighbours are just as important for cities as they are for individuals. Intergovernmental cooperation can enable the more effective and efficient use of scarce public resources, particularly during times of natural disasters where help is needed across political boundaries. While a modicum of friendly rivalry can help to improve the quality of life (e.g. when vying for the most liveable city in the region), poor intergovernmental relations can do just the opposite – leading to wastage, political turf wars and a decline in the quality of public goods. This could result in a serious problem being neglected because no jurisdiction is willing to take responsibility (adapting to the impacts of climate change is a case in point). The purpose of this chapter is to characterise the political interactions between the Gold Coast local council and other governments with a view to identifying how they have helped to shape the city. The first section explains the underlying structure and dynamics of the Australian political system within which the city is embedded. Section two then offers a brief explanation of how governing institutions developed as the region grew. In section three the main resources, powers and organisation of the local council are summarised. Section four then briefly considers examples of relationships between the councils of the Gold Coast, Brisbane, the Sunshine Coast and Tweed. Section five explores how the relationship between the council and the Queensland Government has changed over time. The final section considers interactions with the Australian Government.

A complex system of government

The Gold Coast is embedded within the somewhat complex Australian system of government, with power divided according to both level and function. In terms of level, there are three tiers of government (Fig. 8.1): the first, national Commonwealth (also known as the federal or Australian Government); the second, the six states (e.g. Queensland) and two territories (for convenience this will be referred to as the state level of government); and, the third, 560 local councils (e.g. the City of Gold Coast).

The powers of the Commonwealth Government are defined by the Australian Constitution (Parliament of Australia 2012). These include the power to regulate international trade and commerce, control migration, make provisions for national defence, regulate

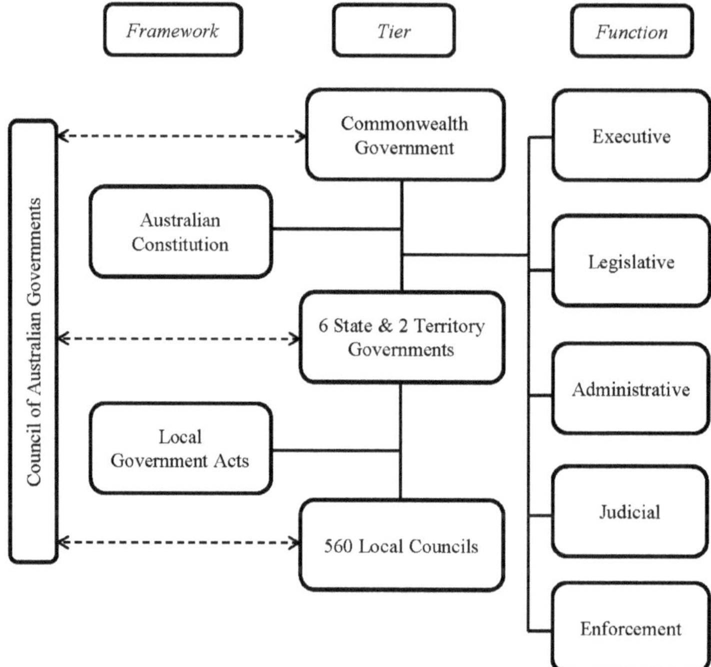

Fig. 8.1. The Australian system of government

banking and money supply, construct railways (in conjunction with the states), acquire property by compulsion, impose taxes, etc. Anything not specified as a power of the Commonwealth is deemed to be a residual power and falls to the state level of government. Since the environment and planning are not mentioned as Commonwealth powers they have fallen largely to the states (Toyne 1994; Howes 2005; Brown 2006). As a consequence, the Commonwealth has adopted three strategies: leaving some issues to the states; cooperating with the states on other issues; or selectively intervening by creatively interpreting its powers (Howes *et al.* 2015). Local councils are not mentioned in the constitution and therefore exist entirely at the mercy of state governments. They are created, merged or abolished by acts of state parliament, as happened in Queensland in 2007 when the number of councils was reduced from 156 to 72 (ABC News 2007a). Further, any council may be removed by a state government and replaced by an administrator, as happened to the Tweed Shire Council in 2005 (*Sydney Morning Herald* 2005) and the (then) Gold Coast City Council in 1978 (Solomon 2009). This three-tiered system has created ongoing power struggles between the different levels of government and this remains the underlying dynamic of intergovernmental relations (Brown 2006; Rolfe *et al.* 2009; Ghazarian 2012; Heazle *et al.* 2013).

Within each tier, powers are further separated according to function, that is, executive, legislative, judicial, enforcement and administrative (Howes 2005). The executive is elected to make the major policy decisions for each level. Nationally, this is the prime minister and a Cabinet; at the state (territory) level this is the premier (or chief minister) and Cabinet; and at the local level this is the mayor. Cabinet consists of ministers who are members of the elected legislature and have been given specific policy responsibilities (e.g. a portfolio such as environment and heritage protection). Legislatures at the national and state levels have the power to make, amend or rescind laws. Local councils have the power to make, amend or rescind by-laws. Both the national and state levels have an independent judiciary with a system of courts designed to decide whether a law has been breached, impose penalties and resolve disputes. At the national level the High Court is the final court of appeal and also has the responsibility to interpret the constitution and resolve disputes between governments. Enforcement agencies (e.g. the police, customs, the military, etc.) are given the power to use coercive force in implementing laws (Howes 2005). Administrative agencies are those public sector organisations given the task of implementing government policies and programs in a particular portfolio area (e.g. the Department of Environment) (Heazle *et al.* 2013). It has been suggested that the separation of functional powers at the state level in Queensland is not as strong as it should be (Alvey and Ryan 2005). What separation there is, however, tends to encourage turf wars between different departments and agencies (Rolfe *et al.* 2009; Heazle *et al.* 2013).

This mixture of different government levels and functions complicates decision-making. The Gold Coast light rail project, for example, was funded by all three tiers of government and was overseen by an executive group made up of representatives from: (i) the City of Gold Coast; (ii) the Queensland Department of Transport and Main Roads, Queensland Treasury, Queensland's TransLink Transit Authority; and (iii) the Commonwealth Department of Infrastructure and Transport (GoldLinQ 2012a, 2012b). Proposals for such a system were first put forward by the (then) Gold Coast City Council in their 1998 *City Transport Plan*. A joint feasibility study was undertaken in 2004 by Queensland Transport and the council, with funding provided by the Commonwealth (Anderson 2002; GoldLinQ 2012a). Construction of the project was put out to tender, a private contractor was chosen in 2011, and stage one was completed in 2014 (Albanese and Bligh 2011; GoldLinQ 2012c). Further stages, that would extend the rail to Helensvale in the north and Burleigh Heads in the south, are being considered (GoldLinQ 2012d). Hence a significant, and much needed, piece of public transport infrastructure has taken 16 years from proposal to first stage completion under this system of government.

In the absence of major structural changes, all levels of government have moved to find other methods for improving the system. One of the main strategies has been to establish organisations that encourage intergovernmental cooperation. The Council of Australian Governments (COAG), for example, was formed in 1992 and includes the leaders of the Commonwealth, state and territory governments, as well as the president of the Australian Local Government Association (which was formed by the 560 local councils around the country to represent their interests and encourage cooperation). It has played a key role as a forum for negotiating agreements to tackle issues such as the environment, transport, health care and education (COAG 2011). Other joint ministerial councils were established to deal with particular issues, such as the National Environment Protection Council. In addition, local councils are networked nationally through the Australian Local Government Association (ALGA 2011) and its state branches. There are also regional groups such as the Council of Mayors: South East Queensland (2011) and international networks such as Local Governments for Sustainability (2011). The City of Gold Coast is linked into all of these organisations.

Despite such efforts, the Australian system of government still has difficulty in addressing major policy issues (Berwick 2006; Heazle *et al.* 2013). There remains considerable rivalry between the different levels of government that manifests itself in administrative duplication, resource wastage and disputes that undermine collaborative organisations (Ghazarian 2012). In addition, the jurisdictional turf wars between departments and agencies persist (Rolfe *et al.* 2009). These structural problems can impede efforts to find effective, efficient and appropriate responses to complex issues that cut across borders and portfolios. Problems such as climate change exacerbate the situation further because they are difficult to understand, there is a lack of agreement on an appropriate response, they require a whole of government approach, and they need the cooperation of business and the community on a large scale (Australian Public Service Commission 2007; Heazle *et al.* 2013). The Gold Coast is on the front line of such issues, being highly vulnerable to the impacts of climate change and suffering from myriad social, economic and environmental challenges associated with its extraordinarily rapid development over the last half a century.

A short history of government and development

The development of the Gold Coast has been reflected in changes to the institutions designed to govern the region. While Indigenous people lived in the area for tens of thousands of years, Brisbane was founded first as a penal settlement in 1825 and was administered by New South Wales until the colony of Queensland was declared in 1859 (Queensland Government 2011). In 1879, six divisional boards were created in South East Queensland (Beenleigh, Coomera, Nerang, Tabragalba (later renamed Beaudesert), Tingalpa and Waterford) to provide some basic local government to the growing population. Southport was split off from Nerang to form its own divisional board in 1883. In 1901, the six colonies (including Queensland) became states in the Australian federation, with the newly formed Commonwealth providing a national level of government.

In 1903 the divisional boards became shires and the Town of Coolangatta Council was added in 1914 (Gold Coast City Council 2011a; Queensland Government 2011). The councils were amalgamated and reorganised in 1948 so the coastal strip from Southport to Coolangatta became the Town of the South Coast. This was renamed the Gold Coast Town Council in 1958 and then became the Gold Coast City Council in 1959. It was amalgamated with the Albert Shire Council (that abutted its eastern border) in 1995 to form the Gold Coast City Council (Gold Coast City Council 2011a). All local councils in Queensland underwent further round of amalgamations in 2007 (ABC News 2007a). In 2013 the council changed its name to the City of Gold Coast. Today the Gold Coast is governed by an elected local council made up of a mayor and 14 councillors, each elected for four years to represent a specific geographical division (see Fig. 8.2). The residents of the region elect 10 members of the Queensland state parliament (which has 89 seats in total) and five members of the Commonwealth House of Representatives (out of a total of 148). This makes it a politically significant entity, particularly at the state level.

In terms of population, the Gold Coast has experienced exponential growth since the middle of the twentieth century, rising from 20 000 residents in 1954 to 455 000 in 2006 (see Table 8.1). By comparison, Tweed Heads currently has ~52 000 residents and the Sunshine Coast Council just over 287 000 (Sunshine Coast Council 2006; Spearritt 2009). The Gold Coast has grown rapidly to become the second largest city in the region and the sixth largest city in Australia, with a population that exceeds the capital cities of Canberra, Hobart and Darwin. The sheer speed of development and population growth has gener-

Table 8.1. Population growth for the Gold Coast and Brisbane council areas
(Sources: Gold Coast City Council 2006a; Brisbane City Council 2006; Spearritt 2009)

	1954	1976	1991	2006
Gold Coast	20 000	88 000	158 000	455 000
Brisbane	502 000	697 000	751 000	956 000

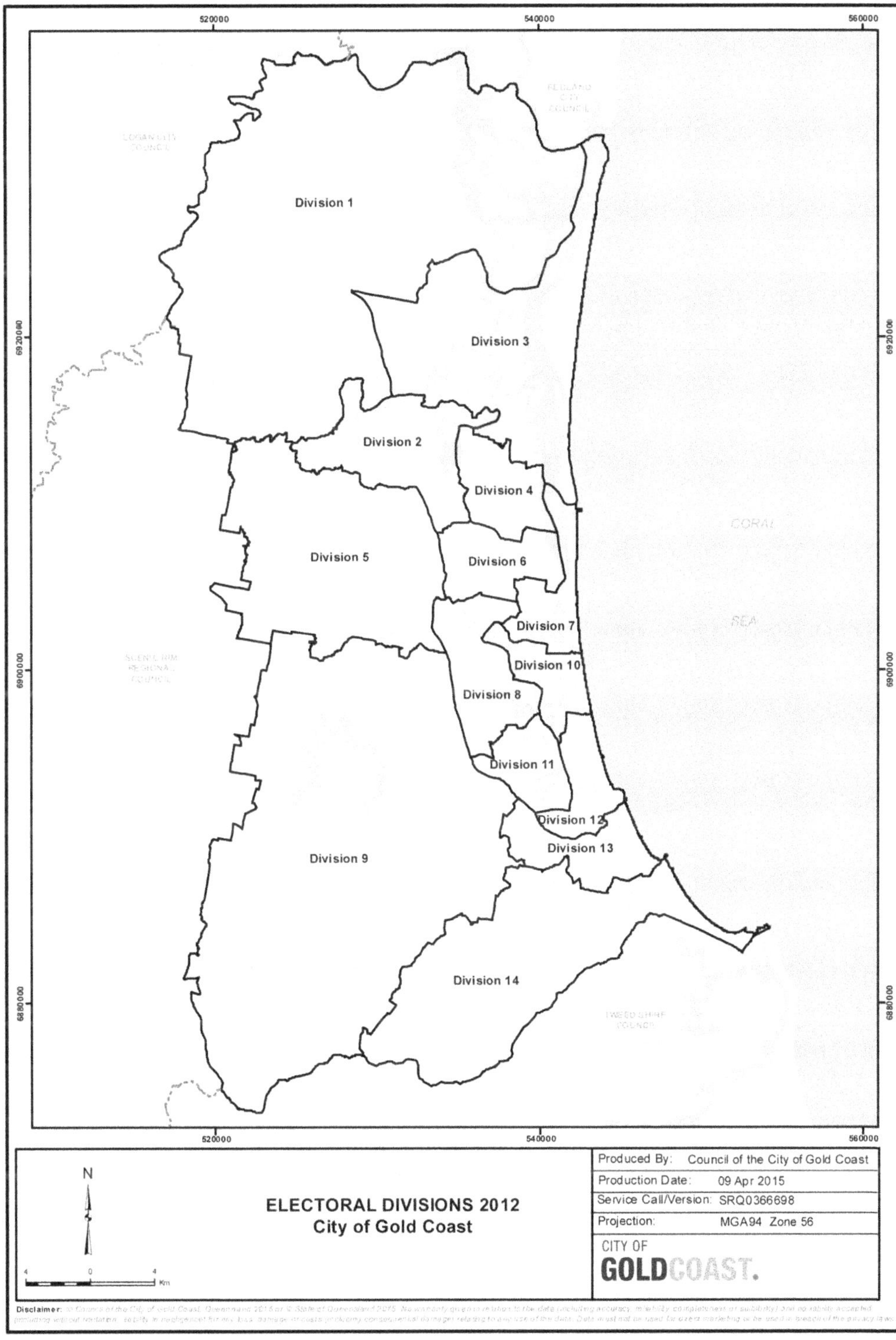

Fig. 8.2. Local council divisions for the City of Gold Coast, 2015 (Map courtesy of the City of Gold Coast)

ated considerable political problems such as traffic congestion, increasing housing costs and overburdened services that challenge all three tiers of government (Berwick 2006). It also means that the region demands considerable public investment in infrastructure from the Queensland and Commonwealth Governments.

In terms of the economy, the Gold Coast has a workforce of over 207 000 people with the traditionally dominant businesses being tourism, hospitality, retail, property development and construction. There are, however, growing local industries involved in manufacturing, education, health care, science and technology (Gold Coast City Council 2006b). The city has been actively seeking to host major events and will be home to the 2018 Commonwealth Games (Whitford 2004; Stannard 2011). Property developers and wealthy business people have played a prominent role in both the growth and politics of the Gold Coast.

The City of Gold Coast

The historical process of local government amalgamations, combined with the rapid population growth, has resulted in the City of Gold Coast Council being the second largest council in Australia, in terms of population and budget (Brisbane being the largest). In 2011 it had a workforce of 2960 staff, a budget of $910.6 million, 541 024 residents and 238 665 rateable properties (Gold Coast City Council 2011b). The council also owned over $10 billion in assets, including: 3006 km of roads; 2162 parks; 213 sporting fields; 105 boat ramps; 39 community centres; 23 jetties; 23 swimming pools; 12 libraries; 11 tourist parks and camping grounds; 8 cemeteries; and 2 art galleries (Gold Coast City Council 2011b).

The council is granted specific powers and responsibilities under the Queensland *Local Government Act 2009* (Gold Coast City Council 2011b). These include the power to make and enforce by-laws as well as issue permits or licences for local recreational or business activities. The areas of responsibility include land and water management, urban design and planning, the maintenance of assets (such as parks and roads), the provision of services (e.g. public transport, waste disposal, water supply, sewerage) and the operation of public facilities (like swimming pools and libraries).

In terms of organisational structure, the elected council is advised by several committees. The chief executive officer provides advice to the council, implements its decisions, and leads an executive leadership team that is responsible for the overall administration of the network of council organisations. Eight directorates (or administrative organisations) answer to this team. They deal with: business improvement; city governance; community services; economic development and major projects; engineering services; organisational services (i.e. administrative support for the council); planning, environment and transport; and water supply reforms (Gold Coast City Council 2011b).

The most recent council election was on Saturday 28 April 2012, and was held only a few weeks after the Queensland state election, which saw a landslide win for the conservative Liberal National Party. On the Friday before the election, the editorial of the *Gold Coast Bulletin*, the main local paper, outlined what it saw as the key issues for the region. These included reviving property development and tourism, relocating Queensland Government departments from Brisbane to the Gold Coast, the need for strong leadership, cutting red tape and reducing the power of the bureaucracy (Gleeson 2012a). On the Monday after the election the editorial endorsed the new mayor (who had strong conservative credentials) but warned that the paper would hold the council accountable for resolving the issues it had promoted. Further, it claimed that 'as other councils like Ipswich, Logan, and Redlands roll out the red carpet for investors, the Gold Coast treats its customers with arrogance and contempt' (Gleeson 2012b, p. 13). These editorials are indicative of three pervasive features of local politics in the region. First, there is a highly vocal pro-business and pro-development lobby. Second, there is a strong distrust of the public sector within sections of business, the media and conservative parties. Third, there is a strong sense of competition between the Gold Coast, the Queensland Government and other local councils. The pro-business policy stance of the council, and the distrust of the public sector, has been shared by conservative governments at the Queensland and Commonwealth levels that embarked on programs designed to reduce the size of the public sector and curb government expenditure.

Relations with other local councils

The City of Gold Coast obviously needs to maintain relationships with other local governments in the region (see Fig. 8.3). There is the need to coordinate key infrastructure, such as roads, water and sewerage. Businesses operate across council jurisdictions and people move freely between them (Spearritt 2009; Abbott 2011). Key services such as health care and education might be provided in one shire, but be used by residents from surrounding areas. A natural disaster in one jurisdiction will inevitably impact on others, with volunteers moving into the impact zone and people affected seeking shelter and support in neighbouring shires (as happened during the 2011 Brisbane floods). Three prominent relationships for the Gold Coast are with Brisbane City Council, Tweed Shire Council and the Sunshine Coast Council. These relations can be characterised as varying between cooperation and competition at different times, depending on the issue (Prideaux and Cooper 2002; Whitford 2004; Spearritt 2008; Abbott 2011; Steele *et al.* 2011).

Brisbane is the largest council in Australia and plays a central role in local government of the South East Queensland region. The Brisbane mayor was instrumental in the formation of the South East Queensland Regional Organisation of Councils (SEQROC) in 1991 and took leadership of the Council of Mayors: South East Queensland that replaced it in 2005. These organisations played an important role in the development of regional planning, first through the voluntary system of cooperation in the 1990s, then in the lead up to the development of the first *South East Queensland Regional Plan 2005–2026* (Queensland Government and SEQROC 2005; Gleeson *et al.* 2010; Abbott 2011). There is also, however, an element of competition between the Gold Coast and Brisbane, particularly when it comes to attracting major events, encouraging development projects and promoting local tourism (Spearritt 2008). Tensions between the two boiled over in May 2006 during the Millennium Drought of 2001–09 when the Gold Coast mayor relaxed water restrictions for a weekend because the local Hinze Dam was still full while the Brisbane reservoirs were at a very low level (Spearritt 2008). The later construction of a water grid connecting reservoirs throughout the region was then seen by some Gold Coast residents as an attempt by Brisbane to steal 'their' water. Such concerns did not manifest themselves in an organised opposition, so the project went ahead. The drought broke shortly after construction was finished, which took the heat out of the issue.

Relations with other councils are less fraught but still double sided. The Sunshine Coast (and its predecessors) was part of the Council of Mayors and cooperated with regional planning process. There is, however, a healthy rivalry with the Gold Coast in the race to attract tourism (Prideaux and Cooper 2002).

Relations with the Tweed Shire Council are complicated by the fact that although it abuts the southern boundary of the Gold Coast, the divide forms part of the border

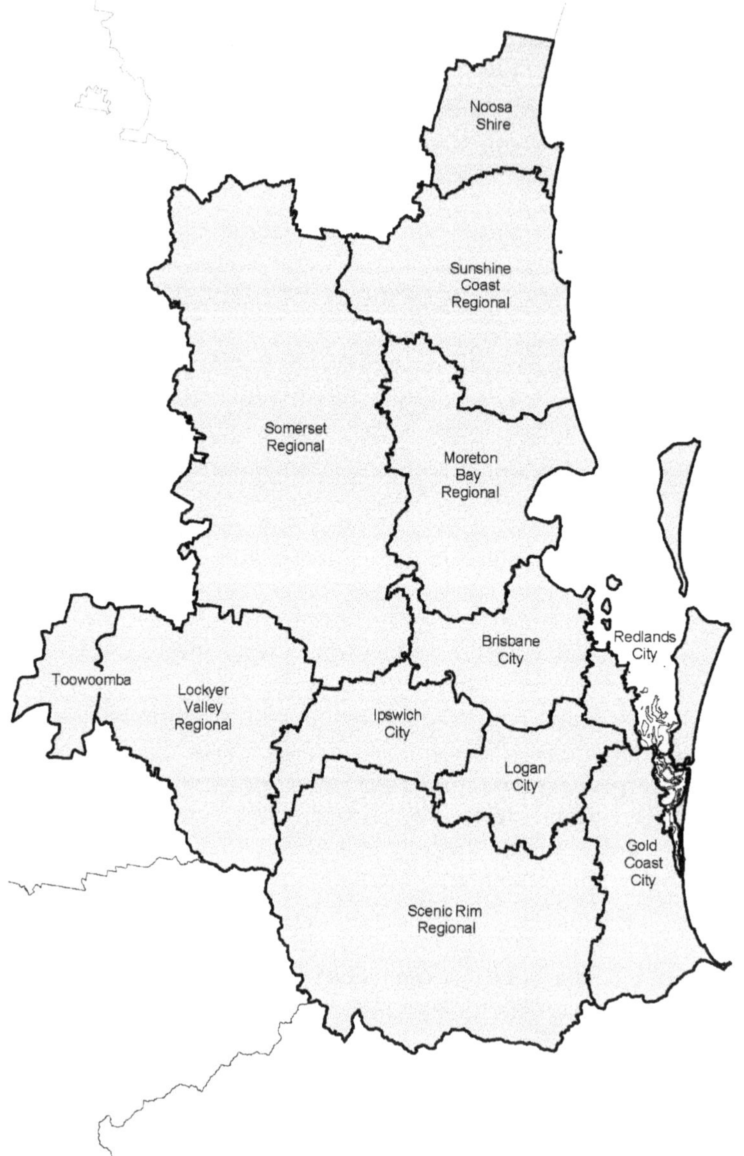

Fig. 8.3. Local government boundaries in South East Queensland, 2015 (Map courtesy of Mariola Rafanowicz)

between the states of Queensland and New South Wales, resulting in some peculiar consequences. Tweed Shire was not part of the regional planning process because it is outside Queensland's jurisdiction and there are no formal agreements on collaborative planning (Spearritt 2009; Steele *et al.* 2011). This also discouraged cooperation and encouraged distrust during the water supply crisis caused by the drought of 2001–09, even though both shires are effectively part of the same city (Spearritt 2008). Further, the Gold Coast Airport straddles the border, so that half the runway is in New South Wales and the other half is in Queensland. But perhaps the most impressive oddity is that only one of the states has daylight saving. As a result, during summer you can stand on Boundary Street in Coolangatta with the time on one side of the road being 8.30 am and on the other 9.30 am – which means that people can effectively travel backwards and forwards in time just by crossing the road – making it very confusing for local residents and businesses. Campaigns by locals to adopt daylight saving have so far proved fruitless because there is no major electoral incentive for the Queensland Government to tackle the issue. There was a brief trial of daylight saving during 1989–92, but a referendum to continue at the end of this period was defeated. Since then, no government has seen any benefit in taking the issue on as it is strongly opposed by residents in northern Queensland.

Relations with the Queensland Government

The most important relationship for the City of Gold Coast is with the Queensland state government. As noted in the previous sections, the council and its predecessors have been created and reorganised by the Queensland Government over more than a century. Indeed, the very structure, operations and powers of the council are determined by the *Queensland Local Government Act 2009* that is administered by the state Department of Local Government and Planning (DLGP 2012). The council depends on the state for the provision of major infrastructure such as main roads, rail, power and water, as well as services such as law enforcement, education and health care.

Historically, forays into particular local projects by the Queensland Government have been on an ad hoc basis and often depended on the preferences of individual ministers. The provision of a rail link between Southport and Brisbane, for example, was completed in 1889 then extended to Tweed Heads in 1903. The link was closed in 1964, but a new line was opened in 1997 from Brisbane to Robina that was extended to Varsity Lakes in 2009 (O'Hare 2008). There is currently some discussion about whether it should be extended to Coolangatta and whether the light rail currently under construction might be connected if a second stage is built (GoldLinQ 2012d).

Apart from intermittent interventions on major projects, local councils such as the Gold Coast were generally left to their own devices on planning and development decisions until the 1990s when successive Queensland governments began to take more of an interest in regional planning. It began with voluntary initiatives designed to encourage intergovernmental collaboration. The state government convened the *SEQ 2001* community conference in 1990 that led to the creation of the Regional Planning Advisory Group in 1991, involving state ministers, mayors and a representative of the Commonwealth. It also led to the aforementioned formation of the South East Queensland Regional Organisation of Councils that later became the Council of Mayors: South East Queensland. The *Regional Framework for Growth Management* emerged from this process in 1995 but by 2003 the process seemed to be stalling. A move was then made towards a statutory approach that led to the *South East Queensland Regional Plan 2005–2026*. While the initial approach was collaborative, the state government had come to dominate the process by the time of the release of the revised *South East Queensland Regional Plan 2009–31* (Marshall *et al.* 2003; Gleeson *et al.* 2010; Abbott 2011). The City of Gold Coast, like all local governments in the region, was compelled by the *Sustainable Planning Act 2009* to abide by this plan in their decision making.

The situation changed again after the 2012 state election. Within a few months the newly elected Newman government introduced amendments to both the *Sustainable Planning Act* and *Local Government Act*. It also started a review of the regional plan and coastal management plan. The overall aim appears to be to hand back powers to the local level of government and reduce delays in development applications. Although it is yet to be seen how this will play out, it is possible that the City of Gold Coast may gain considerable autonomy when these changes come to fruition. A recent change in state government, however, may mean that these proposed changes are less certain than they might have been before the 2015 election.

During the Millennium Drought the Queensland Government moved to intervene further with regards to water supply. Traditionally councils had managed their own water supplies, although the construction of major assets and infrastructure, such as dams, involved the state and Commonwealth governments. In 2006, with a growing water shortage throughout the region, the state government announced the establishment of a Water Commission. They went on to announce the creation of a water grid linking all reservoirs together, the construction of a recycled water plant, the construction of a desalination plant (on the Gold Coast) and plans to build two new dams (Spearritt 2008). After the drought broke in 2009 the proposed dams were shelved, the desalination plant was kept at minimal operating capacity and recycled water was limited to use by industry. Water distribution was transferred to a corporation called Allconnex that was jointly owned by the local councils. In 2011 several councils, including the Gold Coast, were unhappy with the water pricing system so pulled out of Allconnex and took back control of their supplies (*Courier Mail* 2011; Vernon 2011).

This again demonstrates how the relationship between the City of Gold Coast and the Queensland Government has varied in its character over time. First, there has been the ad hoc provision of essential infrastructure such as railways over a century. Second, there has been a shift in regional planning from council independence, through a period of collaboration, to state government ascendency until 2012, then a move to return of some independence. Finally, there has been a shift in the control of water supplies from the council to the state government and back again, all in the space of a decade.

Relations with the Commonwealth

The Commonwealth has played an intermittent but strategically important role in the governance and development of the Gold Coast. It has often been involved in co-funding projects with the Queensland Government and/or the City of Gold Coast. The current light rail construction project is a case in point (GoldLinQ 2012a, 2012b). Since 1990 it has been directly funding Landcare, Coastcare and other environmental rehabilitation projects in the region (NRM 2012). It has given long-term support over several decades to the very successful marketing campaigns that lure international tourists to the Gold Coast (Prideaux and Cooper 2002).

There have been selective interventions of a more systematic nature over time. The Commonwealth funding of urban road systems started back in the 1920s, and it began collaborating with the states on public housing in the 1940s. In 1972, the Department of Urban and Regional Development was established to oversee programs on sewerage, traffic and land management (which had traditionally been the domain of local councils). In the early 1990s the Commonwealth developed national building codes and the *Better Cities* program that helped to fund the Gold Coast rail link (Gleeson 2006).

Changes to the Commonwealth tertiary education system in the late 1980s led to two new universities on the Gold Coast. Griffith University took over the Gold Coast College of Advanced Education in 1988 and turned it into a new campus, while Bond University opened in 1989. This was followed by the construction of campuses by Southern Cross University and Central Queensland University. Griffith was involved in the construction of a new university hospital and medical school at Southport and is a partner in the Queensland Government's Smart Water research facility, all of which are co-located on the Southport campus. These universities rely on Commonwealth funding and administration, and have served to diversify the economy of the Gold Coast in the areas of tertiary education, science, technology and health care.

Conclusions

The Australian political system is complicated, and this has significant implications for governing cities such as the Gold Coast. Getting the relevant approvals and funding for essential projects takes time and managing the intergovernmental relations is often cumbersome. The Gold Coast has grown rapidly over the last half century and the structure of the local council has changed and grown as a result. Throughout its history its relationships with neighbouring councils has been a mixture of cooperation and competition. From 1990 to 2012 the Queensland Government progressively asserted a greater role in regional planning and development, but the Newman government (2012 to 2015) moved back towards more local autonomy. Over the same period there have been intermittent interventions from the Commonwealth on specific environmental, planning and infrastructure projects. The overall outcome has been an economically and socially heterogeneous city with somewhat complicated relations to its political neighbours.

Chapter 9

The changing face of local government on the Gold Coast

Paul Burton

The city of the Gold Coast is renowned in Australia, and to some extent further afield, for the pace of its growth and for the scale of its transformation over the last 70 years from a collection of small seaside settlements and inland towns to one of the country's urban tourism capitals and possibly one of its first knowledge cities. As outlined in Chapter 1, it is home to just over half a million people at present, but is likely to continue to grow by attracting migrants from elsewhere in Australia and from overseas, increasingly from China and India as well as from the more traditional feeder countries of Britain and New Zealand. This transformation has been described by some as the epitome of free-market or neoliberal processes of urbanisation, with only minimal intervention and regulation by any of the three levels of Australian government (Burton 2014). However, governments have always played a role in the establishment and growth of the city and will continue to do so in the future. Whether that role is welcomed by all, whether it represents 'vaulting ambition which o'erleaps itself' or whether a more extensive role will be required in the future are all questions that this chapter attempts to answer. It begins with a brief consideration of the emergence of local government in Australia and its changing role in shaping the development of major cities, and then reviews the growth of the City of Gold Coast through several of the more prominent theoretical perspectives on the role of local government in processes of urbanisation and urban management. The chapter concludes with some informed speculation on the future of Gold Coast local government.

Local government in Australia

The first directly elected local council in Australia was formed in 1840, when the colonial government created the Adelaide Corporation to manage the local affairs of that emerging city and to provide for some of the needs of its citizens. It is worth noting that within three years it had been suspended and was subsequently run by a small group of aldermen commissioned by the colonial government, marking what has been described as a 'continuously abrasive relationship' between local, state and federal governments (Morton 1996). While not always abrasive, the relationship between the three levels of government in Australia has never been entirely harmonious and the latest attempt to secure 'financial' recognition for local government in the Constitution floundered in the aftermath of the election of the new Coalition federal government in 2013.

Local governments in Australia have typically embraced a minimalist position, collecting local rates to provide relatively basic but important local services and facilities, such as roads, bridges, recreational infrastructure such as parks and community centres, as well as the collection and disposal of waste. These could be described as typically property focused rather than social services and reflect the fact that the liability to pay rates and the right to vote were tied initially to property ownership and therefore reflected the interests and needs of property owners. However, throughout the twentieth century the role and scope of local government grew, initially through the acquisition of powers to regulate development and then to provide more in the way of social services to meet the needs of a greater range of local citizens. Nevertheless, there remains a tension between those wishing to limit the powers, and therefore the revenue raising obligations of local government, and those promoting greater local government intervention across a broader spectrum of activities.

Local governments in Queensland have been subject to processes of amalgamation over the years, the last being in 2007–08 which resulted in the creation of 74 local government areas represented by councils typically consisting of several councillors and a directly elected mayor. Following a limited process of de-amalgamation in 2012, Queensland now has 77 local governments, which vary considerably in terms of population served and land coverage and, related to both, in terms of fiscal base and capacity to provide services. Queensland is markedly different to most other states and territories in having relatively few, larger councils (New South Wales, for example, has 152 local governments, most of which are small shire areas) and Brisbane is the only capital city in which the jurisdiction of the city council extends over most of the built up area of the city. Queensland councillors are remunerated and, except for the smaller councils, are typically expected to work full time in the role.

By using their zoning powers and through providing important infrastructure such as roads, reticulated water and sewerage systems, local governments have played an important role in determining the shape and the pace of urban growth in Australia. Although the relationship between the development industry and local government has sometimes lacked transparency and propriety, by and large local government has been seen (by the development industry at least) as a brake on development, either consciously through the maintenance of growth boundaries or more indirectly through the bureaucratic and financial burdens it imposes during the exercise of its planning and development assessment powers. But in the last few years there has been a concerted effort in many parts of Australia to transform local government land-use planning and regulation into something that more explicitly supports and promotes economic growth. Along with a strong ideological commitment to reduce red and 'green' tape by removing unnecessary regulatory regimes, many local governments, especially in South East Queensland, are also proclaiming themselves 'open for business' and using this as a slogan to signify their new attitude to planning and other interventions. In this respect many local governments have now adopted a much more self conscious and explicit role as promoters as well as regulators of growth, which of course brings with it new political challenges in striking an appropriate balance between what are often conflicting (but certainly not novel) imperatives of growth and sustainability.

Finally, a perennial problem confronting local government in Australia is how it manages its relationship with state and federal levels. As noted above, there is not yet any constitutional recognition for local government, which means, in effect, that it can be difficult for the Commonwealth Government to provide direct support and policy guidance to local governments, which remain creatures of their respective state governments. The complexities and complications of this three-way relationship and the political turbulence it creates have been a distinctive feature of Australian federalism for over 100 years and show no sign of becoming simpler or calmer in the immediate future. This, then, is the backdrop against which we must consider the changing role of local government in trying to manage the growth of the City of Gold Coast over the last 50 years.

Local government and the shaping of the Gold Coast

There are many different theoretical perspectives on the role and function of local government in contemporary political systems but they can to some extent be grouped into two broad camps: conventional and critical. The conventional group typically accepts the self-definition of all levels of government as capable of delivering the benefits they claim as part of their raison d'être and assumes they are amenable to reform if the ways in which they deliver these benefits in practice are sub-optimal. Those in the critical group tend to be less convinced of the stated benefits of government intervention and to detect a range of less obvious and acknowledged motivations which run counter to the public rationale of government. Neither group has an especially sophisticated explanation of the specificity of local government vis-a-vis other levels of government, and both typically adopt a rather parochial stance in assuming that local government is like national or state level government writ small in respect of its democratic organisation, but with a particular remit in respect of its scope and sphere of intervention. Saunders' (1986) proposal for a theoretically informed framework for analysing the operations and indeed the specificity of 'the local state' have not been widely adopted in Australia (although see Broomhill 2001).

Conventional perspectives

From a conventional perspective, local government in Australia is presumed to be founded on democratic principles of open election and local accountability, with a functional focus on 'roads, rates and rubbish'. Of course, there is ongoing debate about the best way to manage local democratic processes and systems of accountability, about the most appropriate size of local government jurisdictions in order to strike the right balance between sense of attachment and efficiency in service delivery, and about the proper reach and scope of local government. Nevertheless, local government is generally held to be capable of meeting its promise of delivering a limited range of local services, more or less efficiently by professional officers in accordance with local preferences reflected by locally elected councillors. And in the face of a seemingly inexorable growth in the number of staff employed by local governments, there is an entrenched view that small local government is good and smaller is better.

Within the conventional frame, the emergence and growth of the City of Gold Coast is presented in several different but related ways. One of the more popular and enduring perspectives is that the city is a product of the vision and ambition of a handful of entrepreneurial developers (see for example Jones 1986; Forbes and Spearritt 2003; Burchill 2005), aided and abetted at times by equally visionary and entrepreneurial politicians and in particular by some of its mayors (McRobbie 2000). So, while Thor Jensen and Arthur Blackwood offered parcels of land just north of Broadbeach for sale in 1917 as part of what they called the Surfers Paradise Estate, it was James Cavill's construction of the Surfers Paradise Hotel in 1925 that led soon after to the area being formally renamed Surfers Paradise, despite opposition from the local council concerned at the rapid commercialisation of the area (Moore 2005, p. 192). The local council at that time was the Town of the South Coast and presided mainly over the coastal strip, but in 1959 the state government approved its renaming to the City of Gold Coast. Of greater political significance was the amalgamation in 1995 with the Shire of Albert, which extended west from the coastal strip into the hinterland of the Beechmont–Tamborine mountain ranges from the New South Wales border north to Logan (see Fig. 11.2). This not only expanded the footprint of the new council, but provided substantial new opportunities for suburban residential development. It also created political tensions between those concerned principally with the city as a place of tourism and those more committed to catering for the needs of a rapidly growing resident population – tensions that remain to this day.

Back in 1959, when the city was renamed, Bruce Small settled in the area with the proceeds of a profitable sale of his Melbourne-based Malvern Star bicycle manufacturing business, and acquired 100 acres of mangrove swamp at Nerang, which he set about converting into more valuable real estate. He also brought with him a desire for a more planned approach to development in the belief that it would increase profitability and help make the place more resilient by raising development land above existing flood levels (Small 1978). Small eventually won election as the mayor of the Gold Coast in 1967, campaigning with the slogan 'Think big, vote Small'. Somewhat ironically, within weeks of his election the city was hit by one of its worst cyclones and floods in memory and suffered considerable damage to its canal infrastructure. This boosted its reputation as a place of potentially profitable but high-risk investment. Small also worked hard during his two terms as mayor (1967–73 and 1976–78) to introduce a modern town plan for the city but is perhaps best known for his national and international tours to promote the city and its attractions in which he used the city's infamous bikini-clad Meter Maids to stimulate media interest. He also epitomised the tension between strong political leadership and democratic accountability, never fully accepting the right of his fellow councillors to impose any check on his preferences and plans (McRobbie 2000, p. 323). The end of his mayoralty was also marked by the suspension of the council by the state government for ineptitude, and its temporary replacement by an administrator appointed by the state government in 1978–79. The competency and legitimacy of local politicians remain a popular topic of public debate in the city and elsewhere.

Ten years later, the already fast growing city benefited from another economic stimulation when the state government abolished death duties. This created a tax haven, which succeeded in attracting investors from the southern states looking to retire in a place where their dollar went further and the climate was more congenial than in Sydney or Melbourne. As Small himself put it, 'the Gold Coast … is the loveliest place in the world to live … and it is also the best place to die' (Small 1978, p. 111).

Small's belief in the value of a modern town plan to manage the growth of the city was not realised in practice and by the mid-1980s the balance of power between planners and developers lay clearly with the latter. Jones (1986, p. 62) noted another apparent paradox when he observed that 'the desire for growth has been paramount and developers have far more influence than the town planners', but that this lack of regulation may also have been the key to the city's success and vitality.

Critical perspectives

Critical perspectives usually begin by considering the role in general of the state in capitalist societies and in particular by setting out the ways in which government institutions serve various needs of capitalism: by underwriting the profitability of firms through investment in physical and social infrastructure; by helping to reproduce a skilled and compliant workforce; and by managing the various crises of legitimacy that develop out of the various contradictions of the capitalist mode of production. Variations on this theme have seen a greater emphasis on the social relations of production than on the institutions of the state, and more recently there has been a preoccupation with neoliberalism as a new and possibly distinctive form of state intervention. In order to avoid criticism that such totalising theories attempt to explain each and every local practice as being 'ultimately' or 'in the last instance' supportive of capitalism (Saunders 1986), more empirically grounded approaches have emerged at various points over the last 30 years to critically investigate 'actually existing' forms of neoliberalism (Brenner and Theodore 2002). These new approaches allow the theoretical possibility that some of these local forms allow a degree of material progress for those not typically served by neoliberal forces (Boyle *et al.* 2008) even if most serve to reinforce and reinstate class privileges (Davis 2006).

There have been few accounts of the growth of the Gold Coast as a city or of its structures of governance that apply a critical perspective in a systematic manner, although Burton (2014) presents an exploratory analysis of the neoliberalisation of local government in the city and suggests that several incipient crises appear to be emerging that might challenge the local legitimacy of neoliberal hegemony. Other analytical perspectives that do not sit comfortably with the conventional/critical duality include those that focus on the personalities and contributions of key individuals, on party politics and on the role of the local government bureaucracy.

Personality, party and bureaucratic politics

Personality politics on the Gold Coast has always been connected with the party politics of Queensland and Australia. With one or two notable exceptions – Brisbane City Council and Ipswich, for example – candidates in local elections, including mayoral candidates, are not endorsed by political parties. Indeed, there is typically public hostility to candidates who run as party members as it is felt that local politics should be concerned with parochial issues (in a favourable sense) rather than with party ideologies. For example, while the 2008 local elections for what was then known as Gold Coast City Council included a full slate of candidates endorsed by the Liberal party and another slate of candidates led by former Councillor Rob Molhoek, under the name of UniteGC, the incumbent mayor, Ron Clarke (2004–08) defied the bookmakers and was elected for a second term (2008–12), saying 'party politics rejection is something the Gold Coast has shown time and again … they really don't accept party politics coming into their elections. Neither should they … local government is very different to state and federal governments'. There has never been a plausible political challenge from an endorsed Labor party candidate and the enduring theme of Gold Coast politics has always been about growth: whether it should be encouraged at all costs, how it might be supported by the council and whether there are any plausible limits to growth in and of the city. Although the council led for two terms by Mayor Clarke was often portrayed as an anti-growth and even a 'green' council, this should be seen in the wider context of Queensland and to some extent Australian politics, where 'green' is taken by many to be a self-evident term of political denigration and any attempt to regulate growth in the form of urban development is interpreted as an unfair and unjustified interference with the 'free market'. In fact, the council led by Mayor Clarke planned for considerable growth and provided significant infrastructural support in the form of roads, sewerage and water infrastructure, but it did attempt to introduce a planning scheme that required high standards of design for prominent buildings (and this postmillennial period saw several of these) and expected suburban developers to contribute to the cost of providing infrastructure to new residential areas on the fringes of the city.

Another long standing point of criticism of this and indeed many other local councils in Australia is that its bureaucratic arm comes to dominate the political arm and engages in an inexorable processes of bureaucratic empire building. Launching his mayoral campaign in May 2011, former Councillor and Deputy Mayor David Power summarised this criticism in a series of pithy reflections and electoral promises. He observed: 'We have been let down substantially by our leaders. The Council bureaucracy and the regulations that inhibit business must be brought under control', before promising change: 'A query put to me by many of you here today is whether I will reform the bureaucracy … the answer is an unequivocal yes. Under my mayoralty officers will return to being anonymous and responsive to the people's representatives' (Power 2011). The eventual winner of that electoral contest, Tom Tate (standing this time without the formal endorsement of the Liberal National Party) also promised major reforms of the 'bloated bureaucracy', with the local media predicting the replacement of the chief executive and the number of directorates to be reduced substantially. Neither has transpired, although two long standing directors (of planning and of engineering services) have since left and a new Office of the Mayor has been created to act, among others things, as a counter to the perceived power of the established bureaucracy.

Growth coalitions

In some respects this recent history of the urban politics of the Gold Coast represents a clear case of the growth coalition model articulated first by Molotch (1976) and later by Logan and Molotch (1987) in which the interests of a particular set of people – property developers – are taken to represent the interests of all residents and supported by a coalition led by local government. In this case growth becomes an end in itself rather than a means to another end connected with some conception of the city in an equilibrium or optimal state. In other words, not only does the pursuit of growth become the dominant yardstick for judging all policy proposals and assessing the impact of any regulatory regimes, but there is no logical end to the process. This has long been apparent in the City of Gold Coast and indeed throughout South East Queensland, where any attempt to manage growth through the designation of an 'urban footprint' or growth boundary is constantly challenged both in principle and in detail by representatives of the development industry using the marvellously circuitous argument that an urban footprint limits the availability of land and hence the provision of affordable housing; without affordable housing new migrants will not be attracted to the city; without new migrants who will buy the houses that the development industry needs to build?

The analytical challenge made to growth coalition models is, however, the tendency to treat this coalition of developer interests as monolithic and to ignore or underplay any sets of interests that may well be broadly 'pro-business' but have nevertheless a set of their own distinct interests. In the City of Gold Coast this distinction is most apparent in the tension between developers focused on providing low-density residential housing on greenfield sites in the suburban fringes and hinterland, and those catering for more up-market and tourist schemes closer to the coastal strip. While both may be opposed to the imposition on developers of infrastructure charges for water supply, waste and stormwater facilities, recreational facilities and transport, and to what are seen as unnecessary delays in securing development approvals, the former are more concerned with land supply policies and the latter with height restrictions, parking standards and urban design obligations.

Throughout the mayoralty of Ron Clarke, the council did pursue a political agenda that paid greater attention to notions of sustainability and to the principles of growth management rather than growth promotion. This agenda was not, of course, uncontested either within or beyond the council, but political instability and conflict among councillors allowed the officers to play a more prominent role than might otherwise have been the case in constructing a planning scheme and related policy measures based on principles of sustainable development. But it should also be noted that this was also driven to a great extent by the provisions of the Labor state government's *Integrated Planning Act 1997* which sought to achieve 'ecologically sustainable development' through the implementation of a coordinated and coherent set of state, regional and local plans. There was, therefore, a political alignment of state planning legislation with the professional preferences of council planning officials, even if these were not shared by all local councillors.

Bold futures?

Soon after the 2008 local elections for the city council were concluded – in which all incumbent councillors and the mayor were returned – the council embarked on an ambitious process of developing a long-term strategy for the future of the city. This initiative, known as *Bold Future*, was designed to provide an overarching corporate strategy that would guide more detailed plans such as the planning scheme, the transport strategy and so on. In its 2007/08 annual report (Gold Coast City Council 2008, p. 3) the initiative was described as representing 'a turning point in the city's history. It aims to create a socially, environmentally and economically sustainable city for the next three decades by pinpointing residents' priorities for their city and how they want it to look in 2037'. The process was noteworthy for it put the management and oversight of the process into the hands of a semi-autonomous committee of individuals from a variety of sectors (business, community groups, environmental organisations, developers, academics and planners from elsewhere). Although endorsed by council, the committee did not include councillors as formal members, even if a number attended regularly and contributed to debates.

The *Bold Future* process paid particular attention to two facets in its work: the creation of a long-term vision for the future and the widespread involvement of local residents. Expert witnesses were called to provide advice on future trends that might affect the social, economic and environmental development of the city, and several briefing sessions for councillors were held with a noted futurist, Sohail Inayatullah, an adjunct professor at the University of the Sunshine Coast. Various community forums, online surveys and structured opinion polls were also conducted to gauge the views of residents and led the mayor to describe it as 'the most extensive community consultation process ever undertaken in Australia' (Gold Coast City Council 2008, p. 6). The process attracted a mix of responses, although there was a notable degree of consistency in the issues of most concern to the public and their priorities in addressing them. But it also attracted some criticism for its approach, including from the main local newspaper, the News Limited-owned *Gold Coast Bulletin*. Some members of the committee failed to attend many or any meetings, in some cases because of work pressures but in others because of an unwillingness to work alongside members from outside their usual peer group. The committee included, for example, two young women still attending high school and a representative of a prominent environmental action group – neither of whom were widely recognised as members of the local elite growth coalition! Somewhat paradoxically the process, or rather its outcome, was also criticised for being insufficiently bold, although it was never made entirely clear which elements could or should have been extended in this way. Thus, although the *Bold Future* represented an innovative approach to long-term strategic planning for the city and proposed a set of broad commitments that commanded a reasonably high degree of public support, it did not comprise the usual exercise in closed and relatively elite planning among unequivocal members of the growth coalition. For this reason it was treated as a symbolic product of the 'green' mayoralty of Ron Clarke and dismissed by many of the city's unofficial leaders (some of whom had even been members of the Bold Future Committee). However, unlike many long-term vision documents produced by other cities, this one was used by the council's administration as the foundation for a more systematic application of its principles to all of council's other strategic plans, including the planning scheme, the corporate and community plans and the transport strategy. Somewhat ironically, a plan decried by many among the development elite in the city has continued to influence day-to-day policy and practice through bureaucratic rather than political channels.

Agency and structure: great men and the neoliberal project

From a conventional perspective the growth of the city, and the role of the city council in this process, has been framed primarily in terms of the actions of 'great men', entrepreneurs and developers as well as politicians supporting (or occasionally thwarting) them. From the perspective of agency-structure debates (e.g. Giddens 1984) the balance of explanation and understanding lies clearly on the agency rather than the structural side of the equation. Ongoing attempts to bolster a narrative of growth and development as being unequivocally good for all have always been met by a political undercurrent of resistance, not always strong or effective but always there. This resistance takes many forms: sometimes opposition to specific development proposals; sometimes as part of a broader campaign to retain aspects of both the ambience (its relaxed lifestyle for example) and the build form (the fibro shack or 'iconic' landmarks such as the neon sign of the former Pink Poodle Motel) of the city (see Fig. 9.1). And while this resistance has in recent years been associated with some avowedly environmental groups, such as the Gold Coast and Hinterland Environment Council (GECKO) and the various Save Our Spit campaigns, it has also come from some sectors of the business community in general and the development sector in particular. In other words, somewhat nostalgic attempts to preserve or recreate a mythic past exist across the political spectrum.

Although this complexity can be difficult to accommodate within conventional analytical frameworks, it is more comprehensible within more critical frameworks, which recognise the existence of competing interests and contradictory imperatives even within larger class formations. While the growth coalition model at least allows for the possibility of significant political interests remaining outside any coalition, some of the more crude applications of the neoliberal analytical framework fail to void the pitfalls encountered in earlier crude Marxist frameworks whereby each and every policy intervention is seen as self-evidently part of the 'neoliberal project'. Thankfully some contemporary case studies of local government in practice adopt a more critical stance and are open to the conceptual and empirical possibility that some policies and interventions serve the interests of, or are at least a response to, political pressure from groups other than a dominant group. For example, Blanco's (2009) analysis of the success of the so-called 'Barcelona model' uses detailed empirical analysis to explore what have become taken-for-granted assumptions about the nature of successful urban planning and regeneration. This is especially apposite for the Gold Coast, which in many respects is built on hyperbole and myth.

A contemporary example of a less than coherent and consistent approach to a major development project for the city is the proposal to build a cruise ship terminal and related

Fig. 9.1. Pink Poodle Motel neon sign at night, *c.* 1975 (Photograph by John Gollings. Image reproduction courtesy of the Gold Coast City Council Local Studies Library, image number LS-LSP-CD496-IMG0010)

tourism facilities in the Broadwater, a prominent estuary in the city. Proposals to develop this type of facility in this location have been made at various points over the last two decades and while they have typically commanded widespread support from among the business and development industries, they have divided public opinion. Indeed one of the most prominent and successful local political campaigns was organised in 2004 by the Save Our Spit Alliance with the support of GECKO, in opposition to these development proposals. As noted, the current mayor included his prominent support for a terminal in his election campaign, going so far as to promise that if elected he would deliver the project to the city. With the support in principle of the new state government, the Broadwater Marine Project was launched in October 2012, calling initially for expressions of interest from suitable consortia to develop an integrated facility for cruise ships and super yachts, a casino, residential units and retail spaces, along with enhanced community open spaces and recreational facilities. Four of these were shortlisted and invited to develop more detailed proposals, while at the same time a series of environmental impact studies were commissioned. The ASF Consortium was subsequently selected and invited to prepare a detailed case, including an application to the state government for a casino licence, and required as part of the process to set up a comprehensive process of community engagement over its plans. However, the state's Deputy Premier, Jeff Seeney, announced in August 2014 that state-owned land on The Spit would not be made available for the project because of 'a very clear message that the community does not support the development of Doug Jennings Park and wants The Spit retained as a recreational area' (AAP 2014). It is not clear yet what effect this will have on the commercial viability of the ASF Consortium's proposals, but it is unlikely to be favourable. It is clear that even among levels of government that share an 'open for business' ideology and public commitment to this type development, there is some policy tension and different degrees of sensitivity to popular concerns about the environmental, social and economic impacts of the proposed development. With the change in state government in February 2015 support for this project has diminished, raising concern among its proponents.

Critical perspectives therefore place less emphasis on the role and significance of 'great men' and more on the sometimes conflicting and contradictory pressures that arise from a fragmented development industry, which must be managed by the local state. The extent to which the local state is able to perform successfully these sporadic management challenges will influence the extent to which they grow into more substantial crises of legitimacy for local councils, their mayors and for local government more generally.

Local government and the future

The history of the City of Gold Coast has, inescapably, been one steeped in discourses of growth, mainly of its promotion but occasionally of the need to manage it in ways that might be sustainable. Until recently, this notion of growth has been relatively simple and concerned primarily with growth in the resident population of the city and in the number of temporary tourist visitors. It has also focused on the built environment that accommodates these populations, but again primarily on the fact that the construction and development industry has served as one of the main sectors of the local economy. In this respect the dominant political discourse about the city has typically been on the need for the city to keep growing, and only recently has this begun to include any serious consideration of the nature of that growth, whether and how it might be managed and whether indeed there might be any limits to growth.

The local government of the newly formed and developing city has reflected this discursive pattern, with an enduring focus on the need to stimulate and facilitate growth but an emerging appreciation of the complexities of managing a rapidly growing and changing city. It is commonplace and certainly present in Gold Coast debates for some to want to preserve particular landscapes – built or otherwise – as they were at particular moments in time for nostalgic or more economic reasons. And of course there have been advocates of change and progress, again for a variety of reasons. These different dispositions have been reflected in both the membership and leadership of the local council, although it is always difficult for politicians, including local councillors, to balance their long-term aspirations for the city with shorter-term positions of expediency that are often necessary to achieve and retain office. Nevertheless, the last decade has seen a relatively clear distinction, at the ideological level at least, between Mayor Clarke's advocacy of managed growth and the more active promotion of unrestrained growth by Mayor Tate. The day-to-day realities of urban planning in practice, including both land-use regulation and place promotion, may not of course have been so pronounced.

The current mayor, Councillor Tate, campaigned on a clear platform of growth promotion and being 'open for business', and promised to support and indeed to deliver several high profile projects that would symbolise that stance and drive the future growth of the city. The development of a cruise ship terminal and integrated resort development (including a casino) on the Broadwater remains one of the most contentious proposals, not just because it represents both an economic opportunity and an environmental threat which tends to polarise public opinion, but because it symbolises the often fraught relations between local and state government. Under the previous mayoralty, successful opposition to similar proposals could be portrayed as the product of an unholy alliance between the

Labor state government of Premier Anna Bligh and local green activists, epitomised by the Save Our Spit Alliance. Between 2012 and 2014 the local council was politically aligned with the Liberal National Party state government of Premier Campbell Newman, and grassroots opposition broadened in this time to include highly popular local surfing figures. If the proposal does not go ahead – and it is by no means certain to do so – it may well serve to illustrate the practical difficulties of securing any major development projects, especially those with substantial environmental impacts.

Other major projects promoted by the new council and the mayor have been more successful and less contentious. The council published a new culture strategy – one in a line of such projects – in February 2014 which promoted, among other things, the creation of a 'cultural precinct' in the Evandale district to provide a focal point for new cultural facilities, including an art gallery and performing arts spaces, and for what is hoped will be a blossoming cultural economy. Endorsing many of the positive attributes associated with cultural economic development (Florida 2007; Landry 2006), this is a modern interpretation of the much longer standing representation of the Gold Coast as a resort city with tourism as one of the mainstays of its economy. Indeed, when announcing the shortlist of development consortia for the new cultural precinct, Mayor Tate proclaimed, 'When it comes to arts and culture, we mean business'.

In many conventional accounts of local government, certainly of those in European democracies, the changing nature of local politics and city growth is often presented as the outcome of an ongoing struggle between progressive and conservative forces, or between Keynesian advocates of an expanding local state and neoliberal proponents of small government and limited intervention. Until recently, many critical accounts of urban growth have tended to use neoliberal frameworks in crude and simplistic ways which take little account of local empirical realities and to treat local governments as unequivocal participants in the 'neoliberal project'.

The history of local government in the growth of the City of Gold Coast does not follow these patterns, and not just because Australian local politics has its own idiosyncrasies. It is rather that there has rarely been any political pressure in the city for the local council to expand its scope to become a Keynesian welfare state writ small. The long standing preoccupation with 'roads, rates and rubbish' may well have been superseded by a more comprehensive outlook, but an overriding desire to limit the growth of local rates continues to hold these ambitions in check. Furthermore, the traditional left/right party battles of European municipalities simply do not exist on the Gold Coast and if anything, political rivalries between the parties of the conservatism – the Liberal and National (previously Country) parties – have been more significant. As McRobbie (2000, p. 340) notes:

> *the Country Party was not only anti-tourism, it was anti-Gold Coast. Partly this was because successive Premiers ... were all from rural areas north of Brisbane where there was considerable jealousy of the rapid progress and growth of the Gold Coast.*

The city has for most of its existence been led by men confident in their understanding of what was best for the city, and often what was best for them was best for the city. Of course, this is not new in urban politics and as a young city, the Gold Coast is perhaps simply going through similar phases of development that were seen in Paris, New York or London in previous centuries. Until recently the city's leaders have tended not to believe there is much to learn from elsewhere, secure in their belief that they already live in an earthly 'paradise'. This is changing and a less parochial outlook is now evident, especially in looking overseas for new sources of inward investment in the city's economic, social and cultural infrastructure. Nevertheless, the speed with which the city grows up socially and politically, as well as physically, remains the subject of much conjecture. While the expression 'nanny state' is used invariably as a pejorative term, we might do well to remember that nannies are employed to help children grow up safely and that the adolescent city of the Gold Coast may still need the support of 'nanny local state' to help guide and support it through the often turbulent and sometimes dangerous period in the transition to maturity and adulthood.

Chapter 10

Selling the city

Ruth Potts, Sarah Gardiner and Noel Scott

Cities have attempted to differentiate themselves throughout history based on their spatial qualities, inhabitant characteristics, social conditions and historical roots. In the twenty-first century, however, media plays a significantly greater role in shaping the perception of cities than it has previously. City governments are increasingly turning to the tool of branding to differentiate themselves from other cities. This is especially true for tourism-oriented economies such as Queensland's Gold Coast. The local print media, together with local television stations and tourism bodies have historically promoted the image of the Gold Coast as a place that is growing and is desirable to visit, live and work in, and continue to do so.

Throughout the city's development, the media have sold the Gold Coast to outsiders by focusing on the trinity of sun, surf and sand, and in the early years of the new century, with references to modernity, sophistication and culture. The Gold Coast is often portrayed as a resort town and Australia's playground in a narrative designed to attract the visitors on which the tourism industry depends. The greater frame of reference for the media focuses on growth by promoting large events, ease of development, functionality of infrastructure and the city's potential for population growth. Underpinning both these tourist and growth narratives is the media's emphasis on the potential for future residents to have a relaxed and prosperous lifestyle.

Growth and development of the Gold Coast is a goal supported by the power elites, the service workers, the property industry and its boosters. Print and television media have nurtured their special influence on the Gold Coast by supporting this vision. Media support has led to a large number of interstate and international migrants taking up residence and contributed to large-event opportunities such as the 2018 Commonwealth Games choosing the Gold Coast as home.

Molotch (1976) proposes that cities are machines driven by an elite group with a vested interest in the success of the city as fuelled by ongoing economic, social and population growth. This elite group of players includes (but is not limited to) local land and small business owners, politicians, local boosterists and media organisations such as newspapers. They participate actively in organisation, manipulation, structuring and lobbying to influence the growth of the city based on their varied personal and commercial interests. The Gold Coast's progression from a series of small tourist towns to a globalising city with multiple economic drivers has been accompanied by the ongoing reflection and visioning of planners, marketing groups and particularly the media. The diverse mechanisms employed and the various players engaged in promoting the Gold Coast are identified and discussed in this chapter. The chapter discusses the way in which economic development has extended the Gold Coast's image beyond just a place to have fun, to include it as a city that is open for business and growth. In doing so it explores the multiplicity and nuances of the Gold Coast and the multifarious images used by those promoting the city.

Early and informal marketing and media

The Gold Coast evolved from 'a collection of modest towns and villages on the coast and a plain' (Burton 2009, p. 4) with considerable early development of resort towns around Southport, Elston (now Surfers Paradise), Coolangatta and Burleigh Beach during the late 1890s and early 1900s (Holthouse 1982). During this period, and in the subsequent 20 years, various images of the developing townships and later the city were primarily promoted informally by local and regional newspapers. Stories and descriptions of the Gold Coast were often written in a way that supported specific players' interests, particularly personal political aspirations and economic development.

The *Southern Queensland Bulletin* was the Gold Coast's (then called the South Coast) first newspaper and was first issued on 28 March 1885 by Patrick Joseph Macnamara (Galton 1985; McRobbie 2000). Macnamara was the editor and publisher of the *Southern Queensland Bulletin*, producing 100 copies of his newspaper to be distributed to the people of Southport and its surrounding suburbs. At this time Southport consisted of 80 dwellings and 219 ratepayers, most of whom supported or were the region's farmers, cattlemen and timber getters (Galton 1985).

Macnamara was also involved in the local community outside of his work on the newspaper and was the auditor for the Southport Divisional Board (1887–90), Southport Shire Councillor (1891) and Southport Shire President (1892) (Galton 1985). In 1888, Macnamara ran for the newly created seat of Albert and used his newspaper to further his campaign. Stories were run during this time to slander his opposition, while providing an ongoing and highly biased commentary of Macnamara's campaign. Despite his efforts, Macnamara was not elected for the seat of Albert.

During the Gold Coast's youth in the early 1900s, the city (or township as it was then) was almost purely used as a weekend seaside escape by residents of the nearby conurbation of Brisbane (Holthouse 1982; Jones 1988; Longhurst 1994; Prideaux 2004). The first guest house near Coolangatta was built in 1903 by Patrick J. Fagan at Greenmount and was later followed by the construction of several other properties in Coolangatta and Greenmount (Russell and Faulkner 1998). The railway line running from Brisbane to the South Coast was extended to Southport in 1889 (McRobbie 2000). During this period Macnamara promoted this large-scale infrastructure project through the *South Coast Bulletin* (Galton 1985). His articles further emphasised the ongoing growth and increasing accessibility of the Gold Coast to other cities in the region for tourism and business purposes. The *South Coast Bulletin* published similar articles in 1908 by Edward Fass, then editor and later mayor of Southport, surrounding the construction of the Jubilee Bridge (Galton 1985).

The completion of the Jubilee Bridge in 1925 and the increasing popularity of the area as an investment hot spot and seaside escape from the hustle and bustle of Brisbane led to a doubling of readership of the *Bulletin* from 450 in 1918 to 800 at the end of 1925 (Galton 1985). The primary economic driver of the city during this period was local and regional tourism. Consequently, the Gold Coast was promoted particularly to Brisbane residents, with 'sexy' images of sun, surf and excitement contained in advertisements and articles in local newspapers and magazines (Longhurst 1994). Using these advertisements, the newspapers promoted the city as a good place for investment and as a holiday resort, with pictures of smiling women and families enjoying the beach and sunny weather gracing the cover of the paper on 21 December 1928 (Galton 1985, p. 41).

The introduction of the Gold Coast as a new and exciting, but proximate travel destination was well timed as it coincided with the introduction of annual paid leave for Australian workers in the 1930s (Longhurst 1994). This meant that Sydney and Melbourne residents could easily visit the Gold Coast during their annual leave. As a result, the Gold Coast began to be advertised in newspapers and on radio in Victoria and New South Wales during this period (Longhurst 2006). Queensland hotels and pubs were also advantaged by having a later 10 pm bar closing time compared to 6 pm in the southern states, offering a point of differentiation for the destination.

The *South Coast Bulletin* continued to be published throughout World War Two despite staff shortages, and published stories by war correspondents. But 'war news still had to play second fiddle to the all-important local jottings ... even little Miss Shirley Temple often made the lead column of the front page ahead of Hitler, Mussolini or Hirohito' (Galton 1985, p. 54). Following the war the *Bulletin* continued to expand its distribution to keep up with a growing population and an increased readership.

Brisbane newspapers had first used the term 'Gold Coast' as a jibe at the South Coast, referring to the perception that the South Coast was a place for affluent holidaymakers (McRobbie 2000). Local residents interpreted it in a slightly different way, believing it to be a reference to their 'golden lifestyle'. In Australia, in the early to mid-twentieth century, there were many 'South Coasts'. Tourism marketers saw the potential to differentiate the region from others and be the only 'Gold Coast' in Australia. After much discussion, in 1959, the South Coast officially became the City of Gold Coast (McRobbie 2000), demonstrating the integration of promotion into the identity of a geographical place.

Development, real estate and resort-based marketing and media

As early as the 1920s real estate developers joined local newspapers in promoting the city to outsiders. Real estate advertisements in newspapers at the time used slogans like 'the duckiest surf beach on the coast', 'the king of seaside resorts', 'a haven for happiness' and 'the gem of the pacific' (Longhurst 2006). Geographic and lifestyle attributes, such as 'the best fishing, boating and surfing, safe bathing, good fishing' and 'down by the peaceful sea where the atmosphere is exhilarating', were particularly emphasised by developers to sell newly formed estates including Miami, Burleigh Heads and North Burleigh in 1925 (Longhurst 2006). Real estate based tourism gained popularity in the mid to late 1950s and continued until the late 1970s, with advertisements displaying the Gold Coast's development potential featuring in southern state's papers such as *The Sun Herald* (Fig. 10.1). Many developers offered alluring deals to potential property buyers from the southern states of Australia.

Property developers were essential in the unofficial promotion of the Gold Coast between the 1920s and 1970s. Griffin (2004, p. 77) argues that:

> *the white shoe, the mythical must-have item of Gold Coast businessmen and boosterists; the gold bikini made notorious by the meter maids of Surfers Paradise; and ... chunky gold ornamental jewellery ... illustrate all that is tawdry, vulgar and meretricious about the Gold Coast.*

Fig. 10.1 Real estate based advertising of the Gold Coast (*The Sun Herald*, 5 June 1960)

Significant numbers of tourists chose to settle on the Gold Coast after being seduced by its mild climate, professed relaxed lifestyle and location after visiting or hearing about the city through the media (McRobbie 1991). Waterfront properties were in high demand in the sea change and retiree markets. Based on the demand, developers began 'excavating and cashing in on the emerging little Venice' (Vader and Lang 1980, p. 88) of canal estates on the Gold Coast. Previously large flood plains or farmland were cleared and turned into residential waterfront properties. These often came with alluring and sophisticated estate names indicating the source of the developer's inspiration.

The first canal development, Miami Keys, began construction in the mid-1950s, and a flood of canal developments followed suit, including Rio Vista, Anglers Paradise, Palm Beach and Capri Island (Vader and Lang 1980). Holthouse (1982, p. 50) asserts that the flurry of construction of American-style developments (hotels and canal estates) during the mid-1950s was an attempt to further entice interstate and localised tourists by 'reminding [them] … of other fashionable resorts overseas'. Imitation, as always, was the sincerest form of flattery, as well as being a great marketing ploy for the city to promote itself and attract Australians who were not then sophisticated world travellers.

Ownership of the city's only newspaper remained in the hands of Fass, Rootes and Forster until 1959, when it was purchased by the Tweed Newspaper Co. and The Northern Star Limited Group. Rootes remained as managing director of the newly formed Gold Coast Publications and in 1963 the masthead of the paper was changed from the *South Coast Bulletin* to the *Gold Coast Bulletin* to reflect the city's emerging and evolving identity and development as a city.

Organised media and branding activities

Despite the Gold Coast's historical reliance on newspaper and real estate based advertising to attract visitors to the city, it became apparent by the early 1960s that 'professional promotion of the Gold Coast was essential if the communities' desire to continue developing as a major resort was to be achieved' (Prideaux and Cooper 2002, p. 44). Consequently, in 1967 the Gold Coast Tourist Development Association (later called Gold Coast Tourism) was formed as a business organisation with the aim of 'promoting tourism to the Gold Coast and educating the Queensland Government about the economic benefits which tourism could bring to the State' (McRobbie 1991, p. 143). In collaboration with the city's Chamber of Commerce and the Surfers Paradise Progress Association, the Gold Coast Tourist Development Association secured the development of four major attractions to be constructed on the Gold Coast (Holthouse 1982). They included 'a casino, an international hotel, a Hollywood-type movie studio and a major department store, none of which were then located in the area' (McRobbie 1991, p. 144). All four of the tourist attractions were completed by the early 1980s.

Entrepreneurial, sensationalist attractions and high profile public figures enticing tourists to the city were a hallmark of the Gold Coast's media coverage in the late 1960s. A primary example of this was 'the first public appearance of the bikini, which became a powerful promotional image for the Gold Coast, attracting national media coverage over a period of three decades' (Prideaux and Cooper 2002, p. 44). Gold-bikini-clad Meter Maids were icons of the Gold Coast from 1965 and have continued to act as an attraction within the Surfers Paradise tourist district (McRobbie 1991; Coiacetto 2009a) (Fig. 10.2).

Meter Maids were heavily promoted during the late 1960s in the *Gold Coast Bulletin* and they 'quickly became national celebrities and were used as the spearhead of interstate and overseas promotional drives, always backed by the *Bulletin* to attract tourists' (Galton 1985, p. 75). By 1966, the *Bulletin* added lifestyle articles to its repertoire, introducing columns such as 'Lovely Homes of the Coast', 'In My Fashion' and 'Surfers Paradise News Round-up' (McRobbie 2000). These columns provide an insight into what it was like to live on the Gold Coast with stories on local experiences and day-to-day life. In 1969 Northern Star Holdings Limited became the sole owner of Gold Coast Publications (McRobbie 2000).

Portrayal of the Gold Coast in the *Bulletin* became highly sensationalised in the late 1990s. An example of this was a minor shooting that occurred at Main Beach in 1997 that was headlined across eight columns using the title 'Terror on Tedder' (McRobbie 2000). Such stories portrayed the city as a dangerous yet exciting place, while also contributing to its nickname of 'Australia's sin city' in subsequent years. This emphasises the significant influence of the city's media, particularly the *Gold Coast Bulletin*, on the city's image. While local media continues to play a significant role in selling the city's image to outsiders, the 1970s were significant in that a more formalised approach to promoting the city and its image was introduced in the form of specifically created tourism and economic development agencies (Prideaux and Cooper 2002).

Fig. 10.2. Meter Maids in Surfers Paradise, 1960s (Photograph courtesy of Surfers Paradise Meter Maids)

While real estate and growth-focused advertising of the city were dominant from the 1920s until the late 1980s, it was not until the early 2000s that Tourism Queensland and Gold Coast Tourism 'play[ed] down the free-wheeling developer image of earlier times captured best by the image of the "white shoe brigade"' (Burton 2009, p. 11). During the 2000s Gold Coast Tourism used ubiquitous marketing strategies such as advertisement campaigns, major events and improving existing attractions to 'sell' the Gold Coast as a new and improved national and international tourist destination. The key issue with the use of such a tourism strategy was that in the process of creating a new and exciting urban experience, there was a growth of 'sameness in different localities leading to geographies of nowhereness, otherness and a crisis in place-identity' (Carter *et al.* 2007, p. 758) exemplified by the resemblance of the Gold Coast to cities in Florida and California. Clearly today there is a need to improve the differentiation of the region.

Stimson and Minnery (1998) argue that as a culmination of its history and context, the Gold Coast has been marketed as having four identifiable city identities. The city, they suggest, exists simultaneously as a city of leisure, a city of enterprise, a city of tourism and a city in its own right within the South East Queensland region. To this we would add that the type of tourism and leisure offered over time has changed significantly to cater to different markets. Today there appears to be an attempt to extend this image to a city of culture but, to date, promotion of the Gold Coast has used a traditional and relatively vanilla approach, favouring the use of 'idealised images of the region's natural attractions, combined with the promise of sophisticated pleasures of up-market consumerism' (Griffin 2004, p. 80).

Battle of the brands: competing media and marketing organisations

Since the 1970s there have been four key organisations involved in varying degrees in promoting the Gold Coast to outsiders, including Gold Coast Tourism, Gold Coast City Council, Tourism Queensland and Tourism Australia. Gold Coast Tourism is a 'not-for-profit, membership based, destination marketing organisation structured to promote the city as a leisure and business event destination through global consumer, trade, media and travel industry channels' (Gold Coast Tourism 2011, p. 1). The organisation consists primarily of local tourist and service businesses (e.g. accommodation businesses, theme parks, tour operators, etc.) and is supported by the Gold Coast City Council (Gold Coast Tourism 2011). Gold Coast Tourism operates in conjunction with other tourism bodies such as Tourism Queensland and Tourism Australia with the intent of increasing tourism revenue for the Gold Coast on a local, regional, state and national level (Gold Coast Tourism 2011). The Gold Coast City Council appears to be taking a less active role in the continued tourism branding of the city as they support other organisations (such as Gold Coast Tourism) who actively pursue visitors and revenue sources.

The 1980s and early 1990s saw a boom in tourism fuelled by the growth in international visitation, particularly visitors from Japan and other east Asian countries (Faulkner and Tideswell 2006). The Gold Coast tourism industry targeted this growing demand for overseas travel through a close partnership with the state government and prospered on the back on the rapid growth in east Asian economies. At that time, the dominant image used to promote Queensland overseas was essentially that of the Gold Coast. In 1994, the Cairns and the Tropical North tourism manager complained that travel agents in Japan were advertising the region using images of surfboards and beaches (Faulkner and Tideswell 2006). This was despite the fact that the beaches in Cairns had little or no surf. This eventually led to the break-up of Queensland's monolithic destination image into several distinct destination brands.

From 1995, Tourism Queensland began to develop brands for each of the major Queensland tourist destinations including the Gold Coast. In the first brand development process on the Gold Coast, in 1996, the destination tagline 'The Always Changing Ever Amazing Gold Coast' was used to evoke a fun and exciting destination. This campaign was replaced in 2000 with the slogan 'The Coast with the Most' (McRobbie 2000). Both of these different campaigns portrayed the city as offering something exceptional and unique for everyone and, therefore, made it easy for all products and experiences in the destination to fit under the brand's 'umbrella'.

The importance of a destination brand in influencing travel did not go unnoticed by important attractions on the Gold Coast. The main visitor markets to the Gold Coast were in the 1990s (and remain today) domestic visitors, representing 80% of all visitors (Queensland Tourist and Travel Corporation 1997). Domestic visitors fit into two main market segments: families with children, and (younger or older) couples taking a seaside holiday. The family market was the target of Gold Coast theme parks, which collectively out-spent Gold Coast Tourism in the marketing of the destination, and therefore the brand campaign was heavily influenced by the theme parks' needs. McRobbie (2000, p. 401) captures the situation, describing 'promotion by government-funded tourism bodies [as] a drop in the bucket compared with what private enterprise spends, and this has always been so'. The focus of imagery used by Gold Coast Tourism today to market the destination remains families building sandcastles on the beach or riding the thrill rides at the theme parks.

By the late 1990s, two-thirds of the lucrative overnight international visitation to the Gold Coast was from Asia. This left the Gold Coast exposed to the onset of the Asian financial crisis in the late 1990s, which substantially reduced Asian visitor numbers. International visitation to the Gold Coast declined 6.2% between 1997 and 1999, while overall international visitation to Australia increased 1.5%. At this time, domestic overnight visitation continued to grow, increasing 8.9% in 1999 on the previous year, while nationally this market declined 1.5% (Faulkner 2002). Faulkner and other experts from the Sustainable Tourism Cooperative Research Centre (CRC) argued that this growth was fuelled by the discounting of Gold Coast holidays and described this growth as profitless volume. Research undertaken by the Queensland Tourist and Travel Corporation in 1997 indicated that the Gold Coast was perceived as overly commercialised, and Surfers Paradise and theme parks dominated the destination's image (Moore 2002). Accordingly, the Gold Coast was described as a mature destination and the industry was seen to be at a crossroads. The Chair of Gold Coast Tourism at that time, Grant Bowie, commented that the city is:

> *facing massive challenges in meeting the expectations of the next generation of visitors and residents. Increased competition, more discerning markets, reconciling urban growth with a large tourism industry, and new information technologies, are but indicators of why a more sophisticated approach to tourism planning is required. (Faulkner 1999, p. 1)*

Reinventing a mature tourist destination

In 1998, Griffith University Gold Coast tourism academic Professor Bill Faulkner championed the idea of adopting a new, planned approach to tourism on the Gold Coast. He lobbied the Gold Coast City Council to commission a major research project to create a new tourism vision for the Gold Coast. The *Gold Coast Visioning Project* was officially launched on 19 October 1998 (Moore 2002). The project cost almost $1 million and was undertaken as a partnership by research and industry groups, including the CRC for Sustainable Tourism, Conrad Jupiters Casino and Gold Coast Airport (Moore 2002).

Prior to 1998 the Gold Coast brand and marketing activities were based on planning undertaken by Gold Coast Tourism and Queensland Tourist and Travel Corporation/Tourism Queensland. The *Gold Coast Visioning Project* was a significant departure from that approach as external bodies, such as Griffith University, were now examining the Gold Coast tourism industry and how it presented itself to the world. It marked a transition from an entrepreneurial market-driven approach to selling the Gold Coast to a more strategic and structured approach. While this new approach was mostly supported by the tourism industry, there was still debate about its wisdom. One such critic, McRobbie (2000, p. 384) writes in his book on the history of Gold Coast, 'One wearies of the boring academic mantra about planning. The Gold Coast tourism phenomenon has never been planned … You simply cannot plan tourism growth'. Yet, other community leaders had a different perspective. For instance, Moore (2002, p. 7) quoted one such leader as stating, 'It is no longer good enough for the industry to wait for individual flamboyant entrepreneurs to kick start the next wave of development'. Hence, the city's newer and informed approach to marketing and developing tourism in the city was hotly debated but not resolved among business and community leaders in the early 2000s.

The findings of the *Gold Coast Tourism Visioning Project* challenged the Gold Coast to again consider how it was selling its tourism experience to outsiders. Apart from a new, more strategic approach to marketing the city, the project also advocated for a greater emphasis on the city's natural resources, including the rainforest covered mountain range behind the Gold Coast, the hinterland. This was intended to capitalise on increasing consumer demand for ecotourism experiences that were prominent in the 1990s (McRobbie 2000). It was mooted that the city needed to better sell the 'green behind the gold', thus offering new nature-based experiences for visitors beyond the 'sun, surf and sand' of the past.

Gold Coast Tourism's marketing budget increased from $4 million to $10 million in 2004, funded by a tourism levy collected by the Gold Coast Council. The increased resources of Gold Coast Tourism represented a fundamental shift in destination branding and marketing of the city. As a result, Gold Coast Tourism launched a new brand for the Gold Coast in 2005, featuring the slogan 'Very GC: Very Gold Coast' to describe the city and its attractions (Fig. 10.3) (Gold Coast Tourism 2010).

The Very GC brand aimed to attract higher yield, more affluent visitors to the Gold Coast (Gold Coast Tourism 2010). This new brand aimed to improve the perception of the Gold Coast, particularly in the southern market agglomerates of Sydney and Melbourne, as well as to revitalise the Gold Coast's position in key international markets at that time, namely New Zealand and Japan. The brand used a popular 1950s Frank Sinatra song, 'Somewhere Beyond the Sea', to connect with the heritage and ambience of that era and leverage the popularity of classic jazz music that was associated with contemporary artists like Michael Bublé, who were popular at the time.

The initial accompanying images to the Very GC slogan were of impossibly thin people enjoying a coffee club lifestyle and were designed to appeal to 'the luxury market ... and the sophisticated high-end market' and ignored or were not directed towards 'families and leisure travellers' (Meers 2010a). As the branding program developed, the message was expanded to incorporate other perceived attractions, such as 'Very Natural' (describing the Gold Coast as 'Australia's most biodiverse city'), and 'Very Exciting' (focusing on the Gold Coast's theme park attractions) (Gold Coast Tourism 2010). As the Very GC brand devel-

Fig. 10.3. Image from the 'Very GC' advertising campaign, 2006 (Image courtesy of M&C Saatchi)

oped, other key players in the city began to use the brand to target visitor markets based on specific attributes of the city. For example, the Gold Coast City Council's Economic Development Branch launched a sister brand, Business GC, to attempt to link and provide cohesion to the city's national and international tourism marketing efforts and investment in the Very GC brand.

Very GC was radically different from its predecessors and, initially, the local industry was reportedly excited to see this change. However, the initial enthusiasm was short lived, and critics of the brand emerged, claiming it was too narrow and not a true representation of the entire destination and its experiences. Criticism of the cartoon illustrations suggested they portrayed the city as superficial and lacking real life experiences. Accordingly, the cartoon illustrations were phased out of marketing activities and replaced with real photographs of the destination. Following a change in leadership in 2006, Gold Coast Tourism opened several international offices and created a new event, GC Bazaar, to promote the city. GC Bazaar was an umbrella marketing event that included a 30-day calendar of fashion, food and fun events and promotional offers throughout the city. This was the focus of Gold Coast Tourism's marketing efforts in 2007 and 2008, and was promoted to key intrastate and interstate markets through advertising, promotions, public relations and online and direct mail.

The success of the Very GC brand was hampered by several factors. The lack of local industry belief in and support for the brand made it difficult for Gold Coast Tourism to gain industry buy-in to marketing efforts. This was particularly the case for the theme parks on the Gold Coast whose primary market was middle class families from Sydney and Melbourne, rather than the high-end luxury market that was the target of the Very GC campaign. Another factor was the changing economic conditions in Australia and internationally. The onset of the global financial crisis from 2007 onwards created a major shock to economies around the world, including Australia. The strong Australian dollar and an increase in fuel surcharges made Australian, and thus Gold Coast holidays more expensive than previous years. Consequently, other emerging and budget travel destinations in South-East Asia increased in popularity, while domestic travel declined. The positioning of the Gold Coast as a luxury destination became increasingly unsustainable as consumers tightened their spending. Finally, the campaign was not based on market research and instead appears to have been primarily the vision of the Gold Coast Tourism Marketing Manager alone (Marzano 2007).

In 2008, the Gold Coast Tourism board decided to re-focus the marketing of the city towards domestic visitors and re-building partnerships with key tourism agencies and stakeholders, such as Tourism Australia, Tourism and Events Queensland, the airports and the travel trade. Major changes were made to their corporate structure and allocation of their funding and by 2010, Gold Coast Tourism was allocating a greater proportion of their budget to marketing (from $7.8 million in 2009 to $9.2 million in 2010) (Gold Coast Tourism 2010).

In 2010, the Very GC brand was deemed by state and local tourism leaders and the Gold Coast City Council as being 'Very past-its-use-by-date'. To create a 'new' slogan to sell the 'new' Gold Coast, 'key stakeholders unanimously asked for branding that would focus on the family-oriented and unique diversity of the city's attractions' (Meers 2010a). How the previous program had failed to do this was never revealed, but a large number of respondents, including residents, were surveyed for their views by Gold Coast Tourism and Tourism Queensland (Meers 2010a). The chief executive of the Currumbin Wildlife Sanctuary, Jonathan Fisher, opined that 'in the past we have been famous for our beaches and in the past 10–15 years, theme parks, but it's time for the other real jewel, the environment and wildlife, to shine' (Meers 2010a).

By late 2010 and early 2011, Gold Coast tourism industry sentiment started to turn around, becoming more upbeat as the economic environment and tourism numbers improved. At that time, Paul Donovan, Chair of Gold Coast Tourism, stated, 'some of our member businesses are doing it tough ... Our tourism industry is, without doubt, the most active and resilient in Australia' (Gold Coast Tourism 2011, p. 5). Major earthquakes in 2011 in two important visitor source markets, New Zealand and Japan, led to Gold Coast Tourism placing an increasing focus on China. Gold Coast Tourism established a permanent office in Shanghai and employed Mandarin speaking staff (Gold Coast Tourism 2011). These disasters also highlighted the risk in concentrating on single market economies, and Gold Coast Tourism expanded activities in the Middle East, India, South Korea and South-East Asia to reduce this risk (Gold Coast Tourism 2011).

During this international expansion, Gold Coast Tourism claimed it was concentrating on the 'fundamentals' of the Gold Coast tourism industry that they identified as the Australian family holiday. Accordingly, the Very GC campaign was scrapped and 'Famous for Fun' introduced by Gold Coast Tourism and Tourism Queensland in 2010 (Meers 2010b). Lauding this marketing 'break-through', the then Premier of Queensland, Anna Bligh, declared that it 'captures what the Gold Coast stands for' (Meers 2010b). Queensland Tourism Minister, Peter Lawlor, observed that the new slogan was 'a better fit for the city' and noted: 'over the past couple of years the tourism landscape has changed, therefore the way we communicate also needs to change to focus on the genuine experiences, the things the Gold Coast is known and loved for' (Meers 2010b).

The all new Famous for Fun campaign reinforced the fun positioning of the city a using the tag, 'Australia's favourite playground', and described it as, 'a welcoming, vibrant, diverse, fun and entertaining destination' (Gold Coast Tourism 2013, p. 5). The Gold Coast's campaigns returned to imagery of families building sandcastles on the beach and enjoying theme park rides. Diversity was encouraged with hinterland photographs included in the images used to market the city. Promotional events locally and internationally continued to be a major focus of the city's marketing strategy.

The concept or idea of a city being a product of branding or rebranding is in fact a chicken and egg argument – which came first, the identity or the brand, fun or its fame? Queensland Tourism and various commentators and focus groups were surveyed to identify the existing position and find slogans upon which a marketing campaign to national and international tourists could be hung in conjunction with advertising of Queensland (Meers 2010b). As a result, on 1 October 2010, Queensland Tourism launched their statewide slogan as 'Queensland – Where Australia Shines' (Meers 2010b).

Premier Anna Bligh stated that the Gold Coast had 'a strong opportunity to build on the back of both [branding] announcements' (Meers 2010b). Both branding campaigns by Gold Coast Tourism and Tourism Queensland foregrounded images of sun, surf and sand – the more things change, the more they stay the same – which reflects the stability of the marketing product and the success of successive communication strategies to capture shifts in the market itself. These images were critical to the promotion and later success of the city in being awarded the rights to host the 2018 Commonwealth Games in 2011. As a result of the success of the state government led bid, the 2018 Gold Coast Commonwealth Games are estimated to attract:

> *more than 150,000 extra tourists ... with a 50/50 split between international and domestic visitors, injecting at least an extra $250 million in tourism spent into the local economy ... [The] Gold Coast Games will ultimately generate up to $2 billion in economic benefit with up to 30,000 full time-equivalent jobs created between 2015 and 2020. (Gold Coast Tourism 2013, p. 9)*

The Economic Development Branch of the Gold Coast City Council, known also as Business GC, exists separately to Gold Coast Tourism and is involved in the development of industry within the city and strategically manages related concerns and aims to ensure the Gold Coast remains a competitive tourist destination (Business GC 2009). The promotional activities undertaken by the Gold Coast City Council have a much greater economic focus than those of Gold Coast Tourism. The Gold Coast City Council *Economic Development Strategy 2020* provides the council's plan for strengthening the city's economic prosperity through thorough and adaptive economic planning and strategic infrastructure investments. The most recent developments supported by the Gold Coast City Council include the $25 million upgrade of the Surfers Paradise foreshore and the $42 million redevelopment of the Southport Broadwater Parklands (Business GC 2009). Such large-scale community infrastructure projects, while not actively promoting the Gold Coast as a destination, act as attractions to both residents and visitors within the city.

The polish of the website and marketing materials for Business GC is in distinct juxtaposition with the idealism and exaggeration of the Gold Coast Tourism materials. While Gold Coast Tourism focuses on the same clichéd images of sun, surf and sand, Business GC paints a much broader, cosmopolitan (and perhaps more up-to-date or 'realistic') image of the city.

Rebranding the Gold Coast for the 2018 Commonwealth Games

Winning the 2018 Commonwealth Games bid in 2011 prompted the Gold Coast to once again reconsider its image and how it would present itself on the world stage. Building on the excitement in the lead-up to this event, the Gold Coast City Council launched its first city brand, using the slogan 'It's the Gold Coast. Full stop' (see Fig. 10.4). This brand aims to capture 'what the Gold Coast is now and what it aspires to be in the future' (City of Gold Coast 2014b n.p.), and is used to promote the city simultaneously with Gold Coast Tourism's branding of the city as 'Famous for Fun'. Director of Economic Development and Major Projects at City of Gold Coast, Darren Scott, explained that in developing this new brand they held:

> *some focus groups in Sydney, Melbourne and Brisbane to understand what people thought about the Gold Coast and compared that to what the locals knew about the Gold Coast, those that knew the place. What we found was that people outside of the Gold Coast thought quite poorly of the city and when they thought about the Gold Coast they thought of 24/7 party city, crime and shonky businessmen and actually used the term 'shonky businessmen' in the focus groups and yet the locals think about it as a place with fantastic lifestyle, good opportunities and a really great place to live and work. (City of Gold Coast 2014b, p. 1)*

Responding to this challenging division of perspectives, the brand aimed 'to build on the Gold Coast's positive tourism message and develop a more holistic story for the city. One where the Gold Coast is known as a great place to live, work and invest in - as well as holiday' (City of Gold Coast 2014b).

Despite being considered a mature tourist destination (Faulkner and Tideswell 2006), promoters of the city did not identify one common theme, likely due to the Gold Coast being in its adolescence as a city and still in the process of defining itself (Burton 2009). Recognising this complexity, the 2013 Gold Coast City Council branding campaign describes the city as, 'many different things to many different people. But no single sentiment can define it' (City of Gold Coast 2014b). The character of the city is described as:

Fig. 10.4. Banner from the 'Gold Coast Full Stop' campaign, 2014 (Image courtesy of the City of Gold Coast)

The Gold Coast is proud, unapologetic, independent.
It is innovative, entrepreneurial, unconventional.
It is home, an endless summer holiday, a dynamic business location.
It is inspired by lifestyle, driven by opportunity.
There's no other place in the world like the Gold Coast.

(City of Gold Coast 2014b, p. 1)

Key aspects of this city brand tied into the city's history, most notably the concept of the summer holiday and the entrepreneurial, unconventional spirit of the many developers and business people that have advanced the city in the past. The brand employed people from the Gold Coast, celebrities and local Gold Coasters, to sell the city. For example, in television advertisements Australian surf lifesaving champion, Trevor Hendy, was shown as a person from the Coast, and the Burleigh Brewing Co. was used to illustrate the merits of doing business in the city. These characters and stories of the city are reminiscent of the colourful characters who marketed the Gold Coast in the past. This new brand aimed to leverage these events to promote new investment into the city.

The use of the full stop in the City of Gold Coast brand is intriguing. A full stop may indicate that there is nothing more to say on the topic, yet this book emphasises that there is a lot more to say about the Gold Coast and its heritage and future. The city has only begun to form its identity. The hosting of the Commonwealth Games in 2018 will act as a catalyst for the city, challenging the city to actively shape how it wants to see itself and others to see it. Not unlike Sydney and the Olympic Games in 2000, hosting this major sporting event in 2018 will focus the city and allow it to gain greater confidence in itself and strengthen the local residential and business communities. Throughout this process, it is important that the Gold Coast embraces its past, drawing insights that can inform its future.

Alternate reality: Perception is everything and everything changes

Branding exists partly for the purpose of selling an image and partly for creating a unified vision. The brand, as a selling point rather than reflecting reality, seeks to create the vision. Interestingly, the reality of life for most residents is considerably different to the way in which the city is portrayed to outsiders. Burton (2009, p. 11) claims that to Gold Coast residents, life 'is usually neither another day in paradise nor a walk on the wild side'. The rubric that 'image is everything' in branding resonates heavily throughout the branding literature surrounding the new slogan. It is becoming 'crucial for the city to identify its market niches and construct the appropriate images' (Short 1996, p. 437).

At present it appears that the Gold Coast has surpassed its previous identity as a tourist destination. Edwards *et al.* (2007) support the contention that the Gold and Sunshine Coasts' development should be seen through the paradigm of resort centres evolving into cities although this begs the question: what type of city? One particular sign of this growth is that in 2015 the Gold Coast presents itself in different ways to outsiders, residents and industry, rather than solely as a resort or holiday location. This is demonstrated by the frequent and juxtaposing images and words concurrently used to sell and describe the Gold Coast by multiple organisations.

The Gold Coast and its primary tourist precinct, Surfers Paradise, have been 'accused of showing [their] age and being in need of a facelift or makeover in order to reveal [their] charms to new generations of tourists' (Griffin 2004). Resident perceptions appear to be that the Gold Coast's tourist marketing succeeds on the back of Surfers Paradise's image (Griffin 1998). The inexorable tide of high-rise apartments, international hotels and tourist-oriented developments (rides, putt-putt golf, etc.) is washing further north across the Nerang River into the old business heart of Southport. We now see the new phenomenon of high-rise apartments specifically targeting active baby boomers over the age of 55. These factors make it clear that the Gold Coast is in fact in its mature form a fully functioning city that caters for a wide range of users, visitors and residents. Although the city has grown beyond its original tourist mecca purpose, tourism remains significantly important to the city's economy. From 1 July 2009 to 30 June 2010 over 4 million tourists were attracted to the Gold Coast, compared with the residential population of only 518 000 (Meers 2010a).

While an important focus of the greater Gold Coast area is tourism and its service industries, the city has reached the point where it is self-sustaining and developing as a desirable place to live and work. It is the fastest growing conurbation in Australia. The natural attractiveness of a temperate climate, diverse and developing services (Myer, David Jones and other speciality precincts), combined with an expanding housing market and coming off the back of the longest property development boom of its history has drawn large numbers of new residents to the city. They primarily gravitate to burgeoning sleeper suburbs such as Coomera, Ormeau and Nerang, which lie, as the green between the gold, between the so-called 'Glitter Strip' and the hinterland, stretching north along the growth corridor to Brisbane. In these new suburbs, the Gold Coast has a different face to that of the beach and Surfers Paradise.

The Gold Coast's history and those promoting the city have produced a city of juxtapositions. The Gold Coast exists in the eyes of its beholders as 'an area that is simultaneously brash, trendy, sophisticated, relaxed, overdeveloped and overurbanised' (Stimson and Minnery 1998, p. 196). Contemporary media images of the city demonstrate the contrasting faces of the city, leading to the inference that the city is in a state of identity crisis. Perhaps it is a city caught between its past as an organically formed sun, surf and sand tourist resort town and its future as envisaged by the powers that be, a cosmopolitan, cultural and smart 'world class' city. Or perhaps this vision is just bringing the 'fun' image of the Coast into the twenty-first century and making it multi-dimensional. After all, what is a cosmopolitan and cultural city but one that is fun for an older market.

Chapter 11

City with/out a plan

Ayşın Dedekorkut-Howes and Severine Mayere

One of the distinct features of urbanisation of the Gold Coast is its historically ad hoc approach to development with little or no strategic planning to guide it. Many have commented on the lack of planning on the Gold Coast (Hitch 1959; Pigram 1977; Fitzgerald 1984; Jones 1986; Burchill 2005). Juppenlatz (1959, p. 51) called it 'an experiment in freedom', Mullins (1984, p. 44) dubbed it 'free enterprise city', Jones (1986, p. 62) called it 'a free market city'. Fitzgerald (1984, p. 469) quoted the *Australian Financial Review* stating that the Gold Coast 'was borne to pre-eminence in an era devoid of design or planning. Consequently it was destined to be ravaged by inexperienced, selfish and vested interests in their reckless rush to seize their choice of its delightful foreshores'. Following a major restructuring of the region's councils (see Chapters 8 and 9), the 1990s witnessed a shift from ad hoc decision-making to more systematic planning.

This chapter reviews the history of regulatory planning on the Gold Coast, encompassing decisions affecting the form and development of its earliest settlements through to its periods of greatest construction and most streamlined decision-making. It examines the reasons behind the unplanned development, briefly touches on its consequences as they have been detailed elsewhere (see Chapter 2), but focuses mainly on past planning processes, the problems identified in each planning exercise and the interventions introduced, asking whether these were implemented or not and why. The chapter positions the Gold Coast as a physical embodiment of this history of decision-making, assessing the effects on the city as a whole of specific measures either affording freedoms or insisting on accountability to various levels of regulation. It examines how the absence of some planning measures influenced the form of the city and its internal arrangements and considers how the shift towards increased planning affected the city's urbanisation.

Why was the Coast not planned?

Why was so little attention paid to planning on the Gold Coast? Many explanations have been offered on the subject. As early as 1959 *Architecture in Australia* dedicated a special issue to the Gold Coast and its unparalleled growth, and questioned why planning remained so far in the background in the face of such spectacular growth. Kollar (1959, p. 58) therein surmised the chief cause of short-sighted policy and uncontrolled development to be 'a perpetual fear, year after year, that the boom would suddenly stop: all were eager to make the most of it as long as it lasted'. Not only did growth not abate, however, but its rate continued to increase, bringing a parallel increase in land values to the point where 'an overall regional plan is becoming more and more a major financial sacrifice' (Kollar 1959, p. 58). Smith (1991) notes that this type of unplanned growth with an ad hoc planning process is typical for resorts that have evolved predominantly since World War Two.

Another explanation for the minimal government interference evidenced in the growth of the Gold Coast included the pro-growth attitude of local and state governments. On the Gold Coast this attitude is rooted in developers' historical control over local government, either through direct involvement or by presenting local government with a powerful lobby. A brief planning history of the city shows just how much it was tied to local politics. Melbourne entrepreneur, Bruce Small, entered not only urban development on the Gold Coast but also municipal politics. With his election as lord mayor in 1967 'local government and land development became inseparable on the Gold Coast' (Fitzgerald 1984, p. 462). State government did not help the matters as Smith (1985, p. 27) notes, it is a 'well documented contention that Queensland politics are principally about "bread and butter" issues of development, involving reconciliation of competing demands for resources' where politicians usurped the role of town planners in Brisbane and the rest of the state (Fitzgerald 1984). The Bjelke-Petersen government that maintained power from 1968 to 1983, during which major growth occurred on the Gold Coast, was criticised by some for being a 'development-at-any-price government' (Stuart 1985, p. 53). An optimistic pro-development climate supported by the Premier along with Local Government and Main Roads Minister Russell Hinze – both of whom were particularly accommodating to free enterprise and favourably disposed towards Gold Coast's development – contributed to making the city the perfect place for entrepreneurial activity (Russell and Faulkner 1999). A former Albert Shire mayor, Minister Hinze was a partner in several Gold Coast property companies. After the 1974 Australia Day floods that affected both Brisbane and the Gold Coast, development initiatives came directly from Hinze, who no longer regarded a planning advisory committee as necessary and was of the opinion that 'most people are not interested in town planning' (Fitzgerald 1984, p. 453).

The perception of the role of government also affected these attitudes. Mullins (1984, p. 44) notes that:

> *the Coast ... sees government's role as simply aiding private enterprise. As a consequence, detailed planning is not a part of the process. Even the Queensland government, which has played a major interventionist role in the state over the last 20 years, has played a relatively small role on the Coast.*

In fact, throughout the late 1970s and 1980s, during the Hinze Ministry, state planning powers and infrastructure investments were used to support local developer interests (Burton 2014). This period of government in Queensland was marked by corruption. It was not uncommon for 'the state under the notorious National Party governments from the 1960s to 1989' to intervene to remove local council control over major tourist and residential developments or for corruption to occur, resulting in the prosecution and jailing of several former government ministers and developers during the late 1980s and early 1990s (Guhathakurta and Stimson 2007, p. 139).

The close relationship between government and entrepreneurs, rapid legislative changes that allowed for private development even in flood-prone land and the ability (and willingness) of developers to take public office all resulted in a pro-growth coalition on the Gold Coast where the typical opposition of developers and regulators was diluted and the role of the regulators compromised. The city's reputation for unplanned growth is rooted in these circumstances, exacerbating the effects of a period of actual unplanned development dating to the Gold Coast's early settlement history.

Consequences of no planning

Some saw the Gold Coast's lack of planning as its strength. Farwell (1970, p. 78) claimed that Surfers Paradise was 'the proof that a whole town can be run up without benefit of planner or design'. According to Jones (1986, p. 62), having been developed without modern town planning methods might have been the key to the success and vitality of the Gold Coast; in the absence of town planning, the city's real estate economy could respond to sudden changes in demand.

The undesirable consequences of unplanned growth and development, however, were discussed from an early stage in the city's conspicuous urbanisation. Among these the editors of *Architecture in Australia* (1959, p. 47) identified 'a chaos of the worst type of commercialism and a refreshing vitality so sadly lacking in other parts of Australia'. Newell (1959), in particular, noted that erosion had already caused coastal esplanades to disappear, to the extent that they were only visible on maps (see Fig. 11.1).

The editors of *Architecture in Australia* were in 1959 questioning whether it was already too late for the Gold Coast. By the 1970s many shared this sentiment. Ostle (1974, p. 8) claimed that 'in spite of written intention by the Gold Coast City Council "to make sure that development is not won at the expense of natural resources", it's now too late'. A report

Fig. 11.1. Beach erosion in the vicinity of the Palm Beach Surf Life Saving Club, 1954 (Photograph by Max Thomson. Image reproduction courtesy of the Gold Coast City Council Local Studies Library, image number LS-LSP-CD1062-IMG008)

of the Committee of Inquiry (Parliament of the Commonwealth of Australia 1975, pp. 63–65) concluded that 'The 32 km (20 mile) length of the coastline north of Tweed Heads is probably the worst instance in Australia of the results of unplanned foreshore use without consideration for coastal dynamics'. Pigram (1977, p. 538) stated that 'the townscape reflects the hectic pace of development' and listed among the consequences of the unplanned development environmental degradation in an unfortunate mix of old and new structures, innovative yet shoddy architecture, a lack of provision for open space, inadequate roads and parking facilities servicing high-density populations and building right up to the beachfront and in places on the foreshore. Three decades later, Guhathakurta and Stimson (2007, p. 139) agreed, noting that the domination of private sector interests over the planning and development process in local councils up until the 1990s was largely responsible for this outcome.

Early planning efforts: town planning schemes of the 1950s and 1960s

In Queensland, maps and tables of zones formed the main part of the early planning schemes. These schemes also included various legal provisions, such as the rights of non-conforming uses. In essence, these early plans were just a series of basic zoning maps with land-use tables and by-laws (A.A. Heath & Partners 1970, p. 119). The first documented plan of the Gold Coast area was the *1953 South Coast Planning Scheme*, which according to Allom and Jones (1997, p. 362) 'acknowledged the impending growth and introduced zoning to allow for multiple unit buildings amongst other uses and indeed introduced height controls throughout those zones to focus development in strategic nodes along the coastal strip'. During the 1950s and 1960s, however, successive state governments failed to restrict coastal subdivision (Fitzgerald 1984). There were, though, a few ineffective attempts to control the negative consequences of unplanned development. At the height of canal development and in the wake of the 1954 floods the South Coast Council moved to fix safe flood levels, but not before some estates had already been sold. Until the *Canals Act 1958* neither state nor local governments had power over canal estate developers along the Nerang River. The state government continued to encourage the reclamation of coastal wetlands for urban development with the *Crown Lands Development Act 1959* (Fitzgerald 1984).

The *1959 Merrimac Town Plan* was the first planning scheme for a portion of Albert Shire along the boundary of the shire with the Town of Gold Coast designated as the 'Canal Lands'. The plan contained a series of zones and list of uses and occupations that could be carried out variously with and without any special consent of the council for each zone (Albert Shire Council 1959). The Albert Shire minutes of 21 January 1960 reported a discussion on the importance of inflexibility for the plan to protect the council against decisions that might be made under a flexible plan. This was not viewed as an inconvenience because there was nothing preventing the council from amending the plan when necessary:

> *when any new subdivisional proposal is lodged with the council for development of the rural zone ... [the] Council would require the subdivider to submit with his proposal a plan indicating the types of use for which the allotments would be sold. The Council would then amend the Town Plan in accordance with its decision in respect to the zoning of that subdivision. (Albert Shire Council 1960, p. 7)*

The transfer of some of the areas along the boundary from the jurisdiction of Albert Shire to the South Coast Town Council (which would in 1958 become the Gold Coast

Town Council) spurred the council to update the 1953 plan, which was last amended in 1955. The *1963 City of Gold Coast Town Planning Scheme* established height controls and a series of 11 zones, each designated for a specific purpose, such as residential, light industry, etc. Like earlier schemes, this one also identified, according to the nature of the zone, uses that could be made of land without the special consent of council; uses that required special consent and might be subject to specific conditions; and uses that could not be made (Council of the City of Gold Coast 1963). The process for requesting special consent required a written application to Council, which would take objections into account and make a decision. There was no clear indication, however, of what that special consent and those conditions entailed and so the plan did little to guide development. For example:

> *... by then, the pressure for tall buildings was such that despite notional height controls, with Council consent, the sky was the limit. There was little cognisance of the fragility of the natural environment or the efficiency of infrastructure, but within this fairly basic zoning plan, a clear image of the city was emerging. (Allom and Jones 1997, p. 362)*

Both the Gold Coast and Albert Shire early town planning schemes were deemed ineffective in light of the scale of growth that was occurring and the amount of land development proposals received. None of these plans incorporated population projections and they contained only very crude zoning maps. Furthermore, they had no capacity to cope with massive land development proposals. As such, Burchill (2005, p. 32) opined that 'for much of its life, Gold Coast development happened by the random addition of endless new projects'.

First strategic plans of the late 1960s and 1970s

By the early 1970s, development was booming on the Gold Coast. Thirteen high-rise apartment buildings were constructed between 1970 and 1975. Tourist entertainment facilities such as Sea World were also being developed. Parallel to this growth, the late 1960s and early 1970s saw the development of the first strategic plans for both the Gold Coast and Albert Shire. These plans were a new concept for Queensland and were developed as strategic documents that would support town planning schemes. In essence, these plans recognised that previous attempts at dealing with the consequences of rapid urban development had failed.

After the change of local government in 1967 the Gold Coast Council, under the leadership of incoming mayor Bruce Small, commissioned Sydney-based Clarke, Gazzard and Partners to study and provide advice on strategic 'principles, policies and procedures which could best guide and govern the urban development of the Region in the foreseeable future' (Council of the City of Gold Coast 1969, p. 8). The *1969 Gold Coast Urban Region Strategic Plan 1970–1990* and *1969 Town Planning Scheme* were the dual products of this effort. Fitzgerald (1984, p. 465) described this plan as 'among the first comprehensive attempts of its kind in Queensland' and viewed it as one of Mayor Bruce Small's lasting achievements.

This strategic plan recognised the explosive nature of urbanisation that occurred on the Gold Coast between 1947 and 1967 and argued that the consequences of unchecked growth were poorly addressed in the previous plan because of inadequate council powers and amendments (Council of the City of Gold Coast 1969). Criticisms of the previous council administration voiced in the plan included a failure to provide an acceptable open-space network, careless subdivision of state forests and the Coast's ribbon development.

The plan argued that 'the basic step in city planning and financing must be to bring private land development under a process of comprehensive guidance and control' (Council of the City of Gold Coast 1969, p. 8).

The strategic plan was composed of four sections. The first three dealt with regional perspectives on urbanisation and conservation throughout the Gold Coast; projections of future population and urban land space requirements; and the comprehensive planning process. The final section presented the strategic plan itself (Council of the City of Gold Coast 1969). The plan called for comprehensive planning and/or coordinated financing techniques for the city infrastructure including regional networks of roads and open space, and regional systems for water storage, sewerage, flood mitigation and drainage, and airports. Interestingly, although the need to protect recreational and open spaces within the city was acknowledged as a priority, the plan recognised that the Gold Coast hinterland offered a vast variety of landscapes 'capable of virtually unlimited urban expansion' and that there was 'every opportunity for the continued spread of canal estate development' (Council of the City of Gold Coast 1969, p. 12). The continuous explosive growth of the city far outstripped the long-term population projections made by the plan. The short-term 1975 projection of 100 000 was quite accurate, but while the plan projected a 1983 population of 150 000, by 1981 population had already reached 177 264. Similarly, the 1990 projection of 200 000 was reached much earlier as well with the population totalling 279 443 by the 1991 census (ABS 2008).

The *1969 Strategic Plan* was intended to influence the design and location of buildings over the next 20 years. The plan was criticised, however, for being very broad and failing to consider the eventual growth of high-rise development (Jones 1986; Moore 2005). As many as 3147 high-rise units were built between 1970 and 1980 – some even by Clarke, Gazzard and Partners in its 30-floor Harry Seidler-inspired Focus tower at Surfers Paradise, completed in 1974 – and 1311 in 1980 alone (Jones 1986). As a sign of the bubble forming in this market, in 1982, when the property market slumped, 3633 units were under construction. The overproduction of high-rise units and over-urbanisation threatened the natural qualities that attracted people to the area. One of the purportedly vital principles of regional development recommended in this plan was the protection of waterways like the Nerang River and Currumbin and Tallebudgera Creeks. In blatant contradiction to this, however, the boom in canal development resulted in the removal of estuaries and associated wetlands from public access or control (Fitzgerald 1984).

The planning scheme that was supposed to accompany the *1969 Strategic Plan* was not adopted until four years later. The *1973 Town Planning Scheme for the City of Gold Coast* introduced a 25% maximum site coverage requirement near ocean frontage to protect outlook and open space (Council of the City of Gold Coast 1973), but once again the trend of high-rise development thwarted these intentions. Fitzgerald (1984, p. 467) reported that despite overwhelming public disapproval the council could not keep its promises to limit high-rise development, with soaring prices and scarcity of land placing 'constant pressure on council to rezone land for commercial and shopping purposes, and [permitting the] intrusion of multi-storey units into low density residential areas'. During the late 1970s the land boom continued unchecked, and was only fuelled by the lifting of the death duties in 1977, which attracted even more people to the Coast and helped push up land prices. High-rise buildings continued to proliferate on the Gold Coast, prompting debates within the City Council about the need to slow the pace of high-density vertical development (Fitzgerald 1984). This led to the adoption of a moratorium on permits in some beach-front locations in the late 1980s, pending the completion of the next planning instrument.

Because the area of the City of Gold Coast was at this time mostly limited to the coastal strip, land was at a premium and residential development took place outside the city's jurisdiction (see Fig. 11.2). The Nerang township and its surroundings in adjacent Albert Shire, and in particular the Nerang River flood plains, were perfectly located to accommodate the ever expanding development push from the City of Gold Coast (Dedekorkut-Howes and Bosman 2015). Albert Shire was essentially rural until the 1960s but with the introduction of reticulated water and canal developments in the Broadbeach area, the explosive growth of the Gold Coast spilled over its municipal borders. At that time Albert Shire did not have a planning scheme. Land development was controlled by a *Subdivision of Land By-Law,* which was gazetted in 1952 (Land Court 1991). Responding to growth, the shire council commissioned the Brisbane-based consulting firm A.A. Heath & Partners to produce a report in 1970 that served as a foundation for rethinking the Albert Shire's planning scheme, and commented on key aspects of the plan-making process in the Gold Coast region and Queensland. The report observed that the lack of a regional plan for Albert Shire and the surrounding local governments was causing several problems including difficulties around population projections and competition between the local governments. In addition to these issues, it argued that the lag time between the occurrence of development and the (inadequate) financial return to councils was seriously influencing the form of planning proposals themselves. While the form of planning schemes was not clearly set out in legislation, the standard form included clearly defined zones and rigid land-use tables. The report criticised their lack of flexibility in terms of directing development, as well as the difficulty in trying to clearly define within the schemes all the uses that were likely to occur (A.A. Heath & Partners 1970). Interestingly, the report suggested that one way to achieve greater flexibility would be to leave most uses to the discretion of council (for instance, by limiting forbidden uses), but with clear goals and standards so as to be able to assess individual applications. The difficulties of such a process in introducing a town plan for the first time was, however, clearly recognised. The report recommended a more rigid process for the Albert Shire, but with some modifications in the table of zones for those where a greater flexibility was necessary. It also recommended that the town planning scheme be accompanied by a strategic plan to help guide council's decisions.

At this time the northern and southern parts of Albert Shire were in different statistical divisions, with growth pressure exerted on the northern portion by Brisbane and the southern portion by the Gold Coast (A.A. Heath & Partners 1970). Two strategic plans were prepared in parallel, one for the southern portion and one for the northern portion. The *North Albert Shire Strategic Plan* contained only a map and no final report was prepared. According to Taylor (1973) it departed significantly from the 1970 report with vast additional areas zoned for urban development. The *South Albert Shire Strategic Plan 1972* covered the area from the Albert and Logan Rivers in the north to the New South Wales border in the south and was prepared by Canadian planning consultants Project Planning Associates. The selection of consultants was controversial. The council considered appointing A.A. Heath & Partners, who after all had prepared the background report for the strategic plan, but opponents thought that the few specialist planners in Australia did not have the vision necessary for the growth and physical design challenges being faced by the Gold Coast area (Burchill 2005). While opponents to an Australian firm were appeased by the selection of Project Planning Associates, others still were opposed to the Canadian appointment on the grounds of a conflict of interest generated by the firm's previous work in the shire for large landholders. Council favoured the benefits to be brought by their

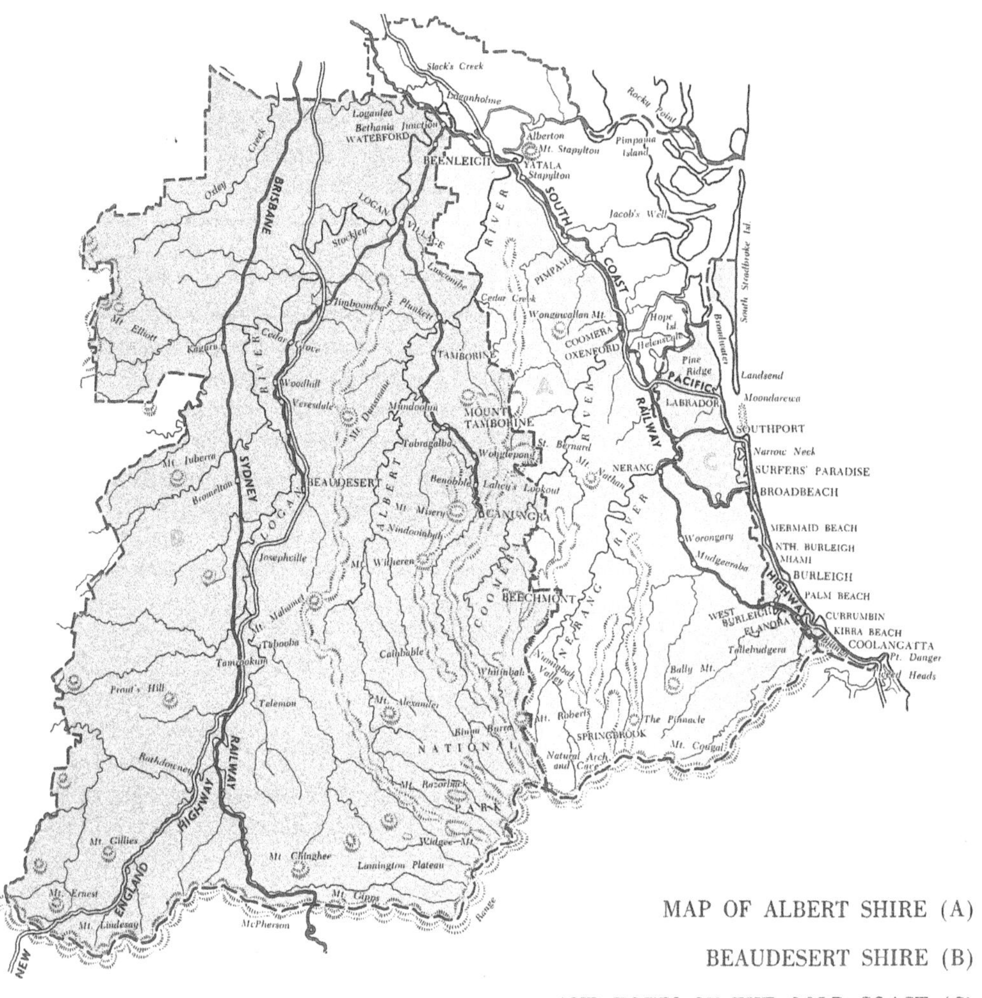

Fig. 11.2. Jurisdictions in the Gold Coast region, 1958 (Keane 1958, p. 2)

knowledge of the shire and their international experience in fast-growing regions of North America over other concerns.

The *South Albert Shire Strategic Plan* did not target a specific time period but was intended to establish a long-range concept of growth and conservation. It warned that 'if a long-range concept of growth, location and strategy for achieving a desirable environmental quality through control and guidance is not established, the result could be the disorder, monotony and abuse of the land so evident in Florida and California' (Albert Shire Council 1972a, p. 12). The plan also emphasised the recognition of the necessity of coordinated planning, consideration of the area's urban growth on a regional scale and integration of urban service systems by both Albert Shire and City of Gold Coast councils. The major elements of the plan included a new satellite community for ~120 000 people at Ormeau and Pimpama with extensive industrial areas adjacent to the cane fields; a new international airport near this community – situated between the two major urban regions of Brisbane and the Gold Coast (this 'logical' location was first proposed in the *Gold Coast Strategic Plan*); expansion of the inland Pacific Motorway to six lanes, connecting the shire to Brisbane and connecting to the Gold Coast Highway at Tugun; a conservation area that would act as a greenbelt and serve as regional open space between greater Brisbane and the Gold Coast/South Albert Shire urban region; major urban expansion adjacent to the Gold Coast communities from Broadbeach down to Burleigh and Currumbin; and lower-density rural residential growth on the urban fringes. It also called for safeguarding of a right-of-way for a rapid transit system along the inland freeway and commented that the loss of the right-of-way of the recently dismantled old railway was 'a pity' in the light of the scale of development that was now occurring (Albert Shire Council 1972a, p. 22). The plan summary argued that a transit link to Brisbane was the only way to avoid 'massive duplication of the road system with its detrimental effects on a sensitive environment' (Albert Shire Council 1972b, p. 4).

The strategic plan also contained a structure plan that depicted proposed major land uses and road network, population allocations and community structures. It also included a section on high-density development, based on expected population growth and rise in land prices, as the alternative development, therefore introducing the concept of high-density housing. A major objective, as stated in the summary of major proposals, was to determine growth projections and population capacities of the major areas identified for urban development. The population projections anticipated 300 000 residents by 2000 in the Gold Coast urban area, which included the City of Gold Coast and part of Albert Shire south of Coomera River. While these projections might have seemed quite exaggerated and ambitious at the time, as in the case of the projections in the *Gold Coast Strategic Plan*, this was far off the mark since population of the somewhat larger Gold Coast–Tweed region, which also included northern Albert Shire and Tweed, reached almost 475 000 by 2001 (ABS 2008).

The Albert Shire strategic plans were severely criticised for not practicing what they preached. In a report prepared for Logan and District Council of Progress Associations, chartered town planner Colin Taylor (1973) claimed that these plans violated both the stated intentions and accepted planning principles and practice. He forecasted that a bleak future with traffic choking the roads, fog obscuring the sun, overcrowded beaches, stinking marshlands and inaccessible National Parks was awaiting shire residents if these plans were implemented. He found the planning process itself to be flawed, from the timeframe set for the task to the lack of data collection such as surveying, growth rates and transportation studies. Taylor agreed with the view conveyed in the *South Albert Shire Plan* that the shire's planning had to be done in a regional context and could not be properly considered in isolation due to its close relations with Brisbane to the north, Beaudesert to the west and the Gold Coast to the east. He noted that with the proposed two-month timeframe to prepare the plan, consultation with neighbouring authorities and government departments would have been impossible.

Although it claimed otherwise, the plan also failed to provide clear direction for the protection of landscape and natural amenities and conservation of the 'diminishing and irreplaceable resources' of the shire unless they already happened to be in public ownership. Not only were there no provisions to protect farmland, but Taylor (1973, pp. 5–6) argued that 'the plan spells the death of farming throughout Albert Shire' and called it 'a blueprint for urban sprawl'. The supposed greenbelt allowed for 25-acre lots on one side of the highway and areas subject to flooding were zoned for 10-acre subdivisions. Previously granted permits served to justify a strategy of gradual transition from rural to urban that prompted Taylor (1973, p. 7) to call the plan 'a sell-out to speculators' and to conclude that they would be the only group benefiting from the plan. Another criticism was of a lack of planning for infrastructure to support the growth of subdivisions, including roads, water supply, sewerage and garbage disposal. Taylor (1973) claimed that even an expanded Pacific Motorway could not serve as both the thoroughfare to Brisbane and the main service road for an urban corridor of a large population of 360 000. Furthermore, the plan made no provision for the railway it promoted.

The resolution to prepare the first planning scheme for Albert Shire was passed in 1964 but the plan was not drafted until 1970, nor approved until 1973 (Albert Shire Council 1982). While the scheme was under preparation and consideration, the council adopted an *Interim Development By-Law* in 1969, which was intended as a holding procedure. According to some (Taylor 1973; Burchill 2005, p. 126), however, it gave council 'unrestricted discretionary means to deal with development applications'. As a result, the number of subdivision proposals for housing development on rural lands without the need for zoning exploded. A 'single' and 'simply granted' development permit was enough to start selling lots without registration of titles (Burchill 2005, p. 126). With the council's 'very liberal' use of its discretionary powers 'to the advantage of developers and speculators' (Taylor 1973, p. 2) many lots in early stages were sold off the plan into a booming speculator's market without consideration for infrastructure issues such as adequate water supply, sewage disposal or roads (Dedekorkut-Howes and Bosman 2015). Because the shire's planning scheme was under review when these proposals were approved, the state returned the scheme to council for revision so that it might take into account the approvals that had been granted in the interim, recognising that these approvals were substantial departures from the planning scheme.

The *1973 Town Planning Scheme for the Shire of Albert* introduced action plans or development control plans to control the development of the urban parts of the shire (Albert Shire Council 1973), but it was put under review after only a year of operation because of the very factors that had seen it returned for revision. The revised 1976 town plan incorporated new zones more aligned with the strategic plan and provided more scope with regards to development control (Albert Shire Council 1982). Development in Albert Shire only slowed with the 1974 flood (see Fig. 11.3), prompting the state government to halt canal development in the Nerang River Valley until the completion of a report commissioned to look at issues associated with development in coastal areas, with a focus on the existing canal estates on the Gold Coast and Sunshine Coast (Burchill 2005). The *1973 Strategic Plan* had alluded to the fact that development in the flood plains would only be possible with expensive flood mitigation measures, but assuming this problem would be overcome the land was shown as urban (Albert Shire Council 1982).

Despite the development and adoption of strategic documents for the long-term development of the Gold Coast region along with town planning schemes, Burchill (2005) argued that the late 1960s and early 1970s were characterised by a lack of effective town planning schemes and strategic planning in both the Gold Coast and Albert Shire, which could not cope with the development pressures borne either by high-rise development or massive subdivision proposals. In that sense, the first strategic plans were tailored to respond to the overwhelming push of new growth and new projects with few planning conventions aiming at limiting development (Burchill 2005). The Albert Shire Council was criticised for confusing subdivisional activity with growth. Taylor (1973, p. 3) argued that the council offered an incentive for speculation by allowing subdivisions in excess of 'reasonable needs'. The accuracy of the population projections was not yet a problem in

Fig. 11.3. Nerang River in flood covering the bridge on Ferry Road, Nerang, January 1974 (Image reproduction courtesy of the Gold Coast City Council Local Studies Library, image number LS-LSP-CD073-IMG0071)

1973, but it certainly became one by the 1990s when the combined population of the Gold Coast and Albert Shire was expected to reach half a million and place immense pressure on existing infrastructure. These projections were a first step towards anticipating rates of growth and change. But each council was still looking after their own issues, with separate goals and responsibilities and the absence of any planning for the region as a whole (Burchill 2005) despite both Gold Coast and South Albert Shire strategic plans emphasising the need to coordinate planning at this level. Another common shortcoming of these documents was the lack of planning for the growth of tourism, illustrated by the lack of guidelines for large-scale attractions.

Integration of the strategic plan and the planning scheme: the 1980s

Continued growth of Albert Shire, the impact of the 1974 floods and alterations to council boundaries necessitated a review of the *1973 Strategic Plan* and *1976 Town Plan*. At the same time the state amended the *Local Government Act* in 1980 and required the incorporation of strategic plans as part of town planning schemes by 1983 (Albert Shire Council 1982).

The *1982 Strategic Plan and Town Plan* for Albert Shire retained much of the form of its predecessors, looking at the long-term development of the shire and laying out the preferred future dominant uses for a progressive development of the area. The basic principles of the previous strategic plan were not altered and the review process undertaken by the council staff was described as 'mainly an updating process and refinement of the some of the broad concepts' (Albert Shire Council 1982, p. 7). The overall concept of the plan was still one of growth. One of its changes was the redefinition of the flood lines along the Albert and Logan Rivers and re-zoning of some land that was classified urban in the previous plan. The airport proposal was also deleted as it became obvious it was not likely to happen and the satellite city of more than 100 000 people was changed to a rural community of 7000. The Pacific Motorway, which was then still four lanes, was once again proposed to be expanded to six lanes; the plan stated that 'road will always be the major transport mode' (Albert Shire Council 1982, p. 85). While the idea of a rail system was kept in the plan, once more no provision was made for it besides the suggestion of possible routes following the existing highway from Beenleigh to Nerang and connecting from there to Broadbeach or Burleigh.

The 1982 plan would not rely so heavily on those development control plans that once filled the gap between the broad strategic plans and day-to-day zoning maps, as they were perceived at the time to prohibit or discourage development and to be unresponsive to change, especially when prepared too early. The new plan intended to 'allow the development industry to have a major input into the detailed design within the broad framework of the Strategic Plan' (Albert Shire Council 1982, p. 8). Rather than directing growth to particular areas, this exercise became one of transferring the actual development into the planning documents post hoc. For instance, the plan report (Albert Shire Council 1982) cited the need to re-align urban development in some rural zoned areas with the strategic documents as one of the reasons for the need of a review.

The City of Gold Coast prepared a new strategic plan to accompany the new planning scheme as well. The 1981 Gold Coast strategic plan, entitled *Looking to the Future*, laid out the aim of the city as being 'to enhance and safeguard the health, safety, convenience, and the economic, cultural, social and general welfare of the people and the amenities of the district and promote developer confidence through consistent development control of the city' (Gold Coast City Council 1981, p. 1). This strategic plan determined preferred land uses and planning objectives, one of which was the establishment of a rail or rapid transit link between Brisbane and the Gold Coast, necessitating the preservation of a corridor for this purpose. Its preferred route would follow the outskirts of existing urban development and connect Brisbane, Southport and Coolangatta, terminating near the airport at Bilinga.

The accompanying *1982 Gold Coast City Council Town Plan* comprised of planning provisions, zoning and height control maps as well as by-laws to implement and administer the scheme (Gold Coast City Council 1982, 1991). As a response to the growth in high rise buildings in the 1970s and early 1980s, the 1982 plan also introduced a series of design measures on height, site coverage, plot ratio and setbacks to protect views and provide ground level amenities. This was intended to oblige developers to supply more land per high-rise unit and limit building heights along the beachfront. Through the creation of highway development zones and facilitation of commercial infill along the main road network, the plan reinforced the characteristic Gold Coast strip development. The 1982 plan recognised 'the real future of the city as a tourist and entertainment centre, supported by an infrastructure of residential, business and light industrial activity' (Allom and Jones 1997, p. 362).

This plan was deemed ineffective because of the wide discretionary powers given to the city council, making the plan a document of convenience rather than a town planning scheme with provisions to limit or manage development (Jones 1986). When the real estate cycle would start again the principles laid out in the plan could be abandoned due to development pressure. Developers furthermore registered its flexibility as lowered certainty and predictability. This illustrates the considerable tension between providing certainty about the future use of land and enabling sufficient flexibility to accommodate unanticipated changes or development proposals that do not conform to expectations (Gurran 2007).

The 1982 Gold Coast plan was put under review in 1988 to address the continuing growth of the city and revise the planning controls put in place earlier. A 1991 planning study, entitled *People, Places and Planning*, acknowledged the limitations of planning to influence the physical, urban, social and economic factors that have shaped the development of the Gold Coast but recognised the need to manage and guide growth in a planned approach rather than the laissez-faire approach of the past (Gold Coast City Council 1991). The report further emphasised the need to develop strategies that would address the main development influences identified: the role of the Gold Coast in the Brisbane–Gold Coast metropolitan corridor; the role of the Gold Coast as a tourist centre; and the need for controlled growth, through urban consolidation for instance, and conservation of open spaces. The report once again acknowledged the need to integrate the future planning for Gold Coast and Albert Shire, and emphasised the need to align basic planning proposals, recognising that major aspects of the development of Albert Shire affect the City of Gold Coast and vice versa. It also recognised the growing importance of other external influences, such as the *Moreton Region Growth Strategy*.

Moving to the planned period: the 1990s

The 1990s saw a more proactive city council adopting and implementing more comprehensive planning schemes and being more assertive in its regulation of development (Burton 2014). The *1994 City of Gold Coast Planning Scheme* (Council of the City of Gold Coast 1994) was presented as a comprehensive strategic document comprising a structure plan expressing the broad planning philosophy for the future development of the Gold Coast, strategic planning statements comprising the planning goals and objectives, and a strategic planning map showing preferred dominant land-use designations. The plan recognised and sought to promote the different images of the Gold Coast that had emerged over several decades: the City of Leisure, the City of Enterprise, the City of Towers and the City in a Metropolitan Region. The structure plan emphasised the promotion of tourism, with the development of facilities in nodes close to tourist attractions, commercial and retail development, and both public and private transport. It was also concerned with the protection and enhancement of residential amenities for Gold Coast residents, as well as the preservation of regional open spaces. Focusing on maintaining and enhancing the elements that contribute to the image of the city, the plan also adopted urban design guidelines and created development control plans in 14 areas that offered bonuses for developers in exchange for streetscaping and landscaping contributions to public areas (Allom and Jones 1997). This plan recognised high-rise buildings as an icon of symbolic value to the city, but with limited aesthetic controls.

Albert Shire prepared a new strategic plan and planning scheme in 1995 to manage ongoing population growth and development pressures, but in that very year the state government amalgamated Albert Shire and the Gold Coast, partially to resolve water supply rights disputes between the two councils (Burchill 2005). This posed the new problem of how the plans of the two areas might sensibly come together as a new plan.

The 1997 strategic plan, *Building Sustainable Communities*, recognised the strong growth experienced by the Gold Coast but also the need to manage this growth to protect the natural environment and support diverse communities (Griffin 1998). It also acknowledged the city as a 'lifestyle destination' (Allom and Jones 1997, p. 363). The strategic plan focused on three basic principles: protection of the natural environment; diversity of communities and their social and economic characteristics; and economic development (Gold Coast City Council 1997). The plan presented a departure from the previous documents in that it emphasised the importance of considering the social, cultural and environmental impacts of any proposed change. It also recognised the importance of social interactions and sensitive and quality urban design (Griffin 1998). The strategic plan and its key themes were supported by the *Gold Coast Urban Heritage and Character Study*, which investigated the characteristics contributing to the Gold Coast's identity and focused on the notion of heritage value for places and objects and the city image and townscape strategy (Allom Lovell Marquis-Kyle *et al.* 1997).

Planning the Gold Coast in the new millennium

In recent years, the Gold Coast City Council has come to embrace a process of community-based, long-term and strategic planning, a departure from the early years of informal and reactive planning (Burton 2009). Post-1990 evolution also indicated a departure from a historic reliance on tourism and real estate development and a new attention to knowledge-based and creative activities, such as information technologies and media, that would render the Gold Coast an Innovation City (Wise 2006).

The *2003 Gold Coast Planning Scheme* is the current plan that governs development in the city. It was adopted in August 2003 after what Burchill (2005, p. 490) called a 'never-ending' consultation period with the community and the state government, replacing the pre-amalgamation individual planning schemes of the Gold Coast and Albert Shire councils. The scheme sought to coordinate and integrate planning dimensions at state, regional and local levels by advancing priority actions and undertaking the relevant lead agency responsibilities for local government contained in the *South East Queensland Regional Framework for Growth Management* through policy and strategy development. It carried forward ecological, economic and social planning concepts from the superseded Albert Shire and Gold Coast planning schemes. It is described as a 'living document' and is periodically reviewed and amended in accordance with relevant state legislation. The current version was amended in November 2011 and contains structure plans as well as local area plans.

The 2003 scheme aimed to recognise and facilitate the development of 'activity clusters' within the city as major locations for employment, investment and productive activity (Gold Coast City Council 2011c). The objective to implement this policy included supporting and encouraging the co-location and agglomeration of industrial and commercial activity into identifiable precincts. The Pacific Innovation Corridor was a key initiative to facilitate the development of a critical mass of knowledge-related industries in several precincts along the corridor, specialised in such fields as creative industries, education, environment, food, health and medicine, information and communications technology, marine and sport. Some of these precincts were later supported by the state government as in the case of the Gold Coast Health and Knowledge Precinct identified in the *South East Queensland Regional Plan 2009–2031* as a major residential and mixed use development node or the Southport Priority Development Area. These two areas are connected to each other through the Gold Coast light rail, which was jointly funded by city, state and Commonwealth.

Even while it was in draft form, some expressed concern that this plan was too daunting and that residents needed to be aware that increased densities would be necessary to address the projected population growth (Burchill 2005). It was also criticised for creating uncertainty for developers and property owners by setting up a review process at regular intervals that would ensure longer delays.

After 2004, under the leadership of Mayor Ron Clarke, there was 'a greater degree of commitment to growth management' (Burton 2014, p. 3240) that was interrupted by the global financial crisis. The latest strategic planning initiative on the Gold Coast called *Bold Future* started in 2007. It involved an extensive program of public participation and community engagement and resulted in a 'high degree of consensus around the key principles to be applied when planning for and managing the future growth of the city' and an overall vision for the future of the city that was 'increasingly green' (Burton 2010, p. 194) (for further details see Chapter 9). A major review of the *Gold Coast Planning Scheme* was undertaken on the basis of the final report of *Bold Future*, delivered in 2009. With a change of both local and state governments to conservative leadership in 2012 *Bold Future* was put aside in favour of a new planning scheme that scaled down development regulation and streamlined the planning regime.

The draft *City Plan 2015* sets out the council's intention for the future development of the city over the next 20-year horizon with a review occurring every decade and consisting of a strategic framework and priority infrastructure plan, as well as planning scheme components such as planning provisions, codes and zoning information (City of Gold Coast 2013c). It seeks to advance state and regional strategies, including state planning policies and the *South East Queensland Regional Plan 2009–2031*, by better taking into account the local context. Its strategic intent is to develop the Gold Coast into a 'world class' city and it thereby represents a major shift from development on the fringe to redevelopment of urban centres and major inner-city neighbourhoods, thus protecting the hinterland and foothills. Its key features therefore include removal of building height restrictions in selected areas, promotion of small lot development and replacement of local area plans with zones. These proposed changes are intended to reduce planning red tape as well as to deal with shortage of land for future development. The draft plan designates a hierarchy of centres supporting the network of larger centres with broad, drive-up catchments providing higher order goods and services with a network of neighbourhood centres based on walking catchments. Major projects like the Southport Central Business District, Commonwealth Games 2018 and light rail network feature prominently. The idea of promoting and facilitating knowledge, innovation and commercialisation through the Pacific Innovation Corridor of the previous plan has evolved into the city's Research Triangle, including Griffith University and the Gold Coast Health and Knowledge Precinct, Bond University and Varsity Central, and the Southern Cross University/Gold Coast Airport. In addition to the three corners of the research triangle, the plan identifies two more specialist centres: the Southport Entertainment Precinct and the Gold Coast Cultural Precinct at Bundall.

The commencement target for the draft *City Plan 2015* has been extended from January 2015 to 31 May 2015 to provide sufficient time to review the 2400 submissions received during the public consultation period. Among the submissions, Urban Development Institute of Australia (UDIA) criticised the lack of connection between the strategic framework and the remainder of the document (UDIA 2014) and expressed concern about the over-reliance on residential growth in infill areas around the coastal strip cautioning against the problems this may cause. UDIA found the population and employment projections in the draft plan too low compared to prior projections produced by the state, whereas Gold Coast and Hinterland Environmental Council (GECKO 2014) argued that the projected gain of 300 000 in population around which the new plan is constructed will only add to infrastructure shortfalls. GECKO further argued that the significant input into the plan's design by the Mayor's Technical Advisory Group favoured the development and construction industries. They also criticised the elimination of details, ostensibly to make the plan easier to understand, arguing that this would open the way to differing interpretations and conflict.

Conclusions

A review of the planning history of the Gold Coast reveals that after the initial laissez-faire development period where there was virtually no planning there were several attempts to control and regulate the development in the city. Several factors, however, hampered their effectiveness. In the early days, the fear that the development boom would suddenly come to an end resulted in virtually uncontrolled development. With continued growth, it became even harder to plan as increasing land values made planning a major financial sacrifice. This situation was aided by the control of local governments by developers, a pro-development state government, corruption in both levels of government and the view that government's role was aiding private enterprise.

When the effects of unplanned rapid development started to be felt, planning entered the picture. Yet growth was just too fast and councils yielded to its pressures. As is typical of fast growing cities, population projections that seemed unrealistically high in planning regularly fell short of the reality of the pace of growth. Some plans were reactive, reflecting past development rather than providing guidance for the future. From 1960s to the draft *City Plan 2015* participation and influence of development interests in local and state government caused critics to argue that the plans produced only served the development interests. While some plans had admirable aims they failed to translate these into implementable actions and planning provisions. From the late 1960s, the earliest strategic plans pointed to the need to coordinate planning in the region, but with no state guidance piecemeal planning continued until the 1995 amalgamations created the 'super council' and the statutory regional plans started to provide guidance from above.

As governments that view planning and government intervention differently change back and forth, there is no long-term, consistent policy trajectory to deal with the challenges cities face. Progressive planning interventions that may take a long time and a lot of effort before they bear fruit are undone easily to 'cut red and green tape', 'streamline the process', 'encourage development', 'create jobs' and 'open cities for business'. In the end, planning on the Gold Coast reflects what is happening in the state, the nation and the world.

Chapter 12

Looking beyond the horizon

Ayşın Dedekorkut-Howes and Caryl Bosman

While many things have changed on the Gold Coast from its early days, some things have remained the same. Development and business interests are still very active in city administration, and local government is pro-business and growth. The sitting mayor, Tom Tate, has a background in the construction, tourism and hospitality industries and still owned the Islander Resort Hotel until very recently. The city's local newspaper the *Gold Coast Bulletin* is no different than its predecessors in being decidedly pro-development (see Chapter 10). The city has great ambitions to grow and this is reflected in the projects pursued in the last decade.

Following the *State of Australian Cities 2013* report, demographer Bernard Salt commented that as the Gold Coast is getting bigger it is normalising and becoming a more sophisticated city (Ardern 2013b) and called it mini-Adelaide. Shortly thereafter, Salt was invited as a guest speaker to the 2013 Regional Leaders' Forum organised by Regional Development Australia (RDA) Gold Coast where the issues and the vision of the Gold Coast was discussed. (RDA is an Australian Government initiative that brings together all levels of government in a partnership to develop regional communities. Each RDA has a volunteer committee drawn from local government, the private sector, education and the community.) Among the issues discussed was the promotion of the Gold Coast (RDA Gold Coast 2014). Soon after, RDA Gold Coast commissioned Salt's firm KPMG to conduct a study into the future of the city and provide a 100-year insight from 1950, especially focusing on the next 35 years to 2050. The *Beyond the Horizon* report resulting from this effort is part of the 12-month *Future Gold Coast* project of the RDA, sponsored by the City of Gold Coast and the Gold Coast business leaders (RDA Gold Coast 2015). The next step of the project involves RDA, the City of Gold Coast and KPMG conducting several road shows in Australia and overseas to communicate the key findings of the report in order to promote a better understanding of the Gold Coast and to attract future investment.

The chapters contained in this book gave a historical account of the city from multiple perspectives and explained some of the factors that shaped the city of today. The purpose was to reflect on the past to inform the future. Therefore, we will now turn our attention to the future of the Gold Coast and overview the population projections and the major projects pursued by the city. The *Beyond the Horizon* report itself builds on the current strategies and opportunities for the city and incorporates and supports the major projects in the draft *City Plan 2015* (see Chapter 11) such as the cruise ship terminal and casino, extension of heavy and light rail to Coolangatta, expansion of the airport, Southport Central Business

District (CBD) and Gold Coast Cultural Precinct. How realistic is the future portrayed in this report and used to market the city to domestic and international businesses?

Population growth and composition

From its humble beginnings as a local seaside resort serving the capital city of Brisbane, who would have guessed the Gold Coast would grow up to be the largest non-capital city in Australia whose population growth consistently surpassed expectations and projections (see Chapter 11)? The *Beyond the Horizon* report projects a population of 1 225 000 by 2050 for the Gold Coast–Tweed area (KPMG 2015). This represents a doubling in size over the next 35 years. Population growth is expected to continue following the trend of the last two decades, adding between 12 000–15 000 new residents annually. Projections show the Gold Coast's growth rate to be normalising to a level consistent with but slightly higher than that of Brisbane.

The ageing of the population is one of the challenges the city will face as 101 000 persons aged 65 and over are expected to be added to the population by 2036, increasing their proportion in the population from the current level of 15% to 20% (Queensland Government Statistician's Office 2014). This figure is parallel to the trend in Queensland. Provision of aged care, health care, social services and infrastructure to support an ageing population will be even more critical for the city. While not at the same rate, the proportion of persons aged 5–19 is also expected to increase. The *Beyond the Horizon* report projects the age structure of the city to shift even further upwards beyond 2036.

Along with the growth and ageing of the population, there are several projects and initiatives started in the new millennium that will shape the Gold Coast in the near future. Some of these projects, while quite controversial, are pursued aggressively by the City of Gold Coast, supported by the local media (namely, the *Gold Coast Bulletin*) and the business community. In addition to the fast approaching Commonwealth Games, the notable ones include several Priority Precinct Projects such as the Parklands and Southport Priority Development Areas, Gold Coast Research Triangle, Gold Coast Cultural Precinct and the proposed cruise ship terminal, as well as major infrastructure projects and proposals such as the extension of light and heavy rail and the expansion of the airport.

Parklands Priority Development Area

The Gold Coast's successful bid for the 2018 Commonwealth Games has provided the opportunity for economic growth and the promotion of the city as a destination. The delivery of a successful Games depends on good organisation through the Queensland Government, involving the ability of urban planners to provide a benchmark for the future development and growth of the city. Sporting events, such as the Gold Coast 600 and the Pan Pacific Masters Games, have been held on the Gold Coast for several years. By hosting an event at the level of the Commonwealth Games, the planning profession has the opportunity to build upon past successes and deliver a refined event. Four key issues have emerged as important planning considerations in the lead up to and during the Games: accessibility, safety, community and legacy.

Traffic congestion emerges as an issue whenever there is a mass movement of people within an area. The Commonwealth Games developments are split into two key areas: the Commonwealth Games Village (CGV) that will accommodate the delegates during the event, and the venues where the sporting events will be held. In the lead up to the Commonwealth Games, planners and decision-makers have a role to play in providing efficient transport services. The sprawled locations of the sporting venues and the CGV present a challenge. It is important that these venues be accessible by both public and active transport, such as walking and cycling. This will help reduce the number of private vehicles on the road during the event and, in turn, will contribute to the overall satisfaction the delegates will feel towards the Gold Coast and improve the quality of life for the wider community. Transporting delegates and attendees to and from the sporting venues and the CGV therefore requires extensive planning in terms of new transport modes and improvement to existing infrastructure.

The Gold Coast light rail has been proposed as a viable means of transportation; however, the increase in demand from delegates and visitors is likely to exceed the current carrying capacity. The light rail system, at the time of the Games, will run from Broadbeach to the Gold Coast University Hospital in Southport. As such, the connectivity to sporting facilities from the light rail is limited to events along this corridor, with TransLink bus services the only public transport option for access to other venues. Therefore, it is crucial to improve current infrastructure and provide alternative transport options during the event.

All major events across the world pose safety concerns for both delegates and the wider community from the vast amount of people congregating in one place. In the lead up for the bid to host the Commonwealth Games, former Queensland Premier Anna Bligh used security as a key endorsement for the Gold Coast. Security and police checks for all Games staff and volunteers and security checks for delegates are standard measures for major events and are managed by event organisers. In comparison, planners are concerned with issues relating to the design of the built environment which can impact on the safety of delegates, event attendees and the wider community. Safety within a community is an important feature as it enables people to connect with their surroundings and each other. From a planning perspective, the design and arrangement of the venue and CGV potentially maximises public security.

Chapter 8 detailed the relationship of the City of Gold Coast with the state government and the role of the state in the development of the city. The area where the CGV is located was declared a priority development area (PDA) by the state on 1 February 2013 giving the state control over the management of land-use planning and development in the site. PDAs are parcels of land within the state identified for 'specific accelerated development with a focus on economic growth' (Department of State Development 2015) where the state government works with local councils to streamline the planning, approval and development processes. Currently, the CGV site is governed by the *Parklands PDA Development Scheme*, which allows development to be fast tracked through Economic Development Queensland (EDQ). The development scheme is the planning document that will assist in planning, carrying out, promoting, coordinating and controlling the development of land in the Parklands PDA. The development of the PDA is intended to promote longer-term development opportunities on the site as well as support the successful delivery of the Games. Upon completion of the Commonwealth Games the site is expected to return to the City of Gold Coast.

The Parklands PDA is located over the old Gold Coast Parklands site, previously home to the Gold Coast Show and Gold Coast Harness Racing Club, in an accessible location ~3.3 km west of the Southport CBD and 3.6 km east of the Pacific Motorway connecting the city to Brisbane. The PDA adjoins the Gold Coast University Hospital on one side and is served by the Gold Coast light rail at the Griffith University Station. Proximity to the transport network, Gold Coast University Hospital and Griffith University can play a key component in ensuring the legacy is achieved.

Fig. 12.1. Artist's impression of Commonwealth Games Village (Image courtesy of the Queensland Government)

As one of the largest urban renewal projects ever undertaken on the Gold Coast, the selection of the site for the CGV was not without controversy. While the redevelopment of the Parklands site was promoted as a big economic boost and more jobs for the Gold Coast (Seeney 2013) a report released after its closure showed that it had been a profitable business and Southport councillor Dawn Crichlow said that the decision to shut the showgrounds down was the worst mistake the government had made (Killoran 2014). With no comparable alternative venue, the fear is that many of the more than 300 events held at the Parklands site each year, such as Big Day Out, would not be coming back to the Coast. On the other hand, the *Gold Coast Bulletin* described the plan for the village, that will host 6500 athletes and officials, 'a Southbank-style residential and retail development' (Ardern 2014) (see Fig. 12.1). And in terms of legacy, the CGV is planned to form the key residential, commercial and retail part of the Gold Coast Health and Knowledge Precinct after the Games.

The Gold Coast Research Triangle

As the pages of this book illustrate, the share of health, education and knowledge sectors in the Gold Coast economy is increasing (Chapter 1) and the local council has been trying to capitalise on this over the years by several different schemes such as the Pacific Innovation Corridor (see Chapter 11). The draft *City Plan* also incorporates the goal of diversifying the economic base of the city, the backbone of the prior economic development strategies, particularly focusing on knowledge economy and expansion of the healthcare and education sectors. To that end, the city's Research Triangle was established as a dedicated Innovation Zone (see Chapter 11) and these specialist centres will be encouraged to grow under the new plan.

The draft *City Plan* proposes health and medical tourism to capitalise on the synergy between the city's driver sector and the rising new sectors. The *Beyond the Horizon* report (KPMG 2015) notes the historically low, but rapidly catching up, levels of skilled and educated work force on the Gold Coast. If the Gold Coast achieves a similar proportion of university students to capital cities, it is expected to host 55 000 university students by 2050; a 162% increase from 2011 levels. The tertiary education sector is responding to this opportunity by expanding their campuses on the Gold Coast or establishing new ones. Growing at an astronomical rate, Griffith University's Gold Coast campus, established back in 1989, has added at least one new building per year for the last decade to its assets and it continues to offer new majors and accept an ever-increasing number of students. The Gold Coast campus passed the old and established Nathan campus in Brisbane several years ago in student numbers, becoming the largest of the university's five campuses and one of the largest employers in the city. At the other end of the city's Research Triangle, Australia's first private university Bond University (also established in 1989) and Southern Cross University Gold Coast campus across the New South Wales border (established in 2010) are also expanding to meet the demand and take advantage of the opportunity provided by the rapid population growth of the city, especially in the education and career formation age group.

Gold Coast Health and Knowledge Precinct on the north corner of the Research Triangle is envisioned to be a mixed use community that includes the Griffith University Gold Coast campus, the brand new Gold Coast University Hospital – the largest in the region – across the street from the university which started operating in 2013, a private hospital that is currently under construction, as well as the Commonwealth Games Village which will form the residential and the commercial areas of the precinct after the Games. This development is viewed as the single-most significant legacy project for the Commonwealth Games, with the Health and Knowledge Precinct expected to create thousands of new jobs and strengthen and diversify the Gold Coast economy.

Southport Central Business District

The Gold Coast is known for not having a CBD (Mullins 1991; Holmes 2006; Dedekorkut-Howes and Bosman 2015). However, the absence of a CBD in the most central and valuable part of the city is not uncommon in resort towns. In fact, Mullins (1991) argues that tourist cities are spatially distinctive by being without traditional CBDs. Instead they have a Recreational Business District (RBD) that is spatially and functionally distinct from a CBD (Stansfield and Rickert 1970). This district is based on a recreational attraction rather than upon the proximity to residential areas or transportation routes, serves an area far beyond the hinterland of the town and is characterised by a distinctive array of pedestrian, tourist-oriented retail facilities. Surfers Paradise fits this description. The reason the city does not have a traditional CBD but several smaller centres around the city lies in its development history of joining of a scattered number of resorts along the beach, like pearls on a string, each of which had a centre of its own (Smith 1991).

In the early years the lack of a CBD worked for the then separate resort centres of Surfers Paradise and Coolangatta because of the 'twinning' that existed with business centres of Southport and Tweed Heads (Pigram 1977; Dedekorkut-Howes 2013). The twin cities in each set played a supporting and complementary role for the other, where Southport and Tweed Heads assumed an administrative and service role with a considerable CBD function to the recreation focused Surfers Paradise and Coolangatta. For the Gold Coast of today, with a population of half a million and ambitions to become a world-class city, having that prestigious part of a city is suddenly critical. Thus, the City of Gold Coast is trying to revitalise Southport as the Gold Coast's CBD in order to enhance and diversify the economy of the region, as well as provide the city with an official CBD. The area has been declared a priority development area under the Queensland Government's *Economic*

Development Act 2012 to 'remove barriers, boost developer confidence and facilitate economic development'. This is another example of using the state's powers for local planning (see Chapter 8).

That the Gold Coast should have a CBD was not contested; however, whether that CBD should be at Southport or not is still causing conflict. The statutory *South East Queensland Regional Plan 2009–2031* identified several regional activity centres, and on the Gold Coast the principal centres were determined as Southport and Robina. In opposition to the Southport CBD initiative, the Robina Group which operates the Robina Town Centre (one of the largest shopping centres in the city) and developed several large housing developments in the area is running its own 'CBD Robina' campaign. While the state and city council backed Southport campaign is comparatively modest, the opposition hosts a dedicated website and pays for regular newspaper advertisements to attract business and investment to Robina. Robina is on a greenfield site and is better connected to Brisbane with a heavy rail station, though the location of that station in relation to the town centre is less than ideal. Land available for development in Southport is scattered, providing mostly infill opportunities. With the opening of the new University Hospital, the old hospital site offers one large block of land but demand for development in Southport is currently not very high.

The business functions of the CBD aside, there are other potential problems for the success of a traditional city centre at Southport. In addition to business and commerce, CBDs usually also include some administrative, cultural and entertainment functions. Even though the mayor symbolically moved his office to Southport, the offices of the second largest local council in Australia are scattered throughout the city. The council and proponents of the CBD project call for government relocations, specifically proposing some state departments to be relocated to the Gold Coast. The proposed Cultural Precinct is not within walking distance to Southport and most of the entertainment functions are located at Surfers Paradise. The newly operating light rail connects Southport to Surfers Paradise and Broadbeach but proposed extensions are necessary to make Southport truly central in the transportation network sense.

On the cultural side, one project to create an attraction for visitors to Southport is the Gold Coast Chinatown. This is viewed as an integral part of the revitalisation of Southport as an international CBD for the Gold Coast. The purpose is to encourage Chinese and Asian tourists and investment, reinforcing the city as a destination to do business, be entertained, to live and be educated. The project is trying to create a sense of home and community for the Chinese and Asian population that permanently reside on the Gold Coast and for international students studying at Gold Coast universities, English language schools and colleges. It is envisioned to be a place for the Gold Coast to celebrate its diversity through culture, design, people and food with an exciting mix of restaurants, cultural festivals and boutiques. Cities want a Chinatown because they are viewed as '"cultural signposts" of any truly international city' (Ip 2005, p. 69) and thus, their 'perceived distinctiveness' becomes appreciated (Anderson 1990). This is consistent with the ambitions of the Gold Coast to become a world-class city. However, wanting something is not enough to achieve it. Brisbane's similar attempt in creating a Chinatown in the late 1980s is viewed as a failure (Ip 2005). Only time will tell whether the Gold Coast will be more successful.

Gold Coast Cultural Precinct

Gold Coast Cultural Precinct is one of the ideas rooted in the *Bold Future* process. A survey conducted as part of that initiative reflected the community's desire for more cultural

Fig. 12.2. Art Tower of the Cultural Precinct designed by ARM Architecture (ARM Architecture 2014)

spaces and with that the idea of expanding the current facilities at Evandale was born. In addition to providing better cultural facilities, the precinct aims to create a civic focal place and be the city's 'new cultural heart' (City of Gold Coast n.d.). The precinct is planned to be an arts and culture corridor that includes civic gardens, a new arts museum and performing arts centre.

The Cultural Precinct is in a very scenic location, almost surrounded by the Nerang River and encompassing the Evandale Lake. However, there are a few problems with the proposal. The source of funding for the $385 million cultural precinct became controversial when what was promised to be paid by the government, gaming levies and private sector was attempted to be passed onto ratepayers through the increase of a levy and disposal of some land (Weston 2015). The design by ARM Architecture + Topotek1, selected through an international competition, has been likened to fruit tingles in the local media (see Fig. 12.2). But the major problem with the project is its location. Far from both the entertainment district of Surfers Paradise and Southport CBD, it is unlikely that the ambition of making it a focal place will become a reality anytime soon. There are plans to connect it to Surfers Paradise through Chevron Island using a green bridge and an arts walk, and vague ambitions of a connection through light rail in the city's transport strategy, but before these are actually in place it will remain a driving-oriented attraction for locals.

Broadwater integrated resort and cruise ship terminal

Development conflicts frequently emerge as a result of change, and as meanings, values and attachments to places alter. The decade long (2005–15) development conflict on the Southport Spit is a case in point. The Spit (see Fig. 12.3, compare to Fig. 3.2) is a permanent landform located at the northern end of the Gold Coast, across the Broadwater from the early settlement of Southport (1880s). It separates the Southport Broadwater and the Pacific Ocean and it is one of the last significant undeveloped public green spaces on the Gold Coast. This landform developed in the late 1800s when the sand dune at the mouth of the Nerang River in Southport was reconfigured by a series of storms. The Southport Spit is an important place within the rapidly changing landscapes of the Gold Coast and it has significant social and cultural meanings and attachments for many Gold Coast residents. The past decade has seen ongoing conflicts surrounding a proposal to develop this piece of public land into a private cruise ship terminal and tourist facilities. The idea, initially proposed in 2005 by the state Beattie Labor Government, was strongly opposed by many in surrounding local communities. The proposed development of the Southport Spit instigated a phase in a long chain of development conflicts that have come to characterise the relationship between large-scale, government-led development projects and community concerns about significant public open space on the Gold Coast. It is the natural environment, more so than the built landscape, that establishes the Gold Coast's essential value as a place or genius loci.

Fig. 12.3. Aerial photo of the Southport Spit looking north, 2008. The Pacific Ocean is to the right and the Nerang River/Southport Broadwater is to the left of The Spit. Sea World is to the bottom left and undeveloped Wave Break Island is to the upper left across from the channel separating The Spit from South Stradbroke Island. (Photograph courtesy of Dianne Dredge)

Fig. 12.4. Cycle of conflict that frames a pattern of development and rapid urban growth on the Gold Coast

The constantly evolving urban landscape on the Gold Coast has come about through a pattern of conflict, change and adjustment to a new 'norm'. This recurring cycle is initiated by the arrival of new players into the development arena. New players invariably bring with them new ideas, concepts, beliefs and place values. Conflict then potentially occurs as a result of the difference in place values between the 'new' and 'old' players/community members. This pattern is immersed within the history of Southport and the Gold Coast as a whole, as discussed in Chapter 6. The cycle can be broken up into five, often difficult to define, phases (see Fig. 12.4).

Several significant conflict cycles are evident in the history of Southport, and the wider area of the Gold Coast. The first was the conflict that followed the arrival of European settlement in the region leading up to the mid-1820s as told in Chapter 2. One of the first to object to development on The Spit, in the 1960s, was the local National Party Member of Parliament at the time, Doug Jennings (the son of Sir Albert Jennings who was the founder of the national housing construction corporation, A.V. Jennings). Jennings's last fight to save The Spit was instigated in 1979 when the Queensland National/Liberal state government, under the Premiership of Sir Joh Bjelke-Petersen, established the Gold Coast Waterways Authority. As a result, by the 1980s the Broadwater and The Spit were 'secured' by the construction of groynes, channel dredging and a sand bypass system. The Waterways Authority was frequently involved in controversy over commercial development rights on public land on the Gold Coast (Condon 2006). In one case a prominent board member obtained 64 ha on the western side of The Spit for tourism urbanisation (now the theme park Sea World). Other tourism-related developments on The Spit were also approved during this time and were subsequently built, renovated and extended: an exclusive shopping precinct, a commercial fishing wharf (that now also accommodates super yacht berths), an exclusive resort complex, and an international hotel and apartment complex. Other development proposals that did not get off the ground included an 'amusement oasis', a mini-city comprising 8000 permanent residents and a golf course (Condon 2006). Development controversy on The Spit ended temporarily in 1992 when a newly elected Labor state government disbanded the Waterways Authority. However, it was not until 1997 that the Labor government set up the Gold Coast Harbours Authority to take a more local approach to the management of the Broadwater and Spit environs.

Notwithstanding the Gold Coast City Council's planning regulations, nor the lengths to which previous National Party government officials had defended The Spit against development, nor the fact that the government had specifically set up the Gold Coast Harbours Authority as a local approach to the management of the Broadwater and Spit environs, on 15 September 2005 the Queensland Labor Government announced its intention of developing an international cruise ship terminal and related services on this valued and valuable piece of public open space. In order to bypass local government planning restrictions (and we argue the views and input of local communities) the state sought absolute control over the planning and development processes by declaring the project a 'Significant Development'. This declaration triggered state legislation that called for an environmental impact study (EIS) which meant the government had direct control over the way the EIS was developed, the criteria by which it was to be assessed and it enabled other legislation to be bypassed if necessary. Importantly, by declaring the project as a 'Significant Development' the local planning authority, the Gold Coast City Council, and local communities ('old' players) were positioned as observers with no authority to provide input into the project other than decreed and regulated by the state government ('new' player).

In December 2005 the Queensland Government created a Gold Coast Marine Development Project Board to act as the proponent for the Spit development. The board was set up to advise the Premier and the Coordinator General and to undertake tasks as required by the government. In effect the state government created its own proponent for the project, a proponent that was also to advise the government. All decisions taken by the government were to be, and in fact were, based upon the advice of the board. To heighten this inbred decision-making process the state government called for expressions of interest from developers at the same time it commissioned an EIS for the site, with the supposition that the advice from the board would be in favour of development. In addition, the state sought direct control over the proposal, feasibility and development of the project.

To provide effective opposition to the state government and its plans for the Southport Spit, a consortium of community groups joined to form the Save Our Spit Alliance. This energetic and dedicated group organised several rallies, delegations and petitions over the next two years and maintained (and continue to maintain) an evocative and resourceful website. By July 2006 (just 10 months into the feasibility studies) the Save Our Spit Alliance had collected over 20 000 signatures as part of their petition to the state government to stop development on The Spit.

A few months after a well attended and enthusiastic protest, and in response to a continued barrage of criticism about the development proposal, the then Deputy Premier, Anna Bligh, herself a Gold Coaster by childhood experiences, summed up the situation by saying 'it would be great if [The Spit] was less environmentally sensitive, if people had less emotional attachment to it – that would make it a lot easier' (Condon 2006). In this statement the Deputy Premier was casting local place attachment as an obstacle to the development process. The government perceived The Spit to be, and valued the site as, a space of economic opportunity. A member of the Parliament at the time in support of the government's Spit development proposal argued that 'The Beattie Government has a duty to provide, amongst other things, economic stability and employment opportunities for the people of this State' (Smith 2006).

Notwithstanding this state level support, on Friday 3 August 2007 (just over two years from the first public announcement) the Premier Peter Beattie proclaimed that the cruise ship terminal on The Spit would not proceed. The Premier did not directly acknowledge that this decision reflected the views of over 22 000 local residents. Instead the argument put forward by the government was that the decision not to proceed was based on the cost to taxpayers; an economic rationale, not an environmental, nor a cultural, and certainly not a social or community rationale. It is important to note, however, that the decision by the government not to proceed was taken at the height of a state government election campaign. At the time a Gold Coast Channel Nine TV news program conducted a poll with the question 'Will the **Beattie Government lose your vote** over its push for a cruise ship terminal at The Spit?' (emphasis in the original) and the published result showed that 86.4% of respondents said YES.

The Southport Spit continues to ride a wave of development abuse. On 11 February 2010 the local Federal Member of Parliament sent out an email survey asking his constituents if they wanted 'a cruise ship terminal on The Spit, the Broadwater or neither?' This email followed in the footsteps of a previous announcement by the state government, in mid-2008, of their (renewed) intention of developing a cruise ship terminal in the vicinity of the Southport Spit. In addition, other smaller private and commercial development proposals continue to be lodged for this section of prime public undeveloped, somewhat raw, open space. The most significant of these was yet another cruise ship terminal proposal in mid-2012, this time emanating from the Gold Coast City Council Mayor Tom Tate. Mayor Tate, backed by the newly elected Newman Liberal National Party state government, put out a call for expressions of interest to develop a range of tourist infrastructure including a casino, hotels and cruise ship terminal on The Spit. By June 2013 the development project was in doubt, primarily on account of fiscal arrangements. In an effort to save The Spit from major development two more rallies took place, in November 2012 (Fig. 12.5) and November 2014 (Fig. 12.6). A recent study indicates that The Spit environs is 'identified as a key environmental asset worth more than $611 million for the city' (Weston 2013). In October 2013 the then Deputy Premier Jeff Seeney announced that the Newman state government would nominate a developer to build a marina in the vicinity of The Spit. With continuing protests over possible loss of Doug Jennings Park at the tip of The Spit, the pro-development interests turned their attention to the man-made Wave Break Island in the

Fig. 12.5. Spit Rally, Southport Spit, November 2012 (C Bosman)

Fig. 12.6. Spit Rally, Southport Broadwater Parklands, November 2014 (C Bosman)

Broadwater across from The Spit, with proposals of a resort-cruise ship terminal complex located there gaining traction (see Fig. 12.3).

To add a new twist to the history of events surrounding development on The Spit, recently elected state Labor Government Premier Annastacia Palaszczuk showed her support to the opposition of the project during her election campaign. The ever pro-development local newspaper *Gold Coast Bulletin* stated that the Premier's view that 'Gold Coasters don't want a cruise ship terminal is based on "dodgy" data' (Skene 2015). So the conflict goes on. The big question remains: will the proposed cruise ship terminal go ahead? It features in the timeline of development in the *Beyond the Horizon* report and is marked as a transportation connection on one of the maps (KPMG 2015), indicating that the council has not given up the idea yet. Even if it is not successful this time around, an asset of such proportions is unlikely to be ignored by the development industry on the Gold Coast. New players and new ideas are likely to result in proposals for the development of The Spit environs time and time again in the future. With every reincarnation proposals get bigger and more ambitious, and what began as a project for a cruise ship terminal, expanded to include a casino, a six-star integrated resort, a super yacht marina and a 50-story tower (Potts and Weston 2014). This pattern confirms opponents' long-held fear that the city's purported need for a cruise ship terminal was just an excuse to privatise and develop the last remaining large scale parcel of coastal public land on the Gold Coast (see Fig. 12.3).

Infrastructure projects

A growing population and economy requires parallel development of infrastructure investments to support it. With growing tourist numbers, direct linkages to major sources of tourists, such as China, are becoming more and more important. Expanded flights are important for achieving the health and medical tourism aims as well. One of the infrastructure developments on the city's current agenda includes an expansion of the Gold Coast Airport. In the short term, the improvements proposed include the building of airbridges. The staging of the future expansion of the current terminal and apron facilities depends on future demand. More importantly, as noted in Chapter 4, this transport precinct includes more than just the airport. The draft *City Plan* lists the airport and Southern Cross University as specialised centres. The city has plans to turn this area into a major business centre on a par with Sydney or Melbourne and make it the region's main logistics and freight hub, bringing more trucks, planes and eventually, trains, to the city's south and making it the city's economic gateway (Potts 2014). This would require re-zoning of the land around the airport at Coolangatta from residential to commercial.

Accessibility becomes the lynchpin to the success of this proposed new development. A business hub envisioned at the scale of Sydney and Melbourne would require much better access, and plans to link the airport to the city through both light and heavy rail have been on the agenda for quite a while now. These transport connections are important for the success of the Commonwealth Games as well. The irony of the Gold Coast bemoaning the loss of its rail link to Brisbane almost as soon as it happened in the 1960s and starting to campaign in order to get it back was highlighted in Chapter 11. Since the reestablishment of the link the intent has always been to extend the heavy rail to Coolangatta thereby connecting both the Brisbane and Gold Coast airports. As we saw in Chapter 4, while the proposed extension remains in the updates of the *South East Queensland Regional Plan* as well as *Gold Coast Planning Schemes*, and although this is supported widely by the Gold Coast community, there are, as yet, no targets, firm dates nor any funding attached to the proposal.

The Gold Coast light rail on the other hand has hopes of a sooner extension using the window of opportunity created by the fast approaching 2018 Commonwealth Games. The idea of a light rail system on the Gold Coast was first proposed in the 1997 *Integrated Regional Transport Plan for South East Queensland.* The 2004 *Gold Coast Light Rail Feasibility Study* recommended a route from Parkwood to Broadbeach which was then determined as a priority in TransLink's 2005 draft *Network Plan.* In the *South East Queensland Infrastructure Plan and Program 2006–2026,* the route proposed for the project was between Helensvale, Parkwood, Broadbeach and Coolangatta. The project was initially conceived as four stages. Stage one between Broadbeach and Parkwood started operation in 2014. Stage two was planned to go north from Gold Coast University Hospital/Griffith University to Helensvale, stage three to the south from Broadbeach to Burleigh Heads and stage four from Burleigh Heads to Coolangatta, connecting to the Gold Coast Airport.

The linking of the heavy rail and light rail at Helensvale station was seen as an imperative for the success of the Commonwealth Games; however, lack of funding and the pre-operation scepticism on the success of the first stage delayed the second stage. The extension to Helensvale was predicted to cost between $800 million and $1 billion. This would require a funding commitment from all levels of government but so far no commitments have been made. In 2013 the *Draft Gold Coast City Transport Strategy 2031* identified an extension of the system from Griffith University to a new heavy rail station at Parkwood as the preferred route (City of Gold Coast 2013b). In early 2013, GoldLinQ, the company which was building the first stage of the light rail, offered to build stage two for free in exchange of extending its operational contract from 15 to 28 years (Ardern 2013a). The $400 million required for construction would be raised by GoldLinQ. The mayor supported this proposal. The finalised transport strategy included several additional stages to connect the system to significant attractions and population centres such as Harbour Town Outlet Mall at Biggera Waters; Sea World and other attractions at The Spit (also the location of the proposed cruise ship terminal); Robina Town Centre through Bond University; and the Gold Coast Cultural Precinct. The extension to Helensvale, it seems, has been completely abandoned. It is the general view that this new route is the only way the light rail will be linked to the heavy rail before the Commonwealth Games. The concern is, this 'saving the day' approach replaces the longer and more expensive route that would ultimately better serve local transportation needs of regular commuters.

Conclusions

Understanding the past is important for shaping the future. This book posed a simple question to which the answers are inevitably complex: what are the historical factors that have conspired, wittingly or otherwise, to produce the Gold Coast as we now know it? Our purpose in doing so was to provide some guidance for the future of a rapidly growing regional city that is unique in many respects in the Australian landscape.

Due to the city's physical amenities and history, tourism will always play a major role in the economy and development of the Gold Coast and physical manifestations of these industries will remain visible in the city. But as this book has shown, along with its population the complexity of the city has also grown such that the Gold Coast is no longer a one-industry town. Still, the position of the Gold Coast is primarily one of fun, interpreted broadly to encompass everything from a family beach outing, to nightclubs and bars, to art galleries and symphony orchestra concerts. As the Gold Coast population ages and as younger generations produce and engage in new trends, so will the Gold Coast's position in relation to fun change. This book then has documented the position of the Gold Coast at a particular time and in relation to the zeitgeist of that time. It also opens up opportunities to imagine the future of the city and possibilities for further research into and of this relentlessly, rapidly evolving urban product that is the Gold Coast.

Bibliography

A.A. Heath & Partners (1970) *Report on the 1970 Town Planning Scheme prepared for Albert Shire Council.* Brisbane.

AAP (2014) Queensland Government backs down on Gold Coast terminal. 26 August, <http://www.traveller.com.au/queensland-government-backs-down-on-gold-coast-terminal-108dbz>.

Abbott C (1987) *The New Urban America: Growth and Politics in Sunbelt Cities.* University of North Carolina Press, Chapel Hill.

Abbott J (2011) Collaborative governance and metropolitan planning in South East Queensland. *Australian Centre of Excellence for Local Government Researchers Forum.* 14–15 December, Sydney.

ABC News (2007a) *Council amalgamation laws pass through Qld parliament.* Australian Broadcasting Commission, Sydney. <http://www.abc.net.au/news/2007-08-10/council-amalgamation-laws-pass-through-qld/636100>.

ABC News (2007b) *First home buyers moving to regions, housing industry says.* Australian Broadcasting Commission, Sydney, <http://www.abc.net.au/news/2007-03-12/first-home-buyers-moving-to-regions-housing/2213978>.

ABS (Australian Bureau of Statistics) (1997) *Regional population growth, Australia 1991 and 1996.* Cat. no. 3218.0. Australian Bureau of Statistics, Canberra.

ABS (Australian Bureau of Statistics) (2007) *Regional population growth, Australia 1996 to 2006.* Cat. no. 3218.0. Australian Bureau of Statistics, Canberra.

ABS (Australian Bureau of Statistics) (2008) *Australian historical population statistics.* Cat. no. 3105.0.65.001. Australian Bureau of Statistics, Canberra.

ABS (Australian Bureau of Statistics) (2010) National Regional Profiles, Canberra.

ABS (Australian Bureau of Statistics) (2013a) 2011 Census Community Profiles, Canberra.

ABS (Australian Bureau of Statistics) (2013b) 2011 Census QuickStats, Canberra.

ABS (Australian Bureau of Statistics) (2013c) National Regional Profile: Gold Coast (Statistical Area Level 4), Canberra.

Adam P (1994) *Australian Rainforests.* Oxford University Press, New York.

Adams D (1994) *Urban Planning and the Development Process.* UCL Press, London.

Albanese A, Bligh A (2011) *Successful bidder named to construct and operate Gold Coast light rail.* Joint media release by the Commonwealth Minister for Infrastructure and Transport and the Queensland Premier, 6 May, Canberra, <http://www.minister.infrastructure.gov.au/aa/releases/2011/May/aa064_2011.aspx>.

Albert Shire Council (1959) *Merrimac Town Plan.* Queensland.

Albert Shire Council (1960) Minutes, 21 January 1960. Queensland.

Albert Shire Council (1972a) *South Albert Shire Strategic Plan 1972.* Queensland.

Albert Shire Council (1972b) *South Albert Shire Strategic Plan 1972: Summary.* Queensland.

Albert Shire Council (1973) *Town Planning Scheme for the Shire of Albert.* Queensland.

Albert Shire Council (1982) *Strategic Plan & Town Plan Review - Part B*. Queensland.
Alfredson G (1984) The Aboriginal use of St Helena Island, Moreton Bay: the archaeological evidence. In *Focus on Stradbroke: New Information on North Stradbroke Island and Surrounding Areas, 1974–1984*. (Eds RJ Coleman, J Covacevich and P Davie) pp. 1–15. Boolarong Publications, Brisbane.
ALGA (Australian Local Government Association) 2011. *About ALGA*. Canberra. <http://www.alga.asn.au/?ID=42&Menu=41,81>.
Allom R, Jones T (1997) 'A nice place to visit': celebrating the superficial and planning for permanence at the Gold Coast. In *Images of the Urban Conference Proceedings*. 17–19 July, Sunshine Coast. (Eds L Finch and C McConville) pp. 360–364. Sunshine Coast University College, Maroochydore, Queensland.
Allom Lovell Architects and The Office of City Architect and Heritage (2010) *Southport Urban Heritage and Character Strategy Review*. Gold Coast City Council, Gold Coast.
Allom Lovell Marquis-Kyle, Henshall Hansen Associates, Context, HJM and Staddon Consulting (1997) *Gold Coast Urban Heritage and Character Study*. Gold Coast City Council, Gold Coast.
Alvey J, Ryan N (2005) The separation of powers in Australia: implications for the state of Queensland. *53rd Australasian Political Studies Association Conference*. 28–30 September. University of Otago, Dunedin.
Amusement Park Journal (1985) Australia's first theme park. **8**(117).
Anderson K (1990) Chinatown re-oriented: a critical analysis of recent re-development schemes of a Melbourne and Sydney enclave. *Australian Geographical Studies* **28**(2), 137–154. doi:10.1111/j.1467-8470.1990.tb00609.x.
Anderson J (2002) *Gold Coast light rail feasibility study*. Media release by the Deputy Prime Minister and Minister for Transport and Regional Services, 14 May, Canberra, <http://www.infrastructure.gov.au/department/statements/2002_2003/media/a13_budget_02.aspx>.
Anonymous (1889) The Southport railway. *The Brisbane Courier*, 25 January.
Anonymous (1958) Land for nothing. *The South Coast Bulletin*, 3 September.
Anonymous (1959) M.H.R. Warns on Coast Morals: Says Some People Don't Know Right from Wrong, *The South Coast Bulletin*, 11 March.
Anonymous (1968) From bora ring to town of the future. *Gold Coast Bulletin*, 24 January.
Anonymous (2000) *S.E.E. the Future: Society, Environment, Ecology. A Local Agenda 21 for the Gold Coast*. Gold Coast City Council, Gold Coast.
Anton Clave S (2007) *Global Theme Park Industry*. CABI, Wallingford.
Archer M, Burnley I, Dodson J, Harding R, Head L, Murphy A (1998) *From Plesiosaurs to People: 100 Million Years of Australian Environmental History*. Environment Australia. Commonwealth of Australia, Canberra.
Architecture in Australia (1959) Editorial. **48**(1), 47–48, 66–69.
Ardern L (2013a) GoldLinQ offers to extend light rail. *Gold Coast Bulletin*, 7 March, pp. 1, 5.
Ardern L (2013b) Salt peppers Coast and says it's boring. *Gold Coast Bulletin*, 1 August, p. 6.
Ardern L (2014) Exclusive first look at South Bank-style Commonwealth Games Athletes Village. *Gold Coast Bulletin*, 24 March.
ARM Architecture (2014) *2014 Gold Coast Cultural Precinct Master Plan Part 1: Design Report*. City of Gold Coast.
Arundell A (2011) *The South Coast Railway: A History of Growth and Transport on the Gold Coast*. Waterstreet Productions, Brisbane.
Australian Bureau of Meteorology (2015) *Climate statistics for Australian locations*. Monthly climate statistics: Gold Coast. <http://www.bom.gov.au/climate/averages/tables/cw_040764.shtml>.

Australian Government (2008) *Australian Civic Aviation.* <http://www.australia.gov.au/about-australia/australian-story/austn-civil-aviation>.

Australian Public Service Commission (2007) *Tackling Wicked Problems: A Public Policy Perspective.* Australian Government, Canberra.

Ball M (1999) Chasing a snail: innovation and house building firms' strategies. *Housing Studies* **14**(1), 9–22.

Ballinger JK (1936) *Miami Millions: The Dance of the Dollars in the Great Florida Land Boom of 1925.* Franklin Press, Miami.

Barnes P (2007) Clarke wants 'green' coast: Council plan to save the planet. *The Gold Coast Sun.* Gold Coast, News Limited/News Corporation.

Berwick M (2006) The challenge of coastal governance. In *Federalism and Regionalism in Australia: New Approaches, New Institutions?* (Eds AJ Brown and JA Bellamy) pp. 83–94. ANU E Press, Canberra.

Best Y, Barlow A (1997) *Kombumerri, Saltwater People.* Heinemann Library, Port Melbourne.

Bishop R (1998) The South Coast Railway: between coach and motor car. *Queensland Review* **5**, 38–51.

BITRE (Bureau of Infrastructure, Transport and Regional Economics) (2013) *Population Growth, Jobs Growth and Commuting Flows in South East Queensland*, Report 134. Department of Infrastructure and Transport, Canberra.

Bitzios Consulting (2013) The Robina link: light rail extension proposal. Unpublished presentation prepared for Bond University, QIC and Robina Group.

Blackman A (2013) *If I Only Had a Heart: A History of the Gold Coast and its Economy from 1823 to 2013.* Fast Proof Press, Gold Coast.

Blanco I (2009) Does a 'Barcelona Model' really exist? Periods, territories and actors in the process of urban transformation. *Local Government Studies* **35**(3), 355–369. doi:10.1080/03003930902854289.

Blunt A, Dowling R (2006) *Home.* Routledge, Milton Park.

Booth D (1994) Surfing '60s: a case study in the history of pleasure and discipline. *Australian Historical Studies* **26**, 262–279. doi:10.1080/10314619408595963.

Bosman C, Dredge D (2011) *Histories of Placemaking in the Gold Coast City: The Neoliberal Norm, the State Story and the Community Narrative.* Griffith University Urban Research Program, Brisbane.

Boyd R (1960) *The Australian Ugliness.* Text Publishing Company, Melbourne.

Boyle M, McWilliams C, Rice G (2008) The spatialities of actually existing neoliberalism in Glasgow, 1977 to present. *Geografiska Annaler* **90**(4), 313–325. doi:10.1111/j.1468-0467.2008.00296.x.

Brenner N, Theodore N (2002) (Eds) *Spaces of Neoliberalism: Urban Restructuring in North America and Western Europe.* Blackwell, Oxford.

Brisbane City Council (2006) *Community Profile: Key Statistics.* Compiled and presented in profile.id by .id, the population experts, <http://profile.id.com.au/Default.aspx?id=327&pg=138&gid=10&type=enum>.

Broomhill R (2001) Neoliberal globalism and the local state: a regulation approach. *Journal of Australian Political Economy* **48**, 115–140.

Brown AJ (2006) Federalism, regionalism and the reshaping of Australian governance. In *Federalism and Regionalism in Australia: New Approaches, New Institutions?* (Eds AJ Brown and JA Bellamy) pp. 11–32. ANU E Press, Canberra.

Brown S, Dovers S, Frawley J, Gaynor A, Goodall H, Karskens G, Mullins S (2008) Can environmental history save the world? *History Australia* **5**(1), 3.1–3.24.

Burchill G (2005) *Passion, Power and Prejudice: A Remarkable Untold Account of a Magic City in the Making.* Golden 12 Pty Ltd, Gold Coast.

Burton P (2009) Growing pains: adolescent urbanism on the Gold Coast. In *State of Australian Cities Conference Proceedings.* 24–27 November, Perth.

Burton P (2010) Business as usual? Responding to the GFC on the Gold Coast. *Journal of Australian Political Economy* **64**, 188–198.

Burton P (2014) From white shoes to bold future: the neoliberalisation of local government in an Australian city. *Urban Studies* **51**(15), 3233–3249. doi:10.1177/0042098014540944.

Business GC (2009) *Economic Development Strategy 2020.* Gold Coast City Council, Gold Coast.

Business GC (2013) Gold Coast Business Precincts. <http://www.businessgc.com.au/pic-precincts>.

Byrne J, Gleeson B, Howes M, Steele W (2009) Climate change and Australian urban resilience: the limits of ecological modernization as an adaptive strategy. In *Planning for Climate Change: Strategies for Mitigation and Adaptation for Spatial Planners.* (Eds S Davoudi, J Crawford and A Mehmood) pp. 136–154. Earthscan Press, London.

Carter J, Dyer P, Sharma B (2007) Dis-placed voices: sense of place and place identity on the Sunshine Coast. *Social and Cultural Geography* **8**(5), 755–773.

Cartier C, Lew A (2005) *Touristed Landscapes: Geographical Perspectives on Globalization and Touristed Landscapes.* Routledge, Oxon.

City of Gold Coast (2013a) *Economic Development Strategy 2013–2023.* Version 2.0. Gold Coast.

City of Gold Coast (2013b) *Gold Coast City Transport Strategy 2031.* Gold Coast.

City of Gold Coast (2013c) *Draft City Plan 2015.* Gold Coast.

City of Gold Coast (2013d) *Gold Coast City Community Profile.* Compiled and presented in profile.id by .id, the population experts, <http://profile.id.com.au/gold-coast>.

City of Gold Coast (2014a) *Gold Coast Destination Tourism Management Plan 2014–2020.* City of Gold Coast, Gold Coast.

City of Gold Coast (2014b) *Behind the Brand* [video and transcript]. Council of the City of Gold Coast, <http://www.goldcoast.qld.gov.au/council/city-brand-14279.html>.

City of Gold Coast (2015) *Gold Coast Economic Profile.* Compiled and presented in profile.id by .id, the population experts, <http://economy.id.com.au/gold-coast>.

City of Gold Coast (n.d.) *Gold Coast Cultural Precinct Vision.* Gold Coast.

Cloutier-Fisher D, Harvey J (2009) Home beyond the house: experiences of place in an evolving retirement community. *Journal of Environmental Psychology* **29**, 246–255. doi:10.1016/j.jenvp.2008.07.002.

COAG (Council of Australian Governments) (2011) *Guide to Intergovernmental Agreements.* Department of Prime Minister and Cabinet, Canberra, <http://www.coag.gov.au/intergov_agreements/index.cfm>.

Coiacetto E (2001) Diversity in real estate developer behaviour: a case for research. *Urban Policy and Research* **19**(1), 43–59. doi:10.1080/08111140108727862.

Coiacetto E (2006) Real estate development industry structure: consequences for urban planning and development. *Planning Practice and Research* **21**(4), 423–441. doi:10.1080/02697450601173355.

Coiacetto E (2007) Residential sub-market targeting by developers in Brisbane. *Urban Policy and Research* **25**(2), 257–274. doi:10.1080/08111140701344833.

Coiacetto E (2009a) Gold Coast development: a special case or same old city factories? In *State of Australian Cities Conference Proceedings.* 24–27 November, Perth.

Coiacetto E (2009b) Industry structure in real estate development: is city building competitive? *Urban Policy and Research* **27**(2), 117–135. doi:10.1080/08111140802499080.

Commonwealth Department of Housing and Regional Development (1995) *Better Cities: National Status Report 1995*. Commonwealth of Australia, Canberra.

Condon M (2003) The Casuarina Forest. *Griffith Review* **2**, 37–49.

Condon M (2006) Spitfight. *The Courier Mail,* 8 April.

Council of Mayors: South East Queensland (2011) *About the Council of Mayors (SEQ)*. Brisbane, <http://www.councilofmayorsseq.qld.gov.au/About/>.

Council of the City of Gold Coast (1963) *The City of Gold Coast Town Planning Scheme 1963*. Gold Coast, Queensland.

Council of the City of Gold Coast (1969) *Gold Coast Urban Region Strategic Plan 1970–1990*. Southport.

Council of the City of Gold Coast (1973) *Town Planning Scheme for the City of Gold Coast*. Queensland.

Council of the City of Gold Coast (1994) *City of Gold Coast Planning Scheme*. Surfers Paradise, Queensland.

Courier Mail (2011) Fight continues over Gold Coast water. Brisbane, <http://www.news.com.au/national/fight-continues-over-gold-coast-water/story-e6frfkp9-1226102391097>.

Cronon W (1992) *Nature's Metropolis: Chicago and the Great West*. W.W. Norton and Company, New York.

CTBUH (Council on Tall Buildings and Urban Habitat) (2011) *The Skyscraper Centre – 100 Tallest Completed Buildings in the World*. Council on Tall Buildings and Urban Habitat, Chicago, <http://skyscrapercenter.com/buildings>.

Daly MT (1982) *Sydney Boom Sydney Bust: The City and its Property Market 1850–1981*. Allen and Unwin, Sydney.

Damanpour F (1991) Organisational innovation: a meta-analysis of effects of determinants and moderators. *Academy of Management Journal* **34**, 555–590. doi:10.2307/256406.

Davidson J, Spearritt P (2000) *Holiday Business: Tourism in Australia since 1870*. Miegunyah Press, Carlton.

Davis M (2006) Fear and money in Dubai. *New Left Review* **41**, 47–68.

Davis M, Monk DB (Eds) (2007) *Evil Paradises*. The New Press, New York.

Dedekorkut-Howes A (2013) City without a plan: how the Gold Coast was shaped. In *State of Australian Cities Conference Proceedings*. 26–29 November, Sydney.

Dedekorkut-Howes A, Bosman C (2011) The unbearable lightness of being Gold Coast. In *State of the Australian Cities Conference Proceedings*. 29 November–2 December, Melbourne.

Dedekorkut-Howes A, Bosman C (2015) The Gold Coast: Australia's playground? *Cities* **42**, Part A, 70–84. doi:10.1016/j.cities.2014.09.005

Department of State Development (2015) *Priority Development Areas*. Queensland Government, <http://www.statedevelopment.qld.gov.au/priority-development-areas/infrastructure-and-planning/priority-development-areas.html>.

Dewar RD, Dutton JE (1986) The adoption of radical and incremental innovations: an empirical analysis. *Management Science* **32**, 1422–1433. doi:10.1287/mnsc.32.11.1422.

DIT MCU (Department of Infrastructure and Transport Major Cities Unit) (2010) *State of Australian Cities 2010*. Commonwealth of Australia, Canberra.

DIT MCU (Department of Infrastructure and Transport Major Cities Unit) (2011) *State of Australian Cities 2011*. Commonwealth of Australia, Canberra.

DIT MCU (Department of Infrastructure and Transport Major Cities Unit) (2012) *State of Australian Cities 2012*. Commonwealth of Australia, Canberra.

DIT MCU (Department of Infrastructure and Transport Major Cities Unit) (2013) *State of Australian Cities 2013*. Commonwealth of Australia, Canberra.

DLGP (Department of Local Government and Planning) (2012) *Local Government*. Brisbane, <http://www.dlgp.qld.gov.au/local-government/index.php>.

Dodson J, Coiacetto E, Ellway C (2006) Corruption in the Australian land development process: identifying a research agenda. *State of Australian Cities Conference*, 30 November–2 December, Brisbane.

Douglas I (1975) Pressure on Australian rain-forests. *Environmental Conservation* **2**(2), 109–119. doi:10.1017/S0376892900001016.

Dovers S (Ed.) (1994) *Australian Environmental History: Essays and Cases*. University Press, Oxford.

Dredge D, Jamal T (2013) Mobilities on the Gold Coast, Australia: implications for destination governance and sustainable tourism. *Journal of Sustainable Tourism* **21**, 557–579. doi:10.1080/09669582.2013.776064.

Drew P (1994) *The Coast Dwellers*. Penguin Books, Ringwood.

Easthope H (2004) A place called home. *Housing Theory and Society* **21**(3), 128–138.

Edwards D, Griffin T, Hayllar B (2007) *Development of an Australian Urban Tourism Agenda*. CRC for Sustainable Tourism, Gold Coast, <http://www.crctourism.com.au/WMS/Upload/Resources/bookshop/Edwards_UrbanTourismAgenda.pdf>.

Ellison N, Burrows R (2007) New spaces of (dis)engagement? Social politics, urban technologies and the rezoning of the city. *Housing Studies* **22**(3), 295–312. doi:10.1080/02673030701253998.

eTourism Holidays (2013) *Gold Coast Theme Parks*. <http://goldcoast.i4u.com.au/page/gold-coast-theme-parks.htm>.

Farwell G (1970) *Sun Country*. Nelson, Sydney.

Faulkner B (1999) *The Gold Coast Tourism Visioning Project*. CRC for Sustainable Tourism, Gold Coast.

Faulkner B (2002) Rejuvenating a maturing tourist destination: the case of the Gold Coast. *Current Issues in Tourism* **5**(1), 472–520.

Faulkner B, Tideswell C (2002) *Gold Coast Tourism Market Analysis*. Common Ground Publishing in association with CRC for Sustainable Tourism.

Faulkner B, Tideswell C (2006) Rejuvenating a maturing tourist destination: the case of the Gold Coast Australia. In *The Tourism Area Life Cycle: Applications and Modifications*, Vol. 1. (Ed. R Butler) pp. 306–338. Channel View Publications, Clevedon.

Fitzgerald R (1984) *From 1915 to the Early 1980s: A History of Queensland*. University of Queensland Press, St. Lucia.

Florida R (2007) *The Flight of the Creative Class: The New Global Competition for Talent*. Collins, New York.

Forbes J, Spearritt P (2003) Rum corps to white shoe brigade. *Griffith Review* **2**, 16–27.

Frawley K (1990) An ancient assemblage: the Australian rainforests in European conceptions of nature. *Continuum* **3**(1), 137–167. doi:10.1080/10304319009388155.

Frost W (2004) Tourism, rainforests and worthless lands: the origins of national parks in Queensland. *Tourism Geographies* **6**, 493–507. doi:10.1080/1461668042000280255.

Galton B (1985) *The Gold Coast Bulletin: A History of a Regional Newspaper (1885–1985)*. Gold Coast Publications Pty Ltd, Southport.

Garcia R, Calantone R (2002) A critical look at technological innovation typology and innovativeness terminology: a literature review. *Journal of Product Innovation Management* **19**(2), 110–132. doi:10.1016/S0737-6782(01)00132-1.

GCAPL (Gold Coast Airport Pty Ltd) (2011) *Gold Coast Airport Master Plan*. Gold Coast Airport Pty Ltd, Gold Coast.

GECKO (Gold Coast and Hinterland Environmental Council) (2014) *Your City, Your Future - Is the Gold Coast being Short Changed?* Media release, 1 July.

Gehl J, Gemzoe L (2004) Close encounters with buildings [Nærkontakt med huse], *Arkitekten* September.

Ghazarian Z (2012) COAG could hurt the Gillard government. *The Conversation,* 13 April. <http://theconversation.edu.au/coag-could-hurt-the-gillard-government-6389>.

Gibson M (2001) Myths of Oz cultural studies: the Australian beach and 'English' ordinariness. *Continuum* **15**, 275–288. doi:10.1080/10304310120086777.

Giddens A (1984) *The Constitution of Society.* Polity, Cambridge.

Gilbert EW (1939) The growth of inland and seaside health resorts in England. *Scottish Geographical Magazine* **55**, 16–35. doi:10.1080/00369223908735100.

Gilbert EW (1949) The growth of Brighton. *The Geographical Journal* **114**, 30–52. doi:10.2307/1789987.

Gleeson B (2006) Rescuing urban regions: the federal agenda. In *Federalism and Regionalism in Australia: New Approaches, New Institutions?* (Eds AJ Brown and JA Bellamy) pp. 71–82. ANU E Press, Canberra.

Gleeson B (2007) The endangered state of Australian cities: climate threat and urban response. Issues Paper 8, Griffith University Urban Research Program, Brisbane.

Gleeson B, Dodson J, Spiller M (2010) Metropolitan governance for the Australian city: the case for reform. Issues Paper 12, Griffith University Urban Research Program, Brisbane.

Gleeson P (2012a) Editorial. *Gold Coast Bulletin.* 27 April, p. 28.

Gleeson P (2012b) Editorial. *Gold Coast Bulletin.* 30 April, p. 13.

Goad P (1997) The Gold Coast: architecture and planning. In *Gold Coast Urban Heritage and Character Study.* (Eds Allom Lovell Marquis-Kyle *et al.*) pp. 37–41. Gold Coast City Council, Gold Coast.

Gold Coast Airport (2010) *About Gold Coast Airport* <http://goldcoastairport.com.au/corporate/about-gold-coast-airport>.

Gold Coast City Council (1981) *Looking to the Future.* Gold Coast, Queensland.

Gold Coast City Council (1997) *Building Sustainable Communities: City of Gold Coast Draft Strategic Plan.* Gold Coast, Queensland.

Gold Coast City Council (2005) *Our Living City Report, 2004–05: A Report to the Gold Coast Community.* Gold Coast, Queensland.

Gold Coast City Council (2006a) *Community Profile: Key Statistics.* Compiled and presented in profile.id by .id, the population experts, <http://profile.id.com.au/Default.aspx?id=292&pg=138&gid=10&type=enum>.

Gold Coast City Council (2006b) *Community Profile: What Industries Do We Work In?* Compiled and presented in profile.id by .id, the population experts, <http://profile.id.com.au/Default.aspx?id=292&pg=112&gid=10&type=enum>.

Gold Coast City Council (2007) *Our Living City Report: A Sustainability Update.* Gold Coast.

Gold Coast City Council (2008) *A Year of Change: 2007–08 Annual Report.* Gold Coast.

Gold Coast City Council (2011a) *History.* City of the Gold Coast, Bundall, <http://www.goldcoast.qld.gov.au/t_standard2.aspx?pid=1442>.

Gold Coast City Council (2011b) *Annual Report 2010–11: Together We Are Creating a Safe City Where Everyone Belongs.* CGC, Bundall <http://annualreport.goldcoast.qld.gov.au/images/downloads/annual-report-2010-11-full.pdf>.

Gold Coast City Council (2011) *Our Living City: Gold Coast Planning Scheme 2003.* Version 1.2. Amended November 2011.

Gold Coast Tourism (2010) *Very Gold Coast, Very GC* <http://www.verygoldcoast.com.au/>.

Gold Coast Tourism (2011) *Gold Coast: Famous For Fun* <http://www.visitgoldcoast.com/>.

Gold Coast Tourism (2013) *Gold Coast Amusement and Theme Parks* <http://www.visitgoldcoast.com/things-to-do/amusement-and-theme-parks/>.
GoldLinQ (2012a) *Funding Partners.* Gold Coast Rapid Transit: Southport <http://goldlinq.com.au/constructing-light-rail/funding-partners>.
GoldLinQ (2012b) *How Is the Project Governed?* Gold Coast Rapid Transit, Southport <http://goldlinq.com.au/faq>.
GoldLinQ (2012c) *Background.* Gold Coast Rapid Transit: Southport <http://goldlinq.com.au/constructing-light-rail/background>.
GoldLinQ (2012d) *Frequently Asked Questions.* Gold Coast Rapid Transit, Southport <http://goldlinq.com.au/faq>.
Graham B (2001) *Tweed Volcanic Region: 360 Million Years Ago to the Present Day.* Norsearch Reprographics, Lismore.
Green A (1982) *Drawn to the Coast: A Sketchbook of the Gold Coast's Heritage.* Boolarong Publications, Brisbane.
Gregory H, McLay D (2010) *Building Brisbane's History: Structure, Sculptures, Stories and Secrets.* Woodslane Press, Warriewood.
Griffin G (1998) The good, the bad and the peculiar: cultures and policies of urban planning and development on the Gold Coast. *Urban Policy and Research* **16**(4), 285–292. doi:10.1080/08111149808727776.
Griffin G (2004) 'The man has gone – the dream lives on': the Palazzo Versace and the re-branding of the Gold Coast. *Queensland Review* **11**(2), 75–88.
Griffiths T (2007) The humanities and an environmentally sustainable Australia. *Australian Humanities Review* **43** (December), <http://www.australianhumanitiesreview.org/archive/Issue-December-2007/EcoHumanities/EcoGriffiths.html>.
Guhathakurta S, Stimson RJ (2007) What is driving the growth of new 'sunbelt' metropolises? Quality of life and urban regimes in greater Phoenix and Brisbane-South East Queensland region. *International Planning Studies* **12**(2), 129–152. doi:10.1080/13563470701453794.
Gurran N (2007) *Australian Urban Land Use Planning: Statutory Planning Practice in NSW.* Sydney University Press, Sydney.
Hajdu J (1993) The Gold Coast, Australia: spatial model of its development and the impact of the cycle of foreign investment in property during the late 1980s. *Erdkunde* **47**(1), 40–51. doi:10.3112/erdkunde.1993.01.04.
Hajdu J (2005) *Samurai in the Surf: The Arrival of the Japanese on the Gold Coast in the 1980s.* Pandanus, Canberra.
Hall HJ (1984) Fishing with dolphins? Affirming a traditional Aboriginal fishing story in Moreton Bay, SE. Queensland. In *Focus on Stradbroke: New Information on North Stradbroke Island and Surrounding Areas, 1974–1984.* (Eds RJ Coleman, J Covacevich and P Davie) pp. 16–22. Boolarong Publications, Brisbane.
Hargroves KC, Smith MH (2005) Towards a deeper understanding. In *The Natural Advantage of Nations: Business Opportunities, Innovation and Governance in the 21st Century.* (Eds KC Hargroves and MH Smith) pp. 217–243. Earthscan, London.
Hart M, Ben-Yoseph M (Eds) (2005) *Psychological, Political, and Cultural Meanings of Home.* Haworth Press, New York.
Healey P, Barrett SM (1990) Structure and agency in land and property development processes: some ideas for research. *Urban Studies* **27**(1), 89–104.
Heather B (1978) 'Bordering on sunshine and sensuality'. Talk to Insite/Outsight, Queensland Chapter Convention of the Royal Australian Institute of Architects, Red Hill, Qld. Gold Coast Architecture Awards Archives, Griffith University.

Heazle M, Tangney P, Burton P, Howes M, Grant-Smith D, Reis K, Bosomworth K (2013) Mainstreaming climate change adaptation: an incremental approach to disaster risk management in Australia. *Environmental Science & Policy* **33**, 162–170. doi:10.1016/j.envsci.2013.05.009.

Herbig P, Golden JE (1993) How to keep that innovative spirit alive: an examination of evolving innovative hot spots. *Technological Forecasting and Social Change* **43**(1), 75–90.

Hinchliffe S (2007) *Geographies of Nature: Societies, Environments, Ecologies*. SAGE Publications, Thousand Oaks.

Hitch J (1959) The spa and the sea resort. *Architecture in Australia* **48**(1), 49–52.

Hofmeister B (1988) *Australia and its Urban Centres*, Urbanization of the Earth Series, Vol. 6. Gebrüder Borntraeger, Berlin.

Holden G (2013) What, if anything, can be made of the Gold Coast Urban Design Awards? In *Proceedings of the Society of Architectural Historians, Australia and New Zealand* **30**(1) *Open*, 2–5 July, Gold Coast. (Eds A Brown and A Leach) pp. 389–403. SAHANZ, Gold Coast.

Holmes D (2001) Monocultures of globalization: touring Australia's Gold Coast. In *Virtual Globalization: Virtual Spaces/Tourist spaces*. (Ed. D Holmes) pp. 175–191. Routledge, London.

Holmes D (2006) The Gold Coast. In *Sociology: Place, Time and Division*. (Eds P Beilharz and T Hogan) pp. 111–115. Oxford University Press, Melbourne.

Holthouse H (1982) *Illustrated History of the Gold Coast*. AH and W Read Pty Ltd, Sydney.

Horton D (Ed) (1994) *The Encyclopaedia of Aboriginal Australia*. Aboriginal Studies Press, Canberra.

Howes M (2005) *Politics and the Environment: Risk and the Role of Government and Industry*. Allen & Unwin, Sydney.

Howes M, Tangney P, Reis K, Grant-Smith D, Heazle M, Bosomworth K, Burton P (2015) Towards networked governance: improving interagency communication and collaboration for disaster risk management and climate change adaptation. *Journal of Environmental Planning and Management* **58**(5), 757–776. doi:10.1080/09640568.2014.891974.

Ip D (2005) Contesting Chinatown: place-making and the emergence of 'ethnoburbia' in Brisbane, Australia. *GeoJournal* **64**(1), 63–74. doi:10.1007/s10708-005-3926-1.

Jenkins L (2013) *Hotdogs and Meatpies: World War II on the Gold Coast*. Gold Coast City Council, Gold Coast.

Johnson RW, Knutson J, Taylor SR (1989) *Intraplate volcanism in eastern Australia and New Zealand*. Cambridge University Press, Cambridge.

Jones M (1986) *A Sunny Place for Shady People*. Allen and Unwin, Sydney.

Jones M (1988) *Country of Five Rivers: Albert Shire 1788–1988*. Allen and Unwin, Sydney.

Joyce RB (1966) Canungra timber. *Queensland Heritage* **1**(4), 3–8.

Juppenlatz M (1959) An experiment in freedom: The Gold Coast. In *Proceedings of Conference Planning for Tourist Development on the North Coast*, p. 51. University of New England.

Keane E (1958) *Gold Coast: The Story of the Gold Coast of Queensland and the Hinterland*. Oswald Ziegler Publications, Sydney.

Kellow A, Niemeyer S (1999) The development of environmental administration in Queensland and Western Australia: why are they different? *Australian Journal of Political Science* **34**(2), 205–222. doi:10.1080/10361149950371.

Killoran M (2014) Report shows Parklands was a sacrificial cash cow and should not have been closed. *Gold Coast Bulletin*. 19 January.

Kilmartin M (1966) The real estate story. In *The Gold Coast Story* (Ed A McRobbie) pp. 35–42. The Gold Coast Annual Company, Surfers Paradise.
Kleinschmidt E, Cooper R (1991) The impact of product innovativeness on performance. *Journal of Product Innovation Management* **8**(4), 240–251. doi:10.1016/0737-6782(91)90046-2.
Knesel KM, Cohen BE, Vasconcelos PM, Thiede DS (2008) Rapid change in drift of the Australian plate records collision with Ontong Java plateau. *Nature* **454**(7205), 754–757. doi:10.1038/nature07138.
Kollar P (1959) The Gold Coast and the principles of regional development. *Architecture in Australia* **48**(1), 57–63.
KPMG (2015) *Beyond the Horizon*. Regional Development Australia Gold Coast Inc.
Land Court (1991) Judgment Re: Claims for Compensation A90–50/51, 15 March. Brisbane.
Landry C (2006) *The Art of City Making*. Earthscan, London.
Laws E, Scott N, Parfitt N (2002) Synergies in destination image management: a case study and conceptualisation. *International Journal of Tourism Research* **4**(1), 39–55.
Lawton LJ (2005) Resident perceptions of tourist attractions on the Gold Coast of Australia. *Journal of Travel Research* **44**(2), 188–200. doi:10.1177/0047287505278981.
Leach A, Rickard K, Jones F (2015) *GC30+: Documenting the Gold Coast Architecture Awards, 1984–2013*. URP Research Monographs 15, Griffith University Urban Research Program, Gold Coast.
Leiper G, Glazebrook J, Cox D, Rathie K (2008) *Mangroves to Mountains: A Field Guide to the Native Plants of South East Queensland*. Queensland, Society for Growing Australian Plants (Queensland Region), Logan.
Licence J (Dir) (2013) *Drawn Here: Architecture of the Gold Coast and Northern Rivers* [video]. Tiger Monkey Productions, <https://www.youtube.com/watch?v=ZEEvMTmtxb0>.
Local Governments for Sustainability (2011) *About ICLEI*. Local Governments for Sustainability (formerly the International Council for Local Environmental Initiatives (ICLEI), Bonn, <http://www.iclei.org/index.php?id=about>.
Logan J (1993) Cycles and trends in the globalization of real estate. In *The Restless Urban Landscape*. (Ed PL Knox) pp. 35–54. Prentice Hall, Englewood Cliffs.
Logan J, Molotch H (1987) *Urban Fortunes: The Political Economy of Place*. University of California Press, Berkeley.
Longhurst R (1991) *The Heart of Paradise: The History of Burleigh Heads*. Gold Coast City Council, Gold Coast.
Longhurst R (1994) *Nerang Shire: A History to 1949*. Albert Shire Council, Moorooka.
Longhurst R (1995) *Gold Coast: Our Heritage in Focus*. State Library of Queensland Foundation, South Brisbane.
Longhurst R (1996) *From Tallebudgera to the Tweed: An Early History of the Southern Gold Coast*. Gold Coast City Council, Southport.
Longhurst R (2001) Southport in the 1890s: Decline and temporary fall from favour. In *Brisbane: Relaxation, Recreation and Rock 'n' roll: Popular Culture 1890–1990*. (Ed. B Shaw) pp. 19–24. Brisbane History Group, Brisbane.
Longhurst R (2006) The power of the poster: pioneering the real estate of the South Coast 1880–1930. In *Sold! The Gold Coast Real Estate Dream*. (Ed. V Rigney). Gold Coast City Art Gallery, Surfers Paradise.
Macnaught TJ (1982) Mass tourism and the dilemmas of modernization in Pacific Island communities. *Annals of Tourism Research* **9**, 359–381. doi:10.1016/0160-7383(82)90019-6.
Maher C, Stimson R (1994) *Regional Population Growth in Australia: Nature, Impacts and Implications*. Australian Government, Canberra.

Marcucci DJ (2000) Landscape history as a planning tool. *Landscape and Urban Planning* **49**(1–2), 67–81. doi:10.1016/S0169-2046(00)00054-2.

Marshall C (2011) It's hot in Brisbane but it's Cool-angatta. ABC Radio, Gold Coast, <http://www.abc.net.au/local/audio/2011/10/19/3345059.htm>.

Marshall N, Dollery B, Witherby A (2003) Regional Organisations of Councils (ROCs): the emergence of network governance in metropolitan and rural Australia? *Australasian Journal of Regional Studies* **9**(2), 169–188.

Marzano G (2007) The effect of stakeholder power on a destination branding process: The Gold Coast VeryGC brand. Unpublished PhD thesis. University of Queensland, St. Lucia.

Mayere S, Dedekorkut A, Sipe N (2010) Resembling Florida: transpacific transfer of ideas from one Gold Coast to another. In *International Planning History Society Conference Proceedings*. 12–15 July, Istanbul, Turkey.

McDonald G (1999) Two-tier markets. *Australian Property Journal* **35**(6), 516–523.

McLeod M (1997) Henri Lefebvre's Critique of Everyday Life: an introduction. In *Architecture of the Everyday*. (Eds S Harris and D Berke) pp. 9–29. Princeton Architectural Press, New York.

McManus P (2004) Writing the palimpsest, again; Rozelle Bay and the Sydney 2000 Olympic Games. *Urban Policy and Research* **22**(2), 157–167. doi:10.1080/0811114042000229627.

McRobbie A (1966) *The Gold Coast Story*. The Gold Coast Annual Company, Surfers Paradise.

McRobbie A (1982) *The Surfers Paradise Story*. Pan News Pty Ltd, Surfers Paradise.

McRobbie A (1984) *The Fabulous Gold Coast*. Pan News Pty Ltd, Surfers Paradise.

McRobbie A (1988) *The Real Surfers Paradise!: From Seaside Village to International Resort*. Pan News Pty Ltd, Surfers Paradise.

McRobbie A (1991) *Gold Coast Heritage: A Multicultural Triumph*. Pan News Pty Ltd, Surfers Paradise.

McRobbie A (2000) *20th Century Gold Coast People*. The Gold Coast Arts Centre Press, Surfers Paradise.

Meers D (2010a) Changing tourism tack. *Gold Coast Bulletin*, 6 October, p. 9.

Meers D (2010b) Beautiful words say it all. *Gold Coast Bulletin*, 9 October, p. 12.

Mepham D (2013) Transitioning from transit oriented development to development oriented transit: a case study of the Gold Coast light rail project. Unpublished PhD thesis, Bond University, Robina.

Merrilees B, Miller D, Herington C, Smith C (2007) Brand Cairns: an insider (resident) stakeholder perspective. *Tourism Analysis* **12**(5–6), 409–417. doi:10.3727/108354207783227975.

Middleton CH, Roberts CR (1968) An introduction to Gold Coast and hinterland agriculture. *Tropical Grasslands* **2**(2), 138–145.

Miles M, Huberman M (1994) *Qualitative Analysis: An Expanded Sourcebook*. SAGE, Thousand Oaks.

Molotch H (1976) The city as a growth machine: toward a political economy of place. *American Journal of Sociology* **82**(2), 309–332. doi:10.1086/226311.

Moore K (2005) Embracing the make-believe: the making of Surfers Paradise. *Australian Studies* **18**(1), 187–210.

Moore S (2002) *Gold Coast Tourism Scoping Study*. CRC for Sustainable Tourism, Altona, Victoria.

Morley I (1981) *Black Sands: A History of the Mineral Sand Mining Industry in Eastern Australia*. University of Queensland Press, St. Lucia.

Morris N (2004) Last post for the Gold Coast: heart of a nation and the Japanese 'colonisation' of Queensland. *Journal of Australian Studies* **28**, 107–120. doi:10.1080/14443050409387942.

Morton P (1996) *After Light: A History of the City of Adelaide and its Council, 1878–1928.* Wakefield Press, Adelaide.

Mullins P (1979) Australia's sunbelt migration: the recent growth of Brisbane and the Moreton region. *Journal of Australian Political Economy* **5**, 17–32.

Mullins P (1984) Hedonism and real estate: resort tourism and Gold Coast development. In *Conflict and Development, Urban Studies Yearbook*, Vol. 2. (Ed. P Williams) pp. 31–50. Allen and Unwin, Sydney.

Mullins P (1988) Is Australian urbanisation different? In *A Sociology of Australian Society.* (Eds JM Najman and JS Western) pp. 517–541. Macmillan, Melbourne.

Mullins P (1990) Tourist cities as new cities: Australia's Gold Coast and Sunshine Coast. *Australian Planner* **28**(3), 37–41. doi:10.1080/07293682.1990.9657471.

Mullins P (1991) Tourism urbanization. *International Journal of Urban and Regional Research* **15**(3), 326–342. doi:10.1111/j.1468-2427.1991.tb00642.x.

Mullins P (2000) Cities of post-industrialism, cities of post modernity. In *A Sociology of Australian Society.* (Eds JM Najman and JS Western) pp. 385–405. Macmillan, Melbourne.

Mulvaney J, Kamminga J (1999) *Prehistory of Australia.* Allen and Unwin, St. Leonards.

New South Wales Government (2012) *NSW Cross-Border Commissioner listening tour report.* NSW Trade and Investment, Armidale.

New South Wales Government Tourist Bureau and NRMA (n.d.) *Official Motor Guide to Northern NSW with Through Routes to and from Brisbane.* Australian Guide Book Company, Sydney.

Newell P (1959) Umbigumbi to the Gold Coast. *Architecture in Australia* **48**(1), 70–73.

Nightingale J (2006) Brisbane, the 200 kilometre city or just another port town. *Urban Policy and Research* **24**(3), 409–421. doi:10.1080/08111140600877073.

Nix H (1994) The Brigalow. In *Australian Environmental History: Essays and Cases.* (Ed. S Dovers) pp. 198–233. Oxford University Press, Oxford.

NRM (Natural Resource Management) (2012) *South East Queensland NRM Region.* Caring for Our Country program. Department of Environment, Canberra, <http://www.nrm.gov.au/about/nrm/regions/qld-seq.html>.

O'Connor J (1997) What is environmental history? Why environmental history? *Capitalism, Nature, Socialism* **8**(2), 3–29. doi:10.1080/10455759709358733.

O'Hare D (2008) *Missing the Gold Coast train? The interaction between private development and three levels of government planning in attempting to co-locate a new railway station and a major new town centre.* Institute of Sustainable Development and Architecture. Bond University, Gold Coast, <http://epublications.bond.edu.au/cgi/viewcontent.cgi?article=1010&context=sustainable_development>.

O'Hare D (2011) Confusion between centrality and remoteness in cross-border regional planning: an Australian case study. In *World Planning Schools Congress Proceedings.* 4–8 July, Perth.

Ostle J (1974) Surfers Paradox. *Walkabout* May, 4–9.

Parliament of Australia (2012) *The Australian Constitution.* Australian Parliament House, Canberra, <http://www.aph.gov.au/About_Parliament/Senate/Powers_practice_n_procedures/Constitution>.

Parliament of the Commonwealth of Australia (1975) *National Estate: Report of the Committee of Inquiry.* Government Printer, Canberra.

Perry DC, Watkins AJ (1977) People, profit and the rise of sunbelt cities. In *The Rise of Sunbelt Cities.* (Eds DC Perry and AJ Watkins) pp. 277–304. SAGE, London.

Pigram JJ (1977) Beach resort morphology. *Habitat International* **2**, 525–541. doi:10.1016/0197-3975(77)90024-8.

Polunin I (1989) Japanese travel boom. *Tourism Management* **10**, 4–8. doi:10.1016/0261-5177(89)90029-0.

Potts A (2014) Gold Coast Airport expansion could see facility expanded and heavy rail links fast-tracked. *Gold Coast Bulletin*. 29 July.

Potts A, Weston P (2014) Gold Coast cruise ship terminal proposal includes making Wavebreak Island three times its current size. *Gold Coast Bulletin*. 6 November.

Potts R, Dedekorkut-Howes A, Bosman C (2013) Gold Coast is not only all that glitters: understanding visitor and resident perceptions of the Gold Coast. *Australian Planner* **50**(4), 316–327. doi:10.1080/07293682.2013.764907.

Power D (2011) Mayoral campaign launch speech, QT Gold Coast Hotel, pers comm.

Prideaux B (2004) The resort development spectrum: the case of the Gold Coast, Australia. *Tourism Geographies* **6**(1), 26–58. doi:10.1080/1461668032000172328.

Prideaux B, Cooper C (2002) Marketing and destination growth: a symbiotic relationship or simple coincidence? *Journal of Vacation Marketing* **9**(1), 35–51. doi:10.1177/135676670200900103.

QGITB (Queensland Government Intelligence and Tourism Bureau) (1927) *From Noosa to the Tweed: Mountain and Seaside Resorts of Southern Queensland*. QGITB, Brisbane.

Queensland Government (2005) *South East Queensland Infrastructure Plan and Program 2005–2026*. Office of Urban Management, Brisbane.

Queensland Government (2009a) *South East Queensland Infrastructure Plan and Program 2009–2031*. Office of Urban Management, Brisbane.

Queensland Government (2009b) *Varsity Station Village Master Plan*. Department of Transport and Main Roads, Brisbane.

Queensland Government (2011) *Creation of a State*. Brisbane <http://www.qld.gov.au/about/about-queensland/history/creation-of-state>.

Queensland Government (n.d.) Tugun bypass project. Brisbane: Department of Transport and Main Roads <http://www.tmr.qld.gov.au/Projects/Name/T/Tugun-Bypass-project.aspx>.

Queensland Government and the South East Queensland Regional Organisation of Councils (SEQROC) (2005) *South East Queensland Regional Plan 2005–2026*. Office of Urban Management, Brisbane <http://www.dlgp.qld.gov.au/regional-planning/past-seq-regional-plan-2005–2026-and-amendment-1.html>.

Queensland Government Statistician's Office (2014) *Queensland Government Population Projections*, 2013 edition. Queensland Treasury and Trade.

Queensland Main Roads Department (1966) *Gold Coast Travel Study*. Main Roads Department with Cooperation of Gold Coast City Council.

Queensland Museum (2007) *Wildlife of Greater Brisbane*. Queensland Government, Brisbane.

Queensland Rail (n.d.) *Gold Coast Railway*, unpaginated brochure. Queensland Rail, Brisbane.

Queensland Tourist and Travel Corporation (1997) *Gold Coast Domestic Leisure Marketing Strategy 1997–1999*. Queensland Tourist and Travel Corporation, Brisbane.

Raitz K (1988) Advantages of place as perceived by sunbelt promoters. *Growth and Change* **19**(4), 14–29. doi:10.1111/j.1468-2257.1988.tb00480.x.

RDA (Regional Development Australia) Gold Coast (2014) *2013 Regional Leaders' Forum*. <http://rdagoldcoast.org.au/news-and-events/news/2013-regional-leaders-forum/>.

RDA (Regional Development Australia) Gold Coast (2015) *Future Gold Coast.* <http://rdagoldcoast.org.au/news-and-events/news/future-gold-coast>.

Rickard K (2013) Run to paradise: the Chevron Hotel, Gold Coast, from foundation to renaissance. In *Proceedings of the Society of Architectural Historians, Australia and New Zealand* **30**(1) *Open.* 2–5 July, Gold Coast. (Eds A Brown and A Leach) pp. 57–66. SAHANZ, Gold Coast.

Rimmer P (1994) Japanese investment in golf course developments: Australia–Japan links. *International Journal of Urban and Regional Research* **18**, 234–255. doi:10.1111/j.1468-2427.1994.tb00264.x.

Rolfe J, Bishop P, Cheshire L, Howes M, Lawrence G, Liebrecht T, Loechel B, Oliver P, Yee S (2009) *Engaged Government: A Study of Government-Community Engagement for Regional Outcomes – Final Report.* Central Queensland University, Rockhampton.

RAIA (Royal Australian Institute of Architects) (2003) *20/20 Vision.* RAIA Gold Coast and Northern Rivers Region, Queensland Chapter. Gold Coast Architecture Awards Archives, Griffith University.

Russell R, Faulkner B (1998) Reliving the destination life cycle in Coolangatta. In *Embracing and Managing Change in Tourism: International Case Studies.* (Eds E Laws, B Faulkner and G Moscardo) pp. 95–115. Routledge, London.

Russell R, Faulkner B (1999) Movers and shakers: chaos makers in tourism development. *Tourism Management* **20**(4), 411–423. doi:10.1016/S0261-5177(99)00014-X.

Russell R, Faulkner B (2004) Entrepreneurship, chaos and the tourism area lifecycle. *Annals of Tourism Research* **31**(3), 556–579.

Saunders P (1986) The dual politics thesis: the argument, its origins and its critics. In *Urban Political Theory and the Management of Fiscal Stress.* (Eds M Goldsmith and S Villadsen) Methuen, London.

Schott D (2004) Urban environmental history: what lessons are there to be learnt? *Boreal Environment Research* **9**, 519–528.

Scott N, Gardiner S, Carlini J (2014) *Experience Gold Coast: Innovative Products for Asian Visitors.* Griffith Institute for Tourism, Gold Coast.

Seeney J (2013) Commonwealth Games milestone. Media statement, 1 October, <http://statements.qld.gov.au/Statement/2013/10/1/commonwealth-games-milestone/>.

Shepherd WS (1997) *The Economics of Industrial Organisation.* 4th edn. Wavell, Illinois.

Short JR (1996) City images. In *The Urban Order: An Introduction to Cities, Culture and Power.* (Ed. JR Short) pp. 414–438. Blackwell, Cambridge.

Skene K (2015) Premier Annastacia Palaszczuk's claim Gold Coasters don't want a cruise ship terminal is based on 'dodgy' data. *Gold Coast Bulletin*, 5 March.

Small B (1978) Resort development. *The Valuer* **25**(2), 108–119.

Smith P (1985) Queensland's political culture. In *The Bjelke-Petersen Premiership 1968–1983.* (Ed. A Patience) pp. 17–32. Longman Cheshire, Melbourne.

Smith RA (1991) Beach resorts: a model of development evolution. *Landscape and Urban Planning* **21**(3), 189–210. doi:10.1016/0169-2046(91)90018-H.

Smith M (2006) Queensland Parliamentary Debates (Member for Burleigh, ALP), 28 February.

Solomon D (2009) *Cabinet Minutes 1978 – Important Decisions.* Short summary of some of the major decisions of the 1978 Queensland Cabinet Released to the public 1 January 2009. Queensland State Archives, Brisbane, <http://www.archives.qld.gov.au/Researchers/CommsDownloads/Documents/1978CabinetMinutesImportantDecisions.pdf>.

South East Queensland Catchments (n.d.) *Nature Conservation and Biodiversity Factsheet.* SEQ. Catchments, Brisbane.

Southern Cross University (n.d.) *Gold Coast campus.* Southern Cross University, <http://scu.edu.au/about/index.php/6>.

Spearritt P (2006) Brisbane. In *Sociology: Place, Time and Division.* (Eds P Beilharz and T Hogan) pp. 59–63. Oxford University Press, Melbourne.

Spearritt P (2008) The water crisis in Southeast Queensland: how desalination turned the region into carbon emission heaven. In *Troubled Waters: Confronting the Water Crisis in Australia's Cities.* (Ed. P Troy) pp. 19–36. ANU E Press, Canberra.

Spearritt P (2009) The 200 km city: Brisbane, the Gold Coast, and Sunshine Coast. *Australian Economic History Review* **49**(1), 87–106. doi:10.1111/j.1467-8446.2009.00251.x.

Stannard D (2011) 2018 Commonwealth Games to be held at the Gold Coast. *Courier Mail*, Brisbane, 12 November, <http://www.news.com.au/national/decision-on-who-will-host-the-2018-commonwealth-games/story-e6frfkvr-1226193308390>.

Stansfield CA, Rickert JE (1970) The recreational business district. *Journal of Leisure Research* **4**, 213–225.

State of New South Wales (2006) *Far North Coast Regional Strategy 2006–2031.* Department of Planning, Sydney.

Steele JG (1984) *Aboriginal Pathways in Southeast Queensland and the Richmond River.* University of Queensland Press, St Lucia.

Steele W, Crick F, Serrao-Neumann S, Sharma V, Wadsworth J (2011) Governing the Australian Megalopolis: The challenge of the 200km city (and beyond). In *State of Australian Cities Conference Proceedings.* 29 November–2 December, Melbourne.

Stimson R (1995) Processes of globalisation, economic restructuring and the emergence of a new space economy of cities and regions in Australia. In *Cities in Competition: Productive and Sustainable Cities for the 21st Century.* (Eds J Brotchie, M Batty, E Blakely, P Hall and P Newton) pp. 58–87. Longman, Melbourne.

Stimson R, Minnery J (1998) Why people move to the 'sun-belt': a case study of long-distance migration to the Gold Coast, Australia. *Urban Studies* **35**(2), 193–214. doi:10.1080/0042098984943.

Stimson R, Minnery J, Kabamba A, Moon B (1996) *'Sun-belt' Migration Decisions: A Study of the Gold Coast.* Australian Government Publishing Service, Canberra.

Stuart R (1985) Resources development policy: the case of Queensland's export coal industry. In *The Bjelke-Petersen Premiership 1968–1983.* (Ed. A Patience) pp. 53–80. Longman Cheshire, Melbourne.

Sunshine Coast Council (2006) *Community Profile: Key Statistics.* Compiled and presented in profile.id by .id, the population experts, <http://profile.id.com.au/Default.aspx?id=352&pg=138&gid=10&type=enum>.

Sydney Morning Herald (2005) Council sacked after property corruption probe. 25 May, Sydney, <http://www.smh.com.au/news/National/Council-sacked-after-property-corruption-probe/2005/05/25/1116950735308.html>.

Symes C (1994) Not learning from Las Vegas: the Gold Coast as theme park. *Arena Magazine.* Feb–March, 28–31.

Taylor G (1949) *Australia: A Study of Warm Environments and their Effect on British Settlement.* Methuen and Co, London.

Taylor CJ (1973) *Report on Albert Shire Strategic Plan.* St. Lucia. 24 February.

The South Coast Bulletin (1959) Dress circle of the Gold Coast. 16 March, p. 8.

Thomas E (1997) *State of the Environment: City of Gold Coast, Benchmark 97.* Gold Coast City Council, Gold Coast.

Tourism and Events Queensland (2012) 'Gold Coast Regional Snapshot: Year ended December 2012'. Fact sheet.
Tourism and Events Queensland (2013) 'Gold Coast Regional Snapshot: Year ended June 2013'. Fact sheet.
Tourism and Events Queensland (2014) 'Gold Coast Regional Snapshot: Year ended September 2014'. Fact sheet.
Tourism and Events Queensland (2015) 'Gold Coast Regional Snapshot'. Tourism and Events Queensland, Brisbane.
Tourism Queensland (2005) *Gold Coast Destination Management Plan*. Tourism Queensland, Brisbane.
Tourism Queensland (2010) 'Gold Coast Regional Snapshot: Year ended December 2010'. Fact sheet.
Tourism Queensland (2011) 'Gold Coast Regional Snapshot: Year ended December 2011'. Fact sheet.
Tourism Research Australia (2008) *Top Ten Regions: International Overnight Trips for Leisure*. Tourism Research Australia, Sydney.
Tourism Research Australia (2011) *Regional Tourism Profiles 2009/2010 Gold Coast*. Tourism Research Australia, Canberra.
Toyne P (1994) *The Reluctant Nation*. ABC Books, Sydney.
TransLink (2014) *Journey Planner*. <www.jp.translink.com.au>.
UDIA (Urban Development Institute of Australia) (2014) Urban Development Institute of Australia Queensland (Gold Coast Logan Branch) submission to the City of Gold Coast Council in relation to the Draft City Plan 2015, 29 July. Brisbane.
Urry J (1995) *Consuming Places*. Routledge, New York.
Vader J, Lang F (1980) *The Gold Coast Book*. Jacaranda Press, Milton.
Vernon K (2011) *Clarke defends Allconnex opt-out move*. Goldcoast.com, Southport, <http://www.goldcoast.com.au/article/2011/07/01/329155_gold-coast-news.html>.
Village Roadshow Limited (n.d.) *Theme Parks* <http://www.villageroadshow.com.au/Village-Roadshow-Limited—Company-Profile/Theme-Parks.htm>.
Walters I (1992) Antiquity of marine fishing in South East Queensland. *Queensland Archaeological Research* **9**, 35–37.
Walters I, Lauer P, *et al.* (1987) Hope Island: salvage excavation of a Kombumerri site. *Queensland Archaeological Research* **4**, 80–95.
Ward S, O'Regan T (2009) The film producer as the long-stay business tourist: rethinking film and tourism from a Gold Coast perspective. *Tourism Geographies* **11**(2), 214–232. doi:10.1080/14616680902827175.
Watt E (1999) The Gold Coast weekender: a character study. Unpublished BArch dissertation, University of Queensland, St. Lucia.
WCMC/WCU (World Conservation Monitoring Centre/World Conservation Union) (1993) World Heritage Nomination – IUCN Summary: Central Eastern Rainforests Of Australia (Extension). The World Conservation Union.
Weaver D (2005) The distinctive dynamics of exurban tourism. *International Journal of Tourism Research* 7(1), 23–33. doi:10.1002/jtr.521.
Weaver DB (2012) Organic, incremental and induced paths to sustainable mass tourism convergence. *Tourism Management* **33**, 1030–1037. doi:10.1016/j.tourman.2011.08.011.
Weston P (2013) Secret study values Broadwater at $4.1b. *Gold Coast Bulletin*, 12 August.
Weston P (2015) Tate's funding backflip: Levies to help finance $385 million culture centre project. *Gold Coast Bulletin*. 12 March, p. 2.

Whitehead JC (1987) Decision making in the property development industry during a business cycle. Unpublished PhD thesis, University of British Columbia, Vancouver.
Whitford M (2004) *Regional Development through Domestic and Tourist Event Policies: Gold Coast and Brisbane, 1974–2003*. University of Queensland, Brisbane.
Williams DR, McIntyre N (2001) Where heart and home reside: changing constructions of place identity, In *Trends 2000: Shaping the Future: The 5th outdoor recreation & tourism trends symposium*. 17–20 September 2000, Lansing, Michigan. pp. 392–403. Department of Parks, Recreation and Tourism Resources, Michigan State University, <http://www.prr.msu.edu/trends2000/pdf/williams.pdf>.
Wise P (2006) Australia's Gold Coast: a city producing itself. In *Urban Space and Cityscapes: Perspectives from Modern and Contemporary Culture*. (Ed. C Lindner) pp. 177–291. Routledge, London.
Zorbaugh HW (1929) *The Gold Coast and the Slum*. University of Chicago Press, Chicago.

Index

* 9 7 8 1 4 8 6 3 0 1 8 3 6 *